2nd Edition

Criminal Law
A Desk Reference

Paul Bergman, Professor of Law

SECOND EDITION	JANUARY 2014
Editor	MICAH SCHWARTZBACH
Cover Design	SUSAN PUTNEY
Book Design	TERRI HEARSH
Proofreading	ROBERT WELLS
Printing	BANG PRINTING

ISSN: 2331-7027 (Print)
ISSN: 2331-7035 (Online)

ISBN: 978-1-4133-1993-4 (pbk)
ISBN: 978-1-4133-1994- 1 (epub ebook)

This book covers only United States law, unless it specifically states otherwise.

Please note

We believe accurate, plain-English legal information should help you solve many of your own legal problems. But this text is not a substitute for personalized advice from a knowledgeable lawyer. If you want the help of a trained professional—and we'll always point out situations in which we think that's a good idea—consult an attorney licensed to practice in your state.

Acknowledgments

Thank you to Professor Eugene Volokh, Hilary Sossin-Bergman, and Carrie Newman for suggestions and advice. Thank you also to Marcia Stewart, Janet Portman, and the wonderful and thoroughly professional Nolo editorial staff. And a final thank-you to Rich Stim and Micah Schwartzbach, very talented writers who managed to blur the line between editing and authoring while assuring me that this is my book.

About the Author

Paul Bergman is a Professor of Law at the UCLA School of Law and a recipient of a University Distinguished Teaching Award. His books include *The Criminal Law Handbook* (with Sara J. Berman, Nolo); *Nolo's Deposition Handbook* (with Moore, Nolo); *Reel Justice: The Courtroom Goes to the Movies* (Andrews & McMeel); *Trial Advocacy: Inferences, Arguments, Techniques* (with Moore and Binder, West Publishing Co.); *Trial Advocacy in a Nutshell* (West Publishing Co.); *Represent Yourself in Court: How to Prepare & Try a Winning Case* (with Berman, Nolo); *Depositions in a Nutshell* (with Moore, Binder, Light, West Publishing); and *Lawyers as Counselors: A Client-Centered Approach* (with Binder, Tremblay, Weinstein, West Publishing). He has also published numerous articles in law journals.

Get Updates and More Online

When there are important changes to the information in this book, we'll post updates online, on a page dedicated to this book:

www.nolo.com/back-of-book/DRCRIM.html

You'll find other useful information there, too, including author blogs, podcasts, and videos.

Introduction

Criminal Law: A Desk Reference is a comprehensive description of the criminal justice system in the United States. The book explores crimes ranging from curfew violations to first degree murder as well as the panoply of punishments that judges can impose. The book also delves into such topics as defenses to criminal charges, constitutional rights of accused persons and prisoners, police officer practices, victims' rights, pretrial and trial procedures, evidence rules, forensic experts, and the roles of lawyers, both prosecutors and defense attorneys.

Millions of people interact with the criminal justice system, almost always unwillingly but all seeking and hoping for justice. The criminal justice system also consumes vast amounts of public money. For society, widespread understanding of the criminal justice system can help reduce crime, ameliorate its effects, and promote the dignity of crime victims and offenders alike. With these goals in mind, I have tried to make the information in this book accessible to nonlawyers as well as lawyers. For example, I have:

- used "plain English";
- explained unavoidable legal jargon (including Latin terms like *mens rea* and *corpus delicti* that judges and lawyers love to toss around);
- developed illustrative examples of legal concepts; many of the examples are based on actual events, and others are based on classic criminal-law-related films;
- provided a bit of historical background when it is particularly interesting and colorful (to me, at least); and
- included sample statutes and referred to important U.S. Supreme Court decisions both to illustrate legal principles and to facilitate further research by interested readers. ●

A

abuse excuse

Offenders who have been subject to victimization—typically a history of abuse by a spouse, significant other, or parent—may attempt to mitigate punishment or disclaim responsibility for their criminal acts because of this past abuse (the "abuse excuse"). Critics claim that advancing such factors into a criminal prosecution enables offenders to avoid accountability. Proponents, particularly attorneys who represent battered women, point out that the laws regarding self-defense are ineffective for their clients because the danger of harm must be imminent or immediate. Most states have responded by creating a defense of "imperfect self-defense." Imperfect self-defense can apply to various defendants, including those who are victims of previous abuse. For victims of past abuse charged with attacking an abuser, it creates an opportunity to mitigate or even escape criminal responsibility by proving that the history of abuse led them to believe reasonably, if mistakenly, that force was necessary to avoid an imminent attack. Past victimization and abuse is also occasionally put forward as part of an insanity defense. An abuse victim charged with a crime claims that a history of abuse led to an inability to understand the difference between right and wrong. A convicted defendant may also cite a history of abuse during the sentencing process as a mitigating factor in punishment.

Related terms: syndrome evidence; insanity defense; self-defense.

accessories

See accomplices and accessories.

accomplices and accessories

People who assist perpetrators (or "principals") in carrying out criminal acts are categorized either as accomplices (if they participate in the commission of a crime) or accessories (if they are behind-the-scenes participants before or after a crime is committed). Here's how the law distinguishes between them.

Accomplices. Accomplices actively participate in the activity that constitutes a crime and are subject to the same punishment as principals. For example, the driver who waits in the getaway car while the principal robs a bank is an accomplice. An ever-present risk is that accomplices will seek to curry favor with prosecutors by exaggerating other participants' criminal responsibility while downplaying their own. Thus, a common criminal law rule provides that an accomplice's testimony is not by itself sufficient to sustain a conviction. Prosecutors have to offer evidence of defendants' guilt that is independent of accomplices' testimony.

Accessories Before the Fact. Accessories are "behind the scenes" culprits and are categorized as either "before the fact" or "after the fact" (the "fact" referring to the commission of the crime). Accessories before the fact knowingly help principals before a crime is committed but do not participate actively in its commission. Nevertheless, accessories before the fact are as guilty as principals in the eyes of the law.

> EXAMPLE: Archie designed a bank building. Archie gives his friend Willie the blueprints, believing Willie's statement that he needs them to help his child with a school project. In fact Willie uses the blueprints to rob the bank. Archie is not an accessory before the fact because he didn't knowingly help Willie, the principal, commit the robbery. However, if Willie tells Archie, "If you get me the blueprints for the bank, I'll rob the bank and give you a third of the loot," and Archie gives Willie the blueprints, Archie is an accessory before the fact and may be convicted of bank robbery, just the same as if he had joined with Willie in the actual robbery.

Accessories After the Fact. These wrongdoers are the mirror image of accessories before the fact except they knowingly help principals following the commission of crimes. As with accessories before the fact, the party must knowingly assist—that is, the person must be aware that they are assisting someone who has committed a crime. The primary difference between accessories before the fact and after the fact is the punishment. While provisions vary from one jurisdiction to another, commonly the maximum penalty for accessories after the fact is one-half the maximum sentence that a principal can receive.

 Real-Life Illustration

Edman Spangler instructed a theater employee to hold a saddled horse in the alley behind Ford's Theater in Washington, DC, on April 14, 1865. The horse was intended to provide a getaway for John Wilkes Booth after Booth assassinated President Abraham Lincoln inside the theater. When Booth took off, Spangler slapped another theater employee and reportedly said, "Don't say which way he went." Knowing what Booth had done, Dr. Samuel Mudd treated the injuries that Booth suffered while carrying out the assassination. Thomas Jones furthered Booth's escape attempt by helping him to cross the Potomac River. John Hughes hid Booth on his farm until authorities found Booth and shot him dead. Spangler, Mudd, Jones, and Hughes were all accessories after the fact. (As it turned out, Spangler was also involved in the actual assassination and he was convicted as a coconspirator.)

 Legal Authority Examples

Federal: Whoever, knowing that an offense against the United States has been committed, receives, relieves, comforts, or assists an offender in order to hinder or prevent the offender's apprehension, trial, or punishment is an accessory after the fact.

Federal: Except as otherwise expressly provided by Congress, an accessory after the fact shall be imprisoned not more than one-half the maximum term of imprisonment or fined not more than one-half the maximum fine prescribed for the punishment of the principal, or both. If a principal is punishable by life imprisonment or death, the accessory shall be imprisoned not more than 15 years.

California: A conviction cannot be had upon the testimony of an accomplice unless it is corroborated by other evidence that connects a defendant to a crime.

Related terms: conspiracy.

actus reus

(Latin for a "guilty act.") Virtually all crimes consist of physical *actions* accompanied by a *mental state* that a statute deems immoral or flawed (*mens rea*). Together, these Latin phrases form the indispensable touchstones of criminal law.

Voluntary Acts. A physical action must be voluntary to qualify as an *actus reus*. So, for example, if a person experiences a sudden and unanticipated epileptic seizure and injures someone else, the action is not a crime as it was involuntary. Similarly, people who have evil thoughts or who develop wicked plans may be immoral. But the criminal justice system punishes people for their deeds, not for their thoughts or beliefs. For example, someone who simply creates an electronic computer file that outlines a plan to rob a bank has not committed a crime because he has not taken an action in furtherance of his plan.

Statutes creating "status offenses" are unconstitutional because they attempt to punish people for their conditions rather than for their actions. For example, statutes purporting to punish people for being a vagrant or a drug addict are invalid. (*Robinson v. California*, U.S. Sup. Ct. (1962).)

Don't Just Do Something, Sit There. Most of us celebrate heroes who try to save others from physical harm, especially if they risk their own life in the process. But the criminal justice system does not require heroism or even lifting a finger to help a person in distress. As a general rule (see the exceptions, below), people have no legal duty to prevent harm, even if they can do so at no risk to their own safety.

 Real-Life Illustration

In 1964, Kitty Genovese was beaten to death on a street in Queens, New York. None of the at least 38 neighbors who heard her screaming for help came to her aid. The neighbors' failure to act did not constitute a crime.

Don't Just Sit There, Do Something. The general criminal law rule that people have no legal duty to prevent harm is subject to a limited number of exceptions. Individuals may be guilty of a crime if they fail to try to protect victims with whom they have a special and trusted relationship—for example, a parent's neglect of a child would constitute child abuse. In a very few states, Good Samaritan laws also make it a crime to refuse to come to the aid of people in physical distress.

> EXAMPLE: In the 1998 finale of the hugely popular *Seinfeld* TV comedy series, the show's eccentric four main characters were convicted of violating a Good Samaritan law for standing around and laughing instead of giving aid while an overweight man was robbed at gunpoint. Each character was sentenced to a year in jail. In the real world, violation of a state's Good Samaritan law is at most punishable by no more than a small fine.

 Legal Authority Examples

Model Penal Code: To be guilty of a crime, a person must engage in a voluntary act or omit to engage in an act that he has a duty to perform. A reflex or convulsion, a bodily movement during unconsciousness or sleep, conduct resulting from hypnotic suggestion, or a bodily movement that otherwise is not a product of effort or determination does not constitute a voluntary act. Possession is an act if the possessor knowingly received the thing possessed or was aware of his control long enough to have been able to terminate possession.

Vermont: A person who knowingly fails to provide reasonable assistance to another who is exposed to grave physical harm is punishable by a fine not to exceed $100. Failure to provide assistance is punishable only if the person could have provided aid without danger to himself and without interference with important duties owed to others.

Related terms: attempts; disorderly conduct; *mens rea*.

affirmative defense

An affirmative defense is a defense in which the offender does not deny that the activity occurred, but instead offers justification or mitigating factors that excuse or limit liability. Some examples are self-defense, insanity, and entrapment.

Related terms: self-defense; burdens of proof; entrapment; insanity.

aggravated assault

See assault and battery; mayhem.

aggravated offense

A crime committed under circumstances that elevate the seriousness of a conviction is referred to as an aggravated offense. Common aggravating circumstances include the use of a weapon and the infliction of injuries. Example: An assault that causes a victim to suffer a concussion can elevate misdemeanor simple assault to aggravated assault, a felony.

alibi

An alibi is an affirmative defense that a defendant was somewhere other than the scene of a charged crime when the crime occurred. Despite the negative connotations often provided by films and TV shows, an alibi is a perfectly respectable legal defense.

Defendants Needn't Testify. Defendants may offer an alibi defense without giving up their constitutional right to remain silent. Any witness who can place the defendant at a location other than the scene of a charged crime can provide an alibi. For example, a defendant may remain silent and call a witness to testify and provide documentation that the defendant was at a dental appointment when a crime took place a mile away.

Burden of Proof. Defendants who offer alibi defenses do not take on the burden of proving to a judge or jury that the alibi is accurate. The burden of proving a defendant guilty beyond a reasonable doubt remains at all times on the prosecution. Of course, a judge or jury can consider the credibility of alibi evidence when deciding whether the prosecution has met its burden.

Pretrial Notice. In most states, laws called "discovery rules" require defendants to advise prosecutors prior to trial of alibi evidence that they intend to rely on. The rule gives prosecutors time to investigate an alibi and prepare to undermine it.

EXAMPLE: Blaine is charged with a sexual assault crime. He plans to offer an alibi defense that he was at a local theater watching an *X-Men* film at the time the assault occurred. Blaine has to notify the prosecution of this planned defense in advance of trial. The prosecution then has time to investigate the alibi. If the investigation turns up evidence that the theater was showing only *Toy Story 3* on the date of the assault, the prosecutor can undermine Blaine's alibi by calling the theater's manager as a witness.

Legal Authority Examples

New York: Prosecutors have up to 20 days following indictment to serve a "Demand for Alibi" on defendants. Defendants who intend to rely on an alibi defense must respond to the demand within eight days, unless the court grants them more time. The response should identify the place or places where the defendant claims to have been at the time of the crime; the name of every alibi witness other than the defendant; and the home address and place of employment of every alibi witness. Defendants must supplement initial responses with information about additional alibi witnesses as they become known. A judge may exclude the alibi testimony of any defense witness whose identity was not disclosed.

Related terms: burdens of proof; failure of proof.

animal cruelty

Animal cruelty laws punish offenders who abuse, mistreat, or neglect animals. These laws respect the value of animals—as workers, food and fiber sources, experimental subjects, and for companionship and entertainment. Animal cruelty laws also seek to protect the public by recognizing that offenders who mistreat animals may also harm individuals. In some cases, animal cruelty concerns are related to public health and safety. Animal cruelty can be punishable as either a misdemeanor or a felony.

 Real-Life Illustration

Employees of the Westland and Hallmark meat packing plants pleaded guilty in 2007 to violating animal cruelty laws. Undercover videographers had secretly recorded them abusing "downer cows" in order to force them into the slaughter area. The angry public reaction to the images was partly fueled by a concern that since downer cows were more likely to carry diseases, using them for food endangered human health.

Anticruelty rules also apply when animals are presented as entertainment. For example, circus trainers can use only reasonable physical force to prepare animals to perform tricks. Trainers violate animal cruelty laws when they use excessive, noncustomary force or keep animals in squalid and unsanitary pens.

Historical Antecedents. British philosopher and barrister Jeremy Bentham was an early proponent of legal protection for animals. In *An Introduction to the Principles of Morals and Legislation* (1771), Bentham famously wrote, "The question is not, 'Can they reason?' or 'Can they talk?' but 'Can they suffer?'" In the early 1800s, a Vermont law provided for imprisonment for up to five years for anyone who killed, wounded, maimed, or poisoned another person's commercially valuable farm animal; the law did not apply to pets. A Maine statute of 1821 was the first to criminalize abuse of an owner's own commercially valuable animal. An 1866 New York statute was the first to extend animal cruelty laws to the abuse of any kind of animal.

Abuse. Animal cruelty laws in all states forbid the intentional abuse and mistreatment of animals. Animal cruelty laws may specify a variety of actions that constitute abuse. These laws may also simply prohibit abuse and leave it to the judicial system to determine the legality of actions on a case-by-case basis. For example, it is not animal cruelty for a vet to commit euthanasia on an elderly sick cat but it would be animal cruelty to poison a dog whose barking bothered you.

 Real-Life Illustration

Professional football star Michael Vick pleaded guilty in 2007 to a federal felony conspiracy charge for operating an interstate dog fighting business known as Bad Newz Kennels. Vick served almost two years in prison, then resumed his football career.

Neglect. Neglect of an animal, whether intentional or negligent, is another form of cruelty that all states prohibit. For example, a pet owner with ill, flea-ridden, and starving pets would be guilty of animal neglect, as would a dog owner who leaves his pet locked in his car, dehydrated and near death.

Endangered Species. Laws in many states seek to protect endangered species around the world by forbidding their importation or use for commercial purposes. The laws typically extend to body parts as well as to the animals themselves.

Real-Life Illustration

In 2010, the owners of The Hump restaurant in Santa Monica, California, pleaded guilty to violating the federal endangered species act for importing and serving the meat of an endangered species of whale to patrons.

Legal Authority Examples

South Carolina: Knowingly inflicting unnecessary pain or suffering on any animal constitutes a misdemeanor.

Wisconsin: Animal cruelty consists of causing unnecessary and excessive pain or suffering or unjustifiable injury or death to any living creature except a human being. Mistreatment or neglect of any animal, whether it belongs to the offender or to someone else, is a misdemeanor that can result in a fine, incarceration, and forfeiture of an animal. Intentionally mutilating, disfiguring, or killing any animal is a felony. Animal cruelty laws do not prohibit bona fide experiments carried on for scientific research or normal and accepted veterinary practices.

Related terms: *mens rea*; sentencing (punishment options).

appeals

The typical hierarchy of state courts consists of trial courts over which single judges preside; intermediate appellate courts made up of three-judge panels; and highest ("supreme") courts consisting of seven or nine justices. The same hierarchy exists in state and federal courts, with the highest federal court being the United States Supreme Court. Convicted defendants have a right to review by an intermediate appellate court, provided that they comply with statutory time limits for requesting an appeal. Defendants file written "briefs" (which often are far from brief) identifying claimed legal errors that took place during a trial and arguing why those errors warrant reversal of a conviction or at least reduction of a sentence. After the government submits a responding brief, an appellate court may hear oral argument from both sides. Weeks and sometimes months later, the appellate court issues a written decision upholding or reversing a conviction.

If a state's intermediate appellate court upholds a conviction, a defendant can appeal to the state's highest court and then to the U.S. Supreme Court. However, the higher appellate courts (the "supreme" courts) have *discretionary* jurisdiction, which means that they can decide not to review a case.

Finality of Acquittals. The government cannot appeal verdicts of acquittal, whether the trial was to a judge or jury. However, if a trial judge rules that a convicted defendant is entitled to a new trial, the government can appeal the new trial order.

> EXAMPLE: A jury convicts Sampson of murder. The judge grants Sampson's motion for a new trial after deciding that a jury instruction was legally improper. The government can appeal the new trial order. If the appellate court decides that the jury instruction was proper, the appellate court can set aside the new trial order and reinstate the conviction.

Raise It or Lose It. Appellate courts typically review only legal claims that defendants make at trial. If defendants neglect to make legal claims at trial, they usually *waive* those claims. For example, if a defendant asks an appellate court to reverse a conviction because of the prosecutor's unfair argument, the court will consider the point only if the defendant objected to the argument during the trial.

It's a Fact. Appellate courts limit review to claimed legal errors. They do not reweigh trial evidence or substitute their factual beliefs for those of trial judges and jurors.

> **EXAMPLE:** Des is convicted of joyriding based largely on Maggie's testimony. Des's lawyer offered evidence that Maggie had previously been convicted of perjury and is visually impaired. Des asks the appellate court to reverse the conviction on the ground that the jury had no business believing Maggie's testimony. Because the claim asks the judges to reevaluate the evidence, the appellate court will not consider this claim.

No Harm, No Foul. Not every error at trial merits reversal. Defendants are entitled to a fair trial, not an error-free trial. (*Lutwak v. U.S.,* U.S. Sup. Ct. (1953).) Appellate courts do not generally reverse convictions unless a legal error was likely to have contributed to a guilty verdict. Errors that do not contribute to a guilty verdict are considered "harmless." However, errors involving constitutional rights require reversal unless appellate courts determine that they were harmless beyond a reasonable doubt.

> **EXAMPLE:** Arker is convicted of animal cruelty. The appellate court decides that the trial judge erroneously forbade Arker from representing himself. The right of self-representation is so fundamental that this erroneous denial results in automatic reversal of the conviction.

Sentencing. Even when upholding convictions, appellate courts can review sentences. For example, an appellate court might uphold a conviction but reduce the sentence by 30 days if the trial judge neglected to credit the defendant with the month that the defendant spent in jail prior to trial.

Guilty Pleas. Defendants who plead guilty can appeal. But the grounds for appeal are generally very limited. For example, a legal resident can appeal and his conviction will be set aside if his attorney failed to advise him of the effect of a guilty plea on his immigration status. (*Padilla v. Kentucky*, U.S. Sup. Ct. (2010).)

 Legal Authority Examples

Washington: Counsel shall be provided at state expense to an adult offender convicted of a crime who files an appeal as a matter of right.

California: A notice of appeal must be filed within 60 days following sentencing or a final order.

Related terms: Confrontation Clause; defense counsel (defense attorney); right to counsel; hearsay; motion; plea bargaining; sentencing (punishment options).

arraignment

Arraignments are generally short, routine courtroom hearings in which judges formally advise defendants of the criminal charges they face and defendants enter a plea to those charges (typically, guilty or not guilty). Judges may also set bail at an arraignment, or consider a prosecutor's or defendant's request to revise the amount of previously set bail. At an arraignment a prosecutor may also provide a defendant's lawyer with a copy of the written document outlining the charges, which might be called an "information," an "indictment," or a "complaint" according to the custom of a jurisdiction and the process leading to the issuance of charges. A prosecutor may also deliver a copy of the police report to a defendant at arraignment. Defendants have a right to be represented by counsel at arraignment, either privately retained or court-appointed.

Prearraignment Courtroom Hearings. For many defendants, an arraignment is their first appearance in a courtroom following their arrest. But before an arraignment takes place, defendants who remain in jail for as long as 48 hours following arrest may first be taken to court for a bail hearing. Magistrates rather than judges often preside over bail hearings. Defendants who are arrested without a warrant may also be taken to court prior to arraignment for a "*Gerstein* hearing," so-called because its origin is in the 1975 U.S. Supreme Court case of *Gerstein v. Pugh*, in which the Supreme Court held that a defendant cannot be detained prior to trial, unless a court makes a timely court determination of probable cause (concluding it's more likely than not that the defendant committed the crime). In a *Gerstein* hearing, a judge or magistrate determines whether probable cause for an arrest existed.

Courtroom or Train Station? Trial courtrooms are typically sedate, often inhabited only by courtroom personnel, the parties to a case, their lawyers, and a witness. Arraignment courts by contrast can be loud and hectic, not unlike a busy train station. Many cases may be scheduled for arraignment on the same day and the judge must work through all of them. Parties and lawyers filter in and out of the courtroom, often conferring on strategy or scheduling matters. Defendants who bailed out of jail prior to arraignment enter the courtroom through a public entrance, while "custodies" have their own entrance that connects a lockup to the courtroom.

The Next Steps. While the primary business of arraignments is to charge defendants with crimes and record their pleas, arraignments are often a time when prosecutors and defense lawyers establish a roadmap for the proceedings to come. For example they may:

- arrange for the defendant to examine prosecution evidence and if appropriate have it tested by a forensic expert selected by the defense
- set a court date for a preliminary hearing if one will take place, or
- set a date for trial if no preliminary hearing will take place.

No Double Jeopardy. Judges occasionally dismiss charges at an arraignment. In the unusual situations when this occurs, typically the reason has nothing to do with a defendant's guilt or innocence.

Instead, dismissal is based on a technical prosecution error. Dismissal of a case at arraignment is rarely a final victory for a defendant because at arraignment, a defendant is not "in jeopardy" for purposes of the Double Jeopardy clause—a Constitutional provision that prohibits the government from prosecuting individuals for the same crime on more than one occasion. Typically the prosecution manages to get its ducks in order later and refile the charges.

> EXAMPLE: Ed is in custody after having been arrested for assault. Ed bails out, and two weeks later appears in court to be arraigned. When Ed's case is called, the prosecutor announces that she is not prepared to go forward with the arraignment because the charging document was prepared incorrectly. In response to the prosecutor's request for a week's continuance (postponement) of the arraignment so that Ed can be properly charged with assault, Ed objects and asks for the case to be dismissed. Even if the judge grants Ed's request, Ed can still be prosecuted for assault. Ed can be rearrested on the same assault charge, and he might even have to pay the cost of a new bail bond. Ed should probably agree to the continuance.

Pleading Guilty at Arraignment. Though arraignments take place at or near the outset of criminal proceedings, plea bargaining often occurs at that time. Using an arraignment as a chance to conclude a case quickly with a plea bargain is often in everyone's best interests. Quick disposition of cases with defendants pleading guilty or *nolo contendere* (a plea of "no contest"), eases the burden of heavy caseloads on judges and prosecutors, and allows them to focus on the most complex and serious cases. Quick disposition can also reduce anxiety for defendants and victims and help them move forward with their lives. Thus, prosecutorial offices may try to motivate defendants to plead guilty by establishing a policy of offering "good deals" at arraignment. Defendants and their attorneys who aren't sure whether it makes sense to plead guilty so quickly may ask to continue an arraignment so that they can investigate the facts and consider options without losing the opportunity to plead guilty at arraignment.

Bail Challenges. Even if bail has been set at an earlier court hearing, arraignment affords defendants an additional opportunity to ask for lower bail. An argument for lowered bail is more likely to succeed if a defendant can support the request with information about changed circumstances that couldn't have been presented earlier, such as a local employer's willingness to give a defendant a job once the defendant is released on bail.

 Legal Authority Examples

Illinois: Before any person is tried for the commission of an offense he shall be called into open court, informed of the charge against him, and called upon to plead thereto. If the defendant so requests the formal charge shall be read to him before he is required to plead ... Every person charged with an offense shall be allowed counsel before pleading to the charge. If the defendant desires counsel and has been unable to obtain same before arraignment the court shall recess court or continue the cause for a reasonable time to permit defendant to obtain counsel and consult with him before pleading to the charge ... When called upon to plead at arraignment the defendant shall be furnished with a copy of the charge and shall plead guilty, guilty but mentally ill, or not guilty. If the defendant stands mute a plea of not guilty shall be entered for him and the trial shall proceed on such plea.

Related terms: plea bargaining; bail; double jeopardy; jurisdiction; no contest (*nolo contendere*) plea.

arrests

As depicted in countless films and TV shows, the words, "You're under arrest," put an end to a suspect's freedom and set in motion a panoply of procedures and rights, such as a police officer's power to conduct a search and a suspect's right to counsel.

A

Citations. Not all police officer detentions of individuals constitute arrests. Police officers often detain individuals temporarily, just long enough to issue citations. This practice is sometimes referred to as being "cited to court." By signing citations, individuals remain free in exchange for their agreement to post bail or appear in court on or before a certain date. While police officers typically issue citations in lieu of making arrests for motor vehicle violations and minor misdemeanors, states can constitutionally authorize arrests in these situations. (*Atwater v. Lago Vista*, U.S. Sup. Ct. (2001).) A citation does not trigger the police officer's ability to search the individual as if an arrest had occurred.

> EXAMPLE: A police officer breaks up a minor scuffle outside a sports arena. The officer issues a citation to one of the combatants, and then proceeds to search the cited combatant. The search is illegal because the combatant was cited rather than arrested. Therefore, the officer cannot justify the search as "incident to an arrest."

Arrest Warrants. At the time of American independence, a familiar occurrence (continued by some countries today) was the sudden disappearance of individuals whose only crime was to incur the wrath of a ruling elite. The Fourth Amendment was a response to this practice. The amendment requires police officers to have probable cause—that is, to reasonably believe that a person committed a crime—in order to make arrests and obtain warrants from judges. Arrest warrants are court orders that police officers obtain by furnishing judges with written statements signed under oath that provide sufficient information to believe that a suspect committed a crime. However, police officers can often make arrests without obtaining an arrest warrant. Whether police officers need to obtain warrants before arresting suspects depends on a variety of factors.

Misdemeanors. Police officers can arrest suspects for misdemeanor offenses without a warrant, but only if an offense is committed in an officer's presence. Otherwise, police officers need to obtain warrants

A

in order to arrest suspects for misdemeanors. If a police officer does not observe the misdemeanor but is informed about it, the officer can detain the suspect long enough to obtain personal contact information, ask for witness statements, and obtain a warrant by putting the statement before a judge.

Felonies. The general rule is that arrests are valid so long as arresting officers have probable cause to believe that a suspect committed a crime that constitutes a felony. In these circumstances, police officers do not need a warrant to make a valid arrest. However, unless *exigent circumstances* (emergencies) exist, police officers generally need to obtain an arrest warrant in order to arrest suspects in their homes. A home for this purpose can be a Beverly Hills mansion, a homeless dweller's cardboard shack, or a temporary abode like a hotel room.

> **EXAMPLE:** An informant tells Officer Parker that suburban housewife Nancy is dealing large quantities of illegal drugs out of her house. The informant signs an affidavit under oath providing a firsthand account of the illegal operations, including two purchases of illegal drugs. Officer Parker also prepares an affidavit describing other occasions on which the informant's information has been accurate, as well as a stakeout during which the officer personally observed numerous individuals going in and out of Nancy's house in a way that is consistent with purchasing drugs. Officer Parker submits the affidavits to a judge and obtains a warrant authorizing Parker to arrest Nancy in her home.

Knock-Knock, Who's There? In police dramas, officers typically make house arrests by breaking down front doors with guns drawn. Luckily for all concerned, actual arrests are ordinarily far tamer. "Knock and Announce" laws aim to reduce the chance of violence by requiring police officers to knock on a suspect's door and announce that they are there to make an arrest before entering a dwelling. They have to allow a suspect a reasonable time to open the door before taking more aggressive action. But *exigent circumstances* can eliminate this polite requirement.

> **EXAMPLE:** In the earlier scenario, Officer Parker and others knock on Nancy's front door and order her to submit to arrest. They hear footsteps, smashing sounds, and two or three voices yelling loudly. The circumstances suggest danger to the officers and destruction of evidence. The exigent circumstances justify the officers' immediate entry of the residence with guns drawn.

Citizens' Arrests. Citizens (essentially everyone other than police officers) have the power to arrest suspects who commit crimes in their presence. Citizens who make arrests normally notify the police, who complete the arrest process. So long as they have probable cause, police officers are generally immune from civil lawsuits if they arrest suspected felons who turn out to be innocent. Citizens have to be more careful. If they arrest a person who turns out to be innocent, laws do not protect them from civil lawsuits. For example, if a security guard detains a suspect at a store and then calls the police and requests that the suspect be arrested, the suspect can sue the security guard if the arrest is a mistake.

 Legal Authority Examples

California: A peace officer may arrest a person without a warrant whenever the officer has probable cause to believe that the person has committed a public offense in the officer's presence, or has committed a felony, although not in the officer's presence.

Federal: A police officer can break into a house to execute a warrant if, after notice of his authority and purpose, he is refused admittance.

Washington State: An officer in whose presence a traffic infraction was committed may stop, detain, arrest, or issue a notice of traffic infraction to the driver who is believed to have committed the infraction.

Text of the Fourth Amendment: "The right of the people to be secure in their persons, houses, papers, and effects, against unreasonable searches and seizures, shall not be violated, and no Warrants shall issue, but upon probable cause, supported by Oath or affirmation, and particularly describing the place to be searched, and the persons or things to be seized."

Related terms: hierarchy of criminal offenses; probable cause; search and seizure; knock and announce rule (aka knock and notice).

arson

Arson consists of setting fire to someone else's property. In most arson situations, the property set on fire consists of a building, which might be a residence or a commercial structure. However, a wrongdoer who ignites a farmer's haystack or forest land that belongs to the public also commits arson. Statutes typically classify arson as a felony rather than a misdemeanor, because aside from the value of the property that is burned, fires always have the potential to cause injuries or death and to spread to other properties.

Burning One's Own Property. In some circumstances, setting fire to one's own property can constitute arson—the typical example, being a property owner seeking to obtain money under a fire insurance policy. In such cases, the property owner may be guilty of arson and insurance fraud.

Felony Murder Rule. Arson is an inherently dangerous crime. An arsonist who starts a fire that causes a person's death—even if the death was accidental—can be found guilty of murder. This is because of a rule (the "felony murder rule") that makes a perpetrator guilty of murder if someone is killed during the commission of a dangerous felony.

EXAMPLE: Seeking to protest government land-use policies that she disagrees with, Meg sets fire to grassland in a national park. The fire spreads far more than Meg anticipated and kills a homeless man who was sleeping several hundred yards away from where Meg started the fire. Though Meg was unaware of the man's presence and she certainly had no intention of killing him, Meg is guilty of murder because the man's death was the result of the inherently dangerous felony that she committed.

Reckless Arson. Although arson charges are typically based on intentionally set fires, reckless behavior that leads to the destruction of property by fire can also constitute arson. For example, campers who disregard signs prohibiting open fires by starting an open fire in vulnerable park land may be guilty of arson.

Arson or Accident? Even if an intentionally (but not recklessly) set fire destroys another's property, the person who set the fire is not an arsonist if the destruction was accidental. For example, according to myth the Great Chicago Fire of 1871 was started when Mrs. O'Leary's cow kicked over a lantern. Had the story been true, Mrs. O'Leary would not have been guilty of arson. She did not intend to start a fire and probably would not have been judged reckless for failing to prevent her cow from kicking over the lantern.

A problem that frequently arises is that a quick and easy determination of whether a fire is due to accident or arson is not always possible. If fire and police officials are uncertain about a fire's origin they may regard it as a "suspicious fire" and investigate. Whether arson charges result and can be proven in court may then depend largely on the work of forensic arson experts. Unfortunately, arson experts are no less fallible than other types of forensic experts.

 Real-Life Illustration

In 2003 an Ohio woman, Rose Roseborough, was convicted of murder and sentenced to life in prison based largely on the testimony of an arson expert that she had intentionally set the fire that resulted in the deaths of her 11-month-old twin daughters. The expert based his conclusion on evidence that Roseborough's face was covered with "large particle soot," which the expert testified is produced only in the very early stages of a fire. The expert's finding contradicted Roseborough's testimony that she ran into the house to try to rescue her daughters only after the fire was well underway. However, at a court hearing that was held some years after Roseborough began serving her sentence, new defense attorneys presented an expert who convinced the judge that the state's expert testimony had been false, and that large particle soot often forms at the end stages of a fire. In 2009, the judge set aside the conviction and ordered a new trial. (You can read the opinion, at www.truthinjustice.org/Roseborough.pdf.)

In the United States, fire officials regard many thousands of fires each year as suspicious and requiring further investigation by a forensic arson expert.

Vigilante Justice and the Use of Arson. Quite often, arson is a weapon of choice for those who resort to vigilante justice—when citizens punish others without resorting to the legal system. In recent years, for example, the use of arson has increased against registered sex offenders. A classic example of vigilante arson can be seen in the 1934 film, *Fury*. In that film, a stranger in a small town is mistaken for a kidnapper and put in jail. An angry mob burns the jail to the ground. The movie's courageous prosecutor charges about 20 of the town's leading citizens with murder. Made during the Great Depression, the film warned about the dangers of mob rule. (By the way, the film also includes a brilliant courtroom ruse, and an early example of newsreel footage used as evidence in a courtroom.)

 Legal Authority Examples

California: Arson consists of willfully setting fire to any structure, forest land, or property, or aiding in or arranging for the burning of a structure, forest land, or property. Arson is a felony that is punished more severely if a fire results in great bodily injury to a victim or if inhabited property is burned. The burning of one's own personal property is not arson unless it is done with the intent to defraud or results in injury to a person or damage to other property.

assault and battery

Assault consists of intentionally causing another person to fear being struck. The striking itself constitutes battery. Historically, assault and battery were separate crimes, but many modern statutes do not bother to distinguish between the two crimes, as evidenced by the fact that the phrase "assault and battery" has become as common as "salt and pepper." These statutes often refer to crimes of actual physical violence simply as assaults.

Traditionally, the definition of assault recognizes that placing another in fear of imminent bodily harm is itself an act deserving of punishment, whether or not a victim is physically harmed. If the victim is not placed in imminent fear of injury, there is no assault.

> EXAMPLE: Snider is walking down a city street carrying a golf club, a short distance behind Mantle. As Snider gets closer to Mantle, he lifts up the club and waves it menacingly in Mantle's direction. Mantle, however, is unaware of Snider's presence. Snider has not committed an assault because Mantle was unaware of Snider's presence and activity and was not afraid of Snider striking him. If, on the other hand, Snider strikes Mantle with the club, Snider would be punished only for the battery, the more serious offense.

Simple and Aggravated Assault. The criminal laws of many states classify assaults as either simple or aggravated, according to the gravity of the harm that occurs or is likely to occur if the assaulter follows through and harms the victim. Aggravated assault is a felony that may occur when an assault is committed with a weapon or with the intent to perpetrate a more serious crime. An assault may also be defined as aggravated if it occurs in the course of a relationship that the legal system regards as worthy of special protection—for example, a husband and wife, cohabitants of a home, or a caregiver and elderly patient. In the absence of factors such as these, the crime is simple assault, a misdemeanor.

Degrees of Assault. As an alternative to classifying assaults as either simple or aggravated, some states recognize the different levels of harm that assaults can cause by classifying them as first (most serious), second, or third degree assaults.

Sticks and Stones. Words alone don't give rise to assault charges. The general policy against punishing people for "naked threats" recognizes that people often make threats in the heat of the moment that they will never carry out—for example, a bar patron telling another, "I'd like to knock your block off." However, threatening to commit a crime that would seriously harm someone is its own offense, often classified as a "terrorist threat." An example is one person telling another, "I'm going to shoot you."

See terrorist threats.

 Legal Authority Examples

Mississippi: Assault consists of attempting to cause or purposely, knowingly or recklessly causing bodily injury to another; or of negligently causing bodily injury with a deadly weapon or other means likely to produce death or serious bodily harm; or of attempting by physical menace to put another in fear of imminent serious bodily harm. Conviction of assault is punishable by a fine of not more than $500 or by imprisonment in the county jail for not more than six months, or both.

Federal Law: Under Section 117 of Title 7 of the United States Code, domestic assault is "an assault committed by a current or former spouse, parent, child, or guardian of the victim, by a person with whom the victim shares a child in common, by a person who is cohabitating with or has cohabitated with the victim as a spouse, parent, child, or guardian, or by a person similarly situated to a spouse, parent, child, or guardian of the victim."

 RESOURCE
For information on how each state defines and punishes assault and battery crimes, go to www.nolo.com/assault.

Related terms: assault with a deadly weapon; domestic violence.

assault with a deadly weapon

An assault with a deadly weapon occurs when an attacker accomplishes a physical attack with a dangerous physical object. Since the use of a dangerous object creates a risk that a victim will suffer severe physical injury or death, all states classify assault with a deadly weapon as a felony. (Judges and lawyers often refer to the crime as "ADW," partly because specialized occupations often develop shorthand jargon and partly because mysterious abbreviations often seem more intimidating to legal outsiders.) "Deadly weapon" generally refers to a wide range of objects that can inflict mortal or great bodily harm—for example a car or a golf club.

"You Missed Me, You Missed Me!" The crime of assault, whether or not accomplished with the use of a deadly weapon, does not require that a victim suffer actual injury. Attackers commit an assault when they intentionally lead a victim to reasonably fear immediate physical harm. The use of a dangerous object rather than the infliction of actual harm elevates simple assault to assault with a deadly weapon.

Related terms: assault and battery.

attempts

Attempts consist of intentional (but unsuccessful) efforts to commit an act that constitutes a crime. People are guilty of attempt only if they take concrete steps toward committing a crime. Thinking about committing a crime, or even planning to commit a crime, does not constitute an attempt.

> EXAMPLE: Angry that too many urban dwellers are using a public bridge to access a remote wilderness area, Sam plans to blow up the bridge. Sam visits the website of the Acme Explosives Co. for information on how to build a bomb. At

this point Sam is not guilty of attempting to destroy public property because his actions do not amount to substantial concrete steps aimed at accomplishing his plan. However, if Sam assembles the explosives needed to build a bomb and makes a drawing of the bridge that indicates the best location for placement of the bomb, a judge or jury may legitimately convict Sam of attempting to destroy public property, because he took substantial concrete steps toward trying to accomplish his goal.

Justifying Punishment for Attempts. Convictions for attempting to commit a crime typically involve situations in which no actual harm ensues. For example, if we analogize to the Roadrunner cartoons, Wile E. Coyote may be convicted of attempted murder for trying to kill Roadrunner, even if Roadrunner suffered no harm and Roadrunner never knew that Wile E. was trying to blow him up. Nevertheless, it is fair to punish Wile E. because he acted with criminal *mens rea* (state of mind). Another justification for punishment is that Wile E. may act in accordance with the familiar saying, "If at first you don't succeed, try, try again." Thus, criminalizing attempts protects would-be victims against future harms.

To Dream the Impossible Dream (… and to Attempt the Impossible Crime). A person may attempt to commit a crime that cannot possibly be committed. A crime is said to be legally impossible when the acts, regardless of the harm an actor intended to cause, don't constitute a crime. A crime is factually impossible when a person tries to commit a crime but cannot complete it because of some unknown circumstance. Many states' laws reject this distinction and provide that neither kind of "impossibility" is a defense.

EXAMPLE: Believing that too many homeless people are destroying the property values in his neighborhood, Joe shoots a man lying in a doorway and covered with blankets. What Joe did not know was that the man had suffered a fatal heart attack and died earlier. Since dead people cannot be homicide victims, Joe cannot be convicted of killing the vagrant. But, in most jurisdictions he can be convicted of attempted murder even though it was legally impossible to murder the already-dead homeless man. If the man lying in the doorway had been alive at the time Joe pulled the trigger, but the gun didn't fire because Joe forgot to load it, murder would have been factually impossible—you can't shoot someone to death with an unloaded gun. Nevertheless, Joe would have been guilty of attempted murder in this situation too, because he tried to kill the man.

Abandonment. People can sometimes escape punishment for attempt by voluntarily and completely abandoning planned crimes. But if they have already caused too much harm or are coerced into abandonment, they remain guilty of attempt.

EXAMPLE: Fred breaks into a college dorm room and shoves his ex-girlfriend, Ethel, onto a sofa with the intent to rape her. When Ethel cries out Fred apologizes repeatedly and walks away from her. Fred has taken substantial concrete steps toward committing a rape. But if a judge or jury decides that Fred voluntary abandoned his planned course of action without substantially harming Ethel, Fred may be convicted of assault and battery but not attempted rape.

If however, Fred shoves Ethel onto the sofa, Ethel cries out, Fred strikes her in the face repeatedly, and then Fred runs away when he hears people running toward the door, Fred is probably guilty of attempted rape because he inflicted serious harm on Ethel before escaping. A second reason he may be guilty is that he did not voluntarily abandon his plan to rape Ethel. Instead, Fred fled to avoid capture.

Do the Crime, Maybe Do Half the Time. The punishment for attempts varies from one state to another and according to the crime that a person is convicted of attempting to commit. Some states prescribe the same punishment for attempts as for completed crimes, on the theory that assailants should be punished for the harms they intend to cause. Other states offer leniency for all attempt convictions, often providing for a maximum penalty for an attempt that is half the penalty for a completed crime.

 Legal Authority Examples

720 Illinois Compiled Statutes § 8-4: People commit an attempt when, with intent to commit a specific offense, they do any act that constitutes a substantial step toward the commission of that offense. The fine or imprisonment for an attempt may not exceed the maximum provided for the offense attempted. It is not a defense to a charge of attempt that because of a misapprehension of the circumstances it would have been impossible for the accused to commit the offense attempted.

Minnesota Statute 609.17: It is a defense to a charge of attempt that the crime was not committed because the accused desisted voluntarily and in good faith and abandoned the intention to commit the crime.

Related terms: defenses; impossibility; *mens rea*; sentencing (punishment options).

attorney-client privilege

Attorney-client privilege refers to the right of a client to prevent the disclosure or seizure of certain information provided to an attorney.

Background. The criminal justice system seeks to encourage clients to be open and honest with their lawyers. Thus, laws in all jurisdictions create a privilege for private communications between lawyers and clients. The privilege extends to all forms of communications, including oral, written, and electronic. Lawyers cannot disclose the contents of privileged communications without a client's consent.

> EXAMPLE: Bernie tells his lawyer in private, "They've got me. I did sucker all those people into investing in my phony scheme."

At Bernie's criminal fraud trial, the prosecutor cannot call the lawyer as a witness to testify to Bernie's admission of guilt. If Bernie's lawyer responds to Bernie's admission of guilt by telling Bernie, "The more money you can return to the defrauded investors, the lighter your sentence will be," that statement is also privileged because the privilege "works both ways."

Privacy Practice. The privilege exists only if circumstances indicate that a client reasonably intended a communication to be private. So, if in the previous example involving Bernie and his attorney, the statements are made in a crowded restaurant and can be overheard, the client gives up the right to claim that the statement was confidential. A prosecutor could call the waiter and the patrons as witnesses to testify to the client's admission of guilt. This "public" exception does not apply to surreptitious listening—for example, someone using listening devices or placing an ear to a closed door. In that situation the eavesdropper cannot testify as to what the client or attorney said.

Take It From Me. Clients cannot hide evidence or contraband from the police by giving it to their lawyers.

> **EXAMPLE:** In the film *The Letter* (1937), Leslie Crosbie is charged with murdering an intruder, she claims was trying to attack her. Prior to the killing, Leslie had written an incriminating letter threatening to kill the victim if he broke off their love affair. Leslie asks the lawyer to destroy the letter. The lawyer has to turn the letter over to the police.

Although attorneys cannot hide or destroy evidence, they do not have to disclose information about the existence of evidence provided in confidence. For example, if a client privately reveals to his lawyer the location where he hid the loot and the gun that he used in a robbery, the communication is privileged and the lawyer cannot tell the police where the loot and gun are. However, the lawyer cannot take the items or change their location.

Future Crimes. A lawyer's role is to protect a client's legal rights and interests, not to help the client commit crimes. The attorney-client privilege does not extend to a client's communications about future crimes.

> EXAMPLE: In the film *A Time to Kill* (1996), Carl Lee Hailey tells his lawyer Jake Brigance of his intent to kill the two men who brutally raped Carl Lee's daughter. The communication is not privileged. Jake has a duty to report Carl Lee's threat to the police. At Carl Lee's trial for murdering his daughter's attackers, the prosecutor could call Jake as a witness to testify to Carl Lee's statement.

 Legal Authority Examples

Massachusetts: The attorney-client privilege extends to all communications between attorneys and clients pertaining to advice about legal matters. The privilege applies not just to existing clients but also to prospective clients with whom a formal attorney-client relationship is never established.

California: The attorney-client privilege is inapplicable if a client seeks the services of a lawyer for help in committing a crime or fraud.

Related terms: defense counsel (defense attorney); privileges.

automobile searches

Police officers who have probable cause to believe that a car contains contraband or evidence of a crime rarely need to obtain a search warrant before searching it. Judges usually offer two justifications for warrantless car searches. One is that cars' mobility may result in the destruction of evidence before police officers can obtain a warrant. The other is that people should not expect much privacy when they use vehicles on public roads.

Traffic Ticket Stops. Most drivers know from experience that when issuing traffic tickets, police officers usually allow them to remain in their cars and proceed on their way. However, police officers can arrest drivers for violating traffic rules.

 Real-Life Illustration

Texas mother Gail Atwater drove with her two young children in the back seat of her pickup truck. Police officer Turek pulled her over for violating the state's seat belt law because neither Atwater nor her children were wearing seat belts. Instead of issuing a citation to Atwater, Turek arrested her and took her to jail. The U.S. Supreme Court upheld the validity of a state statute that authorized Turek to arrest Atwater for the traffic violation. (*Atwater v. Lago Vista*, U.S. Sup. Ct. (2001).)

Police officers concerned for their safety can also order drivers and other occupants to get out of a car while they issue a ticket. (*Virginia v. Moore,* U.S. Sup. Ct. (2009).) If officers reasonably believe that any of a car's occupants might be armed, officers can frisk them for weapons. However, traffic violations do not give police officers the right to search a car's occupants or the car itself unless the officers have probable cause to believe that they will find contraband or evidence of a crime.

> EXAMPLE: Officer Smith pulled over a car for speeding. Smith ordered the four youthful occupants out of the car and testified that as a matter of routine he patted them down for weapons. In the course of frisking one of the occupants Smith felt a hard object in his jacket pocket. Thinking it might be a weapon, Smith pulled out what turned out to be a packet of illegal drugs. The drugs are not admissible in evidence. The frisk was improper because Smith had no reasonable basis for suspecting that any of the car's occupants were armed. The outcome would be different if Officer Smith testified that he patted down the car's occupants for weapons because he had received a police

radio call informing him that four youths had just robbed a convenience store and escaped in a car similar to the one that Smith had pulled over. In that case, the frisk is valid because Smith had reason to believe that the occupants might be carrying weapons. If Smith felt an object in the jacket pocket of one of the occupants that he reasonably believed was a weapon but turned out to be a packet of illegal drugs, the drugs are admissible in evidence.

Probable Cause Stops. So long as they act based on probable cause, police officers can generally conduct warrantless searches of drivers, passengers, car interiors, and objects they find inside cars. Searches should be reasonably calculated to uncover only those items that police officers have probable cause to look for. Here are two examples:

- **Probable Cause: DUI Leads to Drug Search.** Officer Smith pulled Webster over in order to issue a ticket for a left-turn violation. Smith testified that he observed symptoms suggesting that Webster might be under the influence of alcohol or drugs. Smith also testified that he noticed when speaking to Webster that the car's glove box was open and that there was an empty beer can on the floor directly under it. Webster's poor performance of field sobriety tests confirmed Smith's suspicions of drunk driving. Smith placed Webster in his police vehicle and searched Webster's glove box. Smith found another beer can and packages of Oxycontin. The can and packages of Oxycontin are admissible in evidence because Smith had probable cause to search for evidence relating to a DUI offense.

- **No Probable Cause: Burglary Tools Don't Lead to Drug Search.** Officer Smith pulled Webster over in order to issue a ticket for a left-turn violation. Smith testified that he observed illegal burglary tools sticking out from under the passenger seat. Smith arrested Webster for possession of burglary tools, searched him and placed him in his police car. Smith then searched the car and trunk for other tools, and also searched a small leather coin purse lying on the rear seat. Inside the purse, Smith found illegal drugs. Smith's search of the purse is invalid and the drugs are not admissible in evidence. Smith lacked probable cause to search the purse because it could not reasonably hold burglary tools.

 Legal Authority Examples

Text of the Fourth Amendment. "The right of the people to be secure in their persons, houses, papers, and effects, against unreasonable searches and seizures, shall not be violated, and no Warrants shall issue, but upon probable cause, supported by Oath or affirmation, and particularly describing the place to be searched, and the persons or things to be seized."

Related terms: search and seizure; warrantless searches; stop and frisk.

B

bail

Bail consists of the money or other property that an arrested suspect posts with a court to obtain pretrial release from jail. Bailed-out suspects have to agree to appear in court when ordered to do so, and if they do not appear they are subject to rearrest and forfeit of the bail amount. Factors that judges typically consider when setting bail include the seriousness of a charged offense, a defendant's financial circumstances, the length of a defendant's rap sheet, and a defendant's ties to the community. Because defendants are presumed innocent until they plead guilty or are convicted at trial, the amount and conditions of bail should be no more than necessary to secure a defendant's attendance in court and protect the community.

> **EXAMPLE:** Chitra is charged with operating a fraudulent consumer credit scheme. The police report suggests that Chitra defrauded a dozen victims out of a total of about $50,000. At a bail hearing, the judge tells Chitra, "I don't want you scamming more victims between now and your trial, so I'm setting bail at $250,000." The judge improperly based the amount of bail on an assumption that Chitra is guilty rather than on an assessment of the amount of bail necessary to secure her attendance at future court hearings. Chitra could petition an appellate court for an order overturning the judge's decision.

Catch and Release. Following arrest, police officers may issue citations to suspects advising them to appear in court and release them without taking them to jail (known as being "cited to court"). For suspects who are arrested, taken to jail, and booked, many police stations have bail schedules for common crimes. Suspects or people on their behalf may post the amount indicated on a stationhouse bail schedule and secure their release immediately. However, stationhouse release can be costly. Judges often set lower bail than the amount set forth in a bail schedule, in part because formal charges may be less serious than the charges supporting an arrest. As a result, suspects often have to decide whether to pay a higher amount and bail out from jail quickly, or pay a lower amount but spend a night or two in jail waiting to go to court.

Bail Bonds. Suspects can bail out of jail either by posting the full amount of bail with the court or by purchasing a bail bond. Bail bond companies typically charge a fee of 10% of the bail amount, and may also require collateral, such as a lien on a house, to cover the amount of money the company will have to pay to the court if a bonded suspect fails to show up as ordered. Defendants who post cash bail and make all required appearances are paid back nearly in full once a case is over. Bail bond fees are not refundable. When bonded suspects fail to show up, bail bond companies may hire bounty hunters to locate suspects and return them to the police.

Get Out of Jail Free. Judges sometimes release defendants on their own recognizance (known as "O.R.") and these defendants do not have to post bail (or even leave a wristwatch or their library card with the judge). They simply agree to make all required court appearances. Factors that may influence the judge's decision are similar to those involved in setting bail: whether the defendant has a previous record, the stability of the defendant's home life and job, and the seriousness of the crime.

Conditions of Bail or O.R. Release. Judges typically impose conditions on defendants released on bail. Suspects who violate a condition are subject to rearrest. Common conditions of bail include cooperating in the collection of a DNA sample, checking in monthly with a probation officer, maintaining or actively seeking employment, and agreeing to warrantless searches. Conditions of release may also be offense-specific. For example, in the above example concerning Chitra, the judge might condition her release on her giving up her passport and not engaging in any consumer

B

credit transactions. And conditions of release for DUI suspects may include wearing an alcohol-monitoring ankle bracelet and refraining from the use of alcohol or drugs.

 Legal Authority Examples

Eighth Amendment to the U.S. Constitution: "Excessive bail shall not be required, nor excessive fines imposed, nor cruel and unusual punishments inflicted."

Excerpts From the Federal Bail Reform Act: Prior to trial, judges may release suspects on their own recognizance, may require the posting of bail, may impose conditions on released suspects, or may order them detained. A judge may not impose a financial condition that results in pretrial detention. If a judge concludes that no condition will reasonably assure a suspect's appearance as required and the safety of other people and the community, the judge may refuse to release the suspect on bail.

Related terms: sentencing (punishment options).

battery

See assault and battery.

best evidence rule

This rule provides that a party seeking to prove the contents of a document must ordinarily produce the original document in court; a copy or oral testimony to the contents will not suffice. For example, a prosecutor seeking to prove the contents of a defendant's signed confession must offer the written confession into evidence. At the same time, the prosecutor could ask a police officer to testify to a defendant's oral confession even if the defendant had later signed a written one because the prosecutor would not be seeking to prove the contents of the written confession. The best evidence rule is less important in an era of copy machines and computers; virtually any document is likely to qualify as an original or an equally admissible duplicate.

Related terms: evidence.

beyond a reasonable doubt

See burdens of proof.

blackmail

See extortion.

booking procedures

Booking is the process by which an arrested suspect's entry into a jail or police station holding cell (or "tank") is documented. (The phrase "Book 'em, Dano" was popularized by the TV show, *Hawaii Five-0*.) The term originates from the fact that police officers develop "books" that consist of information that is relevant to a current criminal charge and that may also be useful in connection with other offenses.

Booking In, Bailing Out. Many arrested suspects post "stationhouse bail" and bail out before making an initial court appearance. However, police officers do not release suspects on bail until after the booking process is complete.

Arrest-Related Information. Booking officers compile information relating to suspects and the crimes for which they were arrested. The information that is collected includes personal information (name, aliases, date of birth, Social Security number), physical characteristics (height, facial scars, eye and hair color), arrest and conviction history, witness statements, and lab test reports.

Booking has advantages for police officers. For example, booking includes photographing suspects and creating "mug shots." Because many crimes are committed by recidivists (reoffenders), police officers often show their mug shots to victims and witnesses for past and later crimes for purposes of identifying an arrested suspect as the culprit.

Fingerprints and Mug Shots. Obtaining fingerprints and taking mug shots are routine booking process activities. Forensic experts may rely on fingerprints to connect suspects to crimes. Fingerprints also go into a national database, which may allow police agencies across the country to connect suspects to other crimes. Mug shots document an arrested suspect's identity and physical condition, and often aid victims and witnesses to make identifications that are admissible in evidence to prove a culprit's identity at trial. Mug shots are also available for examination by victims and witnesses in connection with other crimes.

DNA Samples. Taking DNA samples from arrested suspects is a standard part of the booking process; federal and many state statutes authorize this practice. These statutes have withstood court challenges that they violate individuals' right to privacy and the principle that suspects are innocent until they have been proven guilty. In *Maryland v. King* (2013), the U.S. Supreme Court ruled that law enforcement may, without a warrant, take DNA samples from people arrested for serious crimes as part of the booking process. Police agencies enter DNA test results into a national registry called CODIS (Combined DNA Index System), which may aid in the identification of arrestees who have committed past offenses or who commit further offenses.

Searching Arrestees. To prevent items such as illegal drugs, alcohol, and weapons from being smuggled in, guards have the right to conduct random and warrantless strip searches of all arrestees who are booked into jail, even if an offense is minor and even if a suspect was arrested by mistake because of an expired warrant. (*Florence v. Burlington*, U.S. Sup. Ct. (2012).) However, an even more intrusive "body cavity" search is not a routine booking activity. Jailers may conduct body cavity searches only when they have reason to believe that a suspect has concealed contraband or a weapon in a body cavity. For example, suppose that police officers observed a suspect in possession of a balloon filled with a substance suspected to be illegal drugs immediately before making an arrest. If the officers cannot find the balloon after arresting the suspect, jailers

B

may conduct a body cavity search for the balloon when the suspect is brought to jail.

Personal Property Inventory. Booking officers confiscate and inventory suspects' personal property. When they are released, whenever that might be, suspects use the inventory to make sure that the police return to them all of their property (other than evidence and contraband, of course).

 Legal Authority Examples

California: Proposition 69, an initiative measure that voters approved in 2004, authorizes the collection of DNA samples from all convicted felons and from suspects arrested for specified crimes.

Michigan: A person arrested for a misdemeanor offense can be strip searched if reasonable cause exists to believe that the person is concealing a weapon, an illegal drug, or evidence of a crime. The search must take place in a private area and must be conducted by a person whose gender is the same as the arrestee's.

Related terms: arraignment; bail; DNA analysis; eyewitness identification; fingerprint analysis; forensic science.

border searches

See search and seizure.

burdens of proof

Burdens of proof prescribe the degree of certainty that judges or jurors must have in order to decide in favor of a party. The most familiar burden of proof is the prosecution's burden to prove defendants guilty beyond a reasonable doubt. Defendants who raise affirmative defenses typically have the burden of establishing those defenses by either a much less onerous burden of proof called preponderance of the evidence or a somewhat more onerous burden called clear and convincing evidence.

Beyond a Reasonable Doubt. Prosecutors' burden to prove defendants guilty beyond a reasonable doubt is the severest burden of proof that the law imposes on any party in any type of case. The language signifies society's commitment not to impose punishment unless the government convinces judges and jurors to a near certainty that a defendant committed a crime. A familiar maxim that expresses this commitment is that "it is better to set 100 guilty people free than to convict one innocent person." Prosecutors' burden of proof extends to each and every element of a crime.

For example, a common definition of murder is "the killing of one person by another with malice aforethought." This definition creates four elements that a prosecutor must prove beyond a reasonable doubt: (1) the killing of (2) a person (3) by another person (4) with malice aforethought (intent to kill).

Similarly, burglary consists of two elements: (1) illegal entry of a building (2) with intent to commit a serious crime. If jurors in a burglary case agree that a valuable artwork was stolen from inside the house but are not convinced beyond a reasonable doubt that the defendant's entry into the home was without the owner's permission, then the defendant is not guilty of burglary.

Affirmative Defenses. While prosecutors have the burden of proving the elements of a crime beyond a reasonable doubt, defendants who put forward affirmative defenses have the burden of proving them by either the preponderance of the evidence or clear and convincing evidence standard. What this means is that if a judge or jury believes that it is more likely than not that the defendant has proved an affirmative defense, or that the defendant has established an affirmative defense by clear and convincing evidence, then the defendant is not guilty. While rules can vary from one state to another, common affirmative defenses defendants must prove include insanity, alibi, self-defense, mistake of fact, and intoxication. When a case is charged after the statute of limitations has passed, defendants may raise this, too, as an affirmative defense.

Real-Life Illustration

John Hinckley, Jr., was charged with attempted murder for trying to assassinate President Ronald Reagan in 1981. Hinckley was found not guilty by reason of insanity. At the time of the trial, federal law required the government to prove beyond a reasonable doubt that Hinckley was sane. Public outrage over the verdict led Congress to change the law such that now in a federal trial a defendant who pleads not guilty by reason of insanity has the burden of proving insanity by clear and convincing evidence.

Foundational Burdens. In a wide variety of situations, evidence is admissible at trial only if a proper foundation exists. Even if the prosecution has the burden of proving the foundation, the burden is the lower preponderance-of-the-evidence burden, not the higher beyond-a-reasonable-doubt standard. The latter burden applies only to the elements of crimes. So for example, in order for a prosecutor to admit a statement as an exception to the hearsay rule, the prosecutor may have to establish a foundation of evidence demonstrating that the statement was made while the conspiracy was ongoing. The prosecution has the burden of proving that foundation by a preponderance of the evidence.

 Legal Authority Examples

Texas: It is an affirmative defense to prosecution that the actor engaged in the proscribed conduct because he was compelled to do so by threat of imminent death or serious bodily injury to himself or another. The defendant must prove the affirmative defense by a preponderance of evidence.

Related terms: affirmative defense; self-defense; intoxication defense; insanity; statute of limitations.

burglary

Burglary consists of making an unauthorized entry into a building with the intent to commit a crime. Typically, the crime that a burglar intends to commit is a theft, but any crime will satisfy the definition, whether the crime is a felony or a misdemeanor. Burglary generally constitutes a felony. However, when a burglary entails little risk of personal harm to a victim and involves only a small amount of property, burglary may be punished as a misdemeanor. It is not necessary to use force to commit a burglary—for example, unauthorized entry through an open window is sufficient. In addition, it is not essential that the burglar fully "enter" the building—for example, reaching a hand through an open window will suffice.

It is essential, however, that the burglar intend to commit a crime at the time of entry. For example, an art student who breaks into a museum simply to look at paintings is not committing burglary. But breaking into a building in order to vandalize it constitutes burglary.

Caught in the Act. Unauthorized entry into a building plus intent to commit a crime equals burglary, even if the culprit's effort to commit the crime is foiled. So if a would-be thief breaks into a house but at the sound of a burglar alarm runs off without stealing anything, a burglary has occurred.

Degrees of Burglary. Statutes often identify degrees of burglary, punishing burglars more harshly according to the risk that a burglary will result in personal harm to a victim. For example, burglarizing a residence is more serious than burglarizing a shed that is not connected to the residence, because there is more risk that a burglar will encounter a victim inside a house than inside a disconnected shed. For the same reason, the nighttime burglary of a residence may result in a harsher sentence than a daytime burglary of the same residence because of the greater probability that occupants will be inside the residence at night.

Burglary Compared to Similar Crimes. Burglary is often confused with robbery, in that a person who returns home to find that a

B

thief broke into the house and stole property might immediately yell out, "I was robbed." However, the generally more serious crime of robbery requires that a culprit steal property from a victim personally, by force and fear. Somehow, "I was burgled" just doesn't have the same ring to it.

Burglary is also different than other kinds of theft in that it traditionally requires entry into a building, not a car, van, or boat. So, a thief who breaks into a car and steals the radio may be guilty of theft, but not necessarily burglary. A crime that prosecutors typically treat as misdemeanor petty theft can constitute burglary if the prosecutor can prove that the thief entered a building for the purpose of stealing a small amount of property.

> **EXAMPLE:** A clothing store security guard stops a customer just outside the store. Inside the customer's large shopping bag the security guard finds three shirts stolen from the store with the price tags still on them; the shirts' total value is less than $150. Inside the bag the guard also finds various items of merchandise stolen from two nearby stores the same day, with a total value of about $100. In this circumstance the customer might be charged with and convicted of a form of burglary often called commercial burglary. The presence of merchandise stolen from other stores in the customer's large shopping bag supports an inference that the customer entered the clothing store for the purpose of stealing clothing. Though the customer did not make a forced entry into the store, the entry is unauthorized if the customer enters with the intent to steal. However, when the value of stolen items is relatively low, prosecutors typically charge thieves with misdemeanor petty theft rather than with felony burglary.

 **Legal Authority Examples**

Chapter 266 Sections 14 and 15 of the penal laws of Massachusetts provide as follows:

Burglary; armed; assault on occupants; weapons; punishment. Whoever breaks and enters a dwelling house in the night time, with intent to commit a felony, or whoever, after having entered with such intent, breaks such dwelling house in the night time, any person being then lawfully therein, and the offender being armed with a dangerous weapon at the time of such breaking or entry, or so arming himself in such house, or making an actual assault on a person lawfully therein, shall be punished by imprisonment in the state prison for life or for any term of not less than ten years.

Whoever commits any offense described in this section while armed with a firearm, rifle, shotgun, machine gun or assault weapon shall be punished by imprisonment in the state prison for life or for any term of years, but not less than 15 years. Whoever commits a subsequent such offense shall be punished by imprisonment in the state prison for life or for any term of years, but not less than 20 years. The sentence imposed upon a person who, after being convicted of any offense mentioned in this section, commits the like offense, or any other of the offenses therein mentioned, shall not be suspended, nor shall he be placed on probation.

Burglary; unarmed. Whoever breaks and enters a dwelling house in the night time, with the intent mentioned in the preceding section, or, having entered with such intent, breaks such dwelling house in the night time, the offender not being armed, nor arming himself in such house, with a dangerous weapon, nor making an assault upon a person lawfully therein, shall be punished by imprisonment in the state prison for not more than 20 years and, if he shall have been previously convicted of any crime named in this or the preceding section, for not less than five years.

Related terms: larceny; robbery.

capital punishment (capital crime)

See death penalty.

carjacking

See robbery.

chain of custody

A chain of custody consists of foundational evidence—evidence that provides enough proof for judges to admit evidence into the trial record—tracing the whereabouts of a substance or other tangible item following its removal from a crime scene. A chain's links depict what happened to an item of evidence from the time it was taken from a crime scene until it reached a courtroom. For example, evidence may move from a suspect to an arresting officer to a crime scene investigator to an evidence room and finally to the court room. Chain of custody evidence typically assures judges and juries that police officers, lab technicians, and others handled tangible evidence properly during any testing that followed its removal from a crime scene.

"How Do You Know ... ?" During chain of custody foundational questioning, witnesses generally explain how and when they acquired evidence and what they did with it. Attorneys typically ask "how do you know" questions to demonstrate the basis for the testimony.

EXAMPLE: Officer Holmes arrests Smokey for possession of opium. In court, the prosecution's chain-of-custody evidence traces the path of the packet from Officer Holmes to the crime

C

testing lab to the courtroom. Officer Holmes testifies that the packet that the prosecutor hands him is the packet that he found in Smokey's pocket. The prosecutor asks, "Officer Holmes, how do you know this is the same packet that you took from Smokey's pocket?" Holmes replies, "Because I attached an evidence tag to the packet and initialed the tag. The tag with my initials on it is still on the packet."

Any Changes? Many tangible items of evidence do not need to be tested and are not handed back and forth between the time they are removed from a crime scene and the time they are bought to court. Nevertheless, a chain of custody foundation typically establishes that a tangible item of evidence is in substantially the same condition at the time of trial as it was when it was removed from the crime scene.

Foundational Standard. Even prosecutors do not have to prove chain of custody foundations beyond a reasonable doubt. Foundational evidence is sufficient so long as a prosecutor or a defendant proves by a preponderance of the evidence that a tangible item offered into evidence at trial is the one that was removed from a crime scene, that if testing occurred the correct item was tested, and that the item has not undergone substantial changes.

EXAMPLE: In a DUI prosecution, Officer Holmes identifies a partially filled bottle of vodka as the one that he removed from the passenger seat of the defendant's car. Officer Holmes admits that he neglected to attach an evidence tag to the bottle of vodka before placing it in the police evidence locker. Holmes also admits that he saw two other partially filled bottles of vodka in the evidence locker when he removed the bottle to bring to court for trial. However, Holmes testifies that he's confident that he brought the correct bottle to court. The foundation is adequate so long as the judge or jury is convinced by a preponderance of the evidence that the bottle in the courtroom is the one that Holmes removed from the defendant's car.

Legal Authority Examples

Federal Rule of Evidence 104(b): When the relevancy of evidence depends upon the fulfillment of a condition of fact, the court shall admit it upon the introduction of evidence sufficient to support a finding of the fulfillment of the condition.

Related terms: DNA analysis; evidence; best evidence rule; forensic science.

character evidence

Character evidence refers to information suggesting that people's activities are a product of their moral or ethical nature. The idea is that if we want to know whether a defendant committed a crime, we might want to find out whether that person has a propensity to engage in that type of illegal activity. In general, the prosecution cannot offer evidence of a defendant's character at trial—reflecting a tenet of the U.S. criminal justice system that the law aims to "judge the act and not the actor." In other words, people should be punished for doing bad things, not for being bad people.

> EXAMPLE: Clyde is charged with bank robbery. The prosecutor cannot try to convince the jury that Clyde committed the charged robbery by offering evidence of other bank robberies that Clyde committed. Nor can the prosecutor call a witness to testify to an opinion along the lines of, "I've known Clyde for years, and I can tell you he's nasty and violent." Nor can the prosecutor call a witness to testify that Clyde has a reputation for breaking the law. Each type of testimony is character evidence that prosecutors cannot, as a general rule, offer to prove a defendants' guilt.

The discussion below briefly highlights the most important exceptions to this rule. However, beware that character evidence

C

rules are complex, riddled with exceptions, and different from state to state. Thus, this discussion serves only as a general guide.

The Mercy Rule. The so-called Mercy Rule allows defendants charged with crimes to offer evidence of good character that is inconsistent with their committing a charged crime. The idea is that a lifetime of good deeds may be a vital refuge for an innocent person caught in a web of damning but misleading circumstantial evidence. A more cynical view is that the rule developed in Merry Old England so that aristocratic miscreants charged with crimes could cow juries into not-guilty verdicts by bringing powerful friends to court to testify to their nobility.

 Real-Life Illustration

O.J. Simpson was charged with brutally murdering his ex-wife Nicole Brown Simpson and her companion Ron Goldman in a 1995 trial that glued people around the world to their TV sets. During his opening statement, defense attorney Johnny Cochran promised the jurors that the defense would call a psychologist as an expert witness to testify that Simpson did not have the character traits of an abusive spouse. The psychologist never testified, but if she had, her testimony would have been admissible under the Mercy Rule.

Don't Blame Me—He Started It! A second character evidence option for defendants charged with crimes is to attack a victim's character. This situation typically comes into play when a defendant charged with a violent crime claims to have acted in self-defense. For example, a defendant charged with assault may claim self-defense and call a character witness to testify that the victim has a propensity for starting fights.

Impeachment; Whom Do You Trust? Defense and prosecution witnesses typically offer conflicting accounts of the events leading to criminal charges. To help judges and jurors decide whom to believe, character evidence rules allow parties to impeach (attack the credibility of) adverse witnesses with evidence of their propensity to tell lies. A judge may also allow parties to offer evidence of adverse witnesses' felony convictions, and to cross-examine adverse witnesses about dishonest actions even if the acts did not give rise to criminal charges.

Special Rules for Sexual Assault Cases. All states have enacted specialized character evidence rules that increase the likelihood of obtaining convictions in prosecutions for rape and other forms of sexual assault. In some states, these rules have been extended to prosecutions for elder abuse and domestic violence. These special rules allow prosecutors to offer evidence that defendants have committed other similar acts in the past. The judge can admit evidence of the other acts regardless of whether they resulted in criminal charges, and indeed even if the defendant was tried for the other acts and acquitted

 Real-Life Illustration

Michael Jackson was charged with sexually molesting a 13-year-old boy at his Neverland Ranch. During the 2005 trial, the prosecutor called five men who testified that Jackson had also molested them when they were teenagers. Despite the plethora of negative character evidence, the jury found Jackson not guilty.

Although character evidence rules generally allow defendants charged with crimes to attack a victim's character, rape shield laws bar defendants from offering evidence that victim had a propensity to consent to sexual activity.

 Legal Authority Examples

Federal: Federal Rule of Evidence 404 provides that a defendant can defend against a criminal charge by offering evidence of the defendant's good character and/or a victim's bad character. Once a defendant offers such evidence, a prosecutor can respond by offering evidence of a defendant's

C

bad character and a victim's good character. Rule 405 provides that testimony to character may consist either of reputation or of an opinion, but specific good or bad deeds may be referred to only during cross-examination.

Federal: Federal Rule of Evidence 608 provides that a party can attack an adverse witness's credibility with reputation or opinion testimony concerning the witness's bad character for truth-telling. The judge may also allow a party to cross-examine an adverse witness concerning specific acts of untruthfulness. Rule 609 provides that a party may impeach an adverse witness with evidence of a prior felony conviction.

Federal: Federal Rule of Evidence 413 provides that in a criminal case in which the defendant is accused of sexual assault, evidence of the defendant's commission of other sexual assaults is admissible. Rule 414 extends this rule to child molestation cases.

Related terms: rape shield laws; self-defense.

checkpoints

See search and seizure.

child abuse and neglect

Child abuse laws target mistreatment of minors. Child abuse crimes include physical and emotional (psychological) mistreatment of minors as well as failure to provide adequate care. Crimes of child abuse and neglect may be either misdemeanors or felonies. Child abuse and neglect can result in a parent's or custodian's loss of custody as well as criminal punishment. Adults who have a statutory responsibility to report suspected child abuse but fail to do so may also be charged with the crime of failure to report. Failure to report is typically a misdemeanor punishable by a fine rather than incarceration. For example, if a teacher suspects that a child is being abused at home, because the child repeatedly comes to school with bruises and behaves lethargically, the teacher may be guilty of neglect for failing to report the suspected abuse.

Cultural Norms. Child rearing practices vary greatly among cultures. Treatment of children that in some countries is acceptable may constitute abuse in the United States. U.S. courts do not accept a "cultural defense" to child abuse—that is, no matter what their cultural background, parents and caregivers who do not conform their treatment of children to U.S. laws are subject to conviction and punishment. However, depending on the circumstances, counseling may occur before authorities consider criminal charges.

Physical Abuse. In the U.S., parents and caregivers generally have the right to raise children as they see fit. Laws do not punish moderate spanking or other forms of mild physical control and discipline. Illegal abuse occurs when physical discipline causes injury. Judges and jurors often have to decide where to draw the line between reasonable discipline and illegal abuse.

> EXAMPLE: Watching as his 12-year-old son Butch teases and is about to hit a younger boy on a playground, Foote rushes over and forcefully yanks Butch away hard enough to cause him to fall to the ground. Butch is left with a bruised arm and knee lacerations. If Foote is prosecuted for child abuse, a judge or jury would have to consider the seriousness of Butch's injuries and the circumstances leading up to Foote's behavior to decide whether Foote is guilty. If after the playground incident Butch has nightly nightmares and becomes inattentive and withdrawn at school, those psychological symptoms might also constitute injuries that a judge or jury can consider when deciding whether Foote is guilty of child abuse.

Emotional Abuse. While physical abuse may consist of a single act, emotional (or psychological) abuse generally consists of a pattern of criticism, threats, or other behavior that impairs a child's emotional development. Emotional abuse does not leave visible marks and therefore is more difficult to diagnose and prosecute than physical abuse. An example of potential emotional abuse is constant ridiculing of a child that causes severe depression and feelings of lack of self-worth.

Neglect. Criminal neglect occurs when parents and caregivers have the means but fail to provide children with the basic necessities of life. For example, parents' actions constitute criminal neglect if the parents let their children stay home from school, ignoring warnings from school officials and the police to send the children to school or make alternate arrangements.

Contributing to the Delinquency of a Minor. The crime of contributing to a minor's delinquency occurs when adults induce or encourage children to violate the law. For example, a parent who repeatedly uses heroin in front of his teenage children and encourages them to use it, is guilty of contributing to a minor's delinquency regardless of whether the children use heroin.

Legal Authority Examples

Colorado: Child abuse includes injuring a child's life or health, and engaging in a continued pattern of conduct that results in malnourishment, lack of proper medical care, cruel punishment, mistreatment, or an accumulation of injuries that ultimately results in a child's death or serious bodily injury. Intentional abuse is a felony; criminal negligence resulting in serious injury to a child is a misdemeanor.

Connecticut: Child abuse includes malnourishment, emotional maltreatment, and cruel punishment. Intentional abuse by a parent or caregiver is punishable by a fine of up to $5,000 and imprisonment for up to five years or both.

Colorado: Inducing, aiding, or encouraging a person under age 18 to violate a law or a court order is a felony.

California: Child sexual assault includes the intentional touching of the genitals or intimate parts or the clothing covering them, of a child, or of the perpetrator by a child, for purposes of sexual arousal or gratification, unless done in the course of normal caretaker responsibilities, demonstrations of affection for the child, or for a valid medical purpose. Child sexual assault also includes the intentional masturbation of the perpetrator's genitals in the presence of a child.

Child sexual exploitation includes depicting a minor engaged in obscene acts, and aiding or permitting a child to engage in prostitution, a live performance involving obscene sexual conduct, or to be used as a model for an obscene film or photograph.

> RESOURCE
> **For information on how each state defines and punishes child enticement, a term that covers several offenses against minors, go to www.nolo.com/childenticement.**

Related terms: child sexual abuse; child pornography; rape.

child pornography

Child pornography laws make it illegal to visually depict children under the age of 18 engaged in sexually explicit conduct. While sexual intercourse between two minors constitutes an obvious form of illegal sexually explicit conduct, an image of a single naked child can also constitute child pornography. Illegal visual images include photos, films, videotapes, and electronic data. Typical family photos—for example, a mother's photo of her five-year-old daughter washing her hair in the bathtub—do not violate child pornography laws because such photos do not depict explicit sexual conduct. Child pornography is a felony.

A Chain of Illegality. Child pornography involves a variety of processes for creating and distributing sexually explicit images of children. These processes typically begin with the solicitation of minors and end with individuals' possession of sexually explicit images. Child pornography laws usually seek to criminalize each link in the chain.

C

EXAMPLE: In an attempt to convince a 12-year-old girl that sexual behavior by children is normal and acceptable, a producer of child pornography shows the girl photos of other girls engaged in sexually explicit conduct. The producer's conduct violates child pornography laws. The producer also violates child pornography laws if he pays the father of a 14-year-old boy for allowing the boy to pose for sexually explicit photographs. (The father is also guilty.)

The chain of child pornography violations also extends to those who view, store, and transmit sexually explicit images of children. So, for example, storing an image on a hard drive and transmitting it by email both constitute violations.

Virtual Images. Many experts argue that a harm of child pornography is that looking at sexually explicit images of children encourages pedophiles to engage in child sexual abuse. This risk led Congress to pass a law that made it illegal to create computer-generated images of "virtual children" engaged in sexually explicit conduct, and to pass off images of adults engaged in sexually explicit conduct as depicting children. However, such laws are unconstitutional under the First Amendment because they criminalize activities that constitute legitimate forms of speech. (*Ashcroft v. Free Speech Coalition*, U.S. Sup. Ct. (2002).) For example, filmed versions of the Nabokov novel *Lolita* depict romantic and sexual activities between an adult male and the teenage girl who seduces him, but an adult actress plays the part of the teenage seducer. These films do not violate child pornography laws.

Pandering. Offering to provide others with images of children engaged in sexually explicit conduct violates child pornography laws even if no payment is involved and no transmission of images actually occurs. (*U.S. v. Williams*, U.S. Sup. Ct. (2008).) So, for example, a participant in an Internet chat room who offers to provide others with sexually explicit electronic images of young girls in exchange for similar images is guilty of illegal pandering.

No Kidding. Child pornography statutes criminalize activities and images that are otherwise lawful if adults, not children, are involved. Thus, people who reasonably believe that they are working with or viewing images of adults who are in fact children can defend against charges by trying to prove that they unknowingly participated in child pornography.

 Legal Authority Examples

Federal Pandering and Solicitation Statute: Anyone who knowingly uses any means of interstate commerce, including a computer, to receive, distribute, advertise, sell, or possess child pornography shall be fined and imprisoned for not less than 15 nor for more than 30 years. Repeat offenders may be imprisoned for life.

New York: Employing or authorizing a child who is under the age of 17 to participate in a sexually explicit performance is a felony.

 RESOURCE

For information on how each state defines and punishes child enticement, a term that includes child pornography offenses, go to www.nolo.com/childenticement.

Related terms: defenses; rape.

child sexual abuse

Various laws punish offenders (often called pedophiles) who engage in sexual activities or have sexual contact with children. These statutes are gender neutral and offenders and victims can be either male or female. Sexual abuse of children typically constitutes a felony, though the gravity of the offense can vary depending on the ages of offenders and victims and also on their relationship.

Offenders convicted of child sexual abuse may have to register as sex offenders after any period of incarceration ends.

Age of Consent. Child sexual abuse laws deem minors to be legally incapable of consenting to sexual activity. Age of consent laws vary from one state to another. However, virtually all states treat consensual sexual activity involving a minor who is at least 16 years old as a misdemeanor rather than a felony when a sexual partner is also a minor—that is, under the legal age of adulthood, which is typically 18.

> EXAMPLE: Ryan, age 17, and Ali, age 16, are high school sweethearts whose sexual relationship is consensual. While a prosecution of either Ryan or Ali may be unlikely, technically both are guilty of misdemeanor statutory rape. On the other hand, if Ali is only 13 years old, Ryan's conduct constitutes a felony in virtually all states.

Sexual Touching (Molestation). All types of sexual contact with minors that include penetration are illegal. More subtly, child sexual abuse also includes touching a child's intimate parts with sexual intent. This includes placing one's hands on the outside of children's clothing. Abuse can even occur without a minor being touched—for example, when an adult masturbates in a child's presence.

Continuous Abuse. Most criminal charges grow out of events that witnesses testify to with particularity as to times, dates, and other details. Continuous abuse laws recognize that sexual offenders often abuse children over such a lengthy period that child victims are unable to pinpoint specific incidents. Continuous abuse statutes require only that prosecutors prove that a number of illegal acts took place within a designated period of time.

> EXAMPLE: Six-year-old Carla testifies that her stepfather babysat for her while her mom attended evening classes. Almost always, her stepfather would rub his hands all over the front of her pajama tops and bottoms when putting her to bed. Carla can't describe any specific incident in detail, but her mom identifies the two-month period when she attended evening classes two nights a

week. Carla's and her mom's testimony combine to support the stepfather's conviction for violating a continuous abuse law.

Sexual Exploitation. Sexual behavior with minors can be illegal even in the absence of actual physical contact. Showing children sexually explicit visual material, recording children engaged in sexual activity, and allowing children to participate in sexual activity are forms of illegal sexual exploitation.

Reporting Laws. Virtually all states punish adults who are aware of (or who have good reason to be aware of) but fail to report sexual abuse of a child. So, for example, a mother violates reporting laws if she witnesses and fails to report a live-in boyfriend who regularly abuses her young daughter.

Legal Authority Examples

Federal: A parent or other person who has legal custody of a child who permits the child to engage in recorded sexual activity may be fined and imprisoned for not less than 15 nor more than 30 years.

Arizona: Sexually abusing a minor under the age of 14 three or more times during any period of three months or more constitutes continual sexual abuse. Conviction of an offender requires a judge or jury to agree that at least three illegal acts took place during the specified period of time, but they need not agree on which specific acts took place.

Texas: Any sexual contact between an adult and a minor under the age of 17 is indecency and punishable as a felony.

RESOURCE

For information on how each state defines and punishes child enticement, a term that covers several sexual offenses involving minors, go to www.nolo.com/childenticement.

Related terms: child abuse and neglect; child pornography; rape.

C

churning

See securities fraud.

circumstantial evidence

See evidence.

civil compromise

In some states, a court can dismiss a misdemeanor charge if the defendant settles with—that is, pays money to—the victim. This process is called civil compromise because it resolves the case without a criminal conviction. The financial settlement must be directly related to the criminal conduct, and it must compensate for the financial injury the victim suffered. Usually both the judge and victim must consent to the criminal case being resolved by civil compromise.

Same Act. Civil compromise is available only if the same act results in both criminal and civil liability. For example, a defendant who punches another in the face has committed battery, which is both a crime and a tort (an act giving rise to civil liability). In states that allow civil compromise, the misdemeanor battery charge is eligible for compromise if the defendant pays for the medical costs, lost wages, and pain and suffering caused by the attack. That's because the exact same act (hitting) resulted in both civil and criminal liability. On the other hand, if a defendant drives drunk and hits a parked car, the drunk driving charge cannot be compromised by the defendant paying for the damage to the parked car. Drunk driving is its own act—damaging property is incidental to the crime. The "victim" is the public at large rather than a specific person. Because no one individual can accept compensation on behalf of society, no civil compromise is possible.

civil lawsuit

In a civil lawsuit, one party demands compensation—usually money—for some injury; in a criminal prosecution the government seeks punishment for a harm that is considered to have been done to society as a whole. The remedies for a civil lawsuit never result in incarceration, because the goal of civil litigation is to compensate the injured party, not punish the wrongdoer. Examples of a civil lawsuit include a landlord seeking to evict a tenant from an apartment, one driver suing another for personal injuries and property damage resulting from an accident, and a government's antitrust suit seeking to prevent a corporation's takeover of a competitor. (By the way, the use of the term, "civil," does not connote "civility" by the parties or their lawyers.)

A civil lawsuit can be based on the same events as a criminal prosecution. That is, a criminal prosecution by the government doesn't prevent a victim from seeking financial compensation from the same defendant. If, for example, Bruce beats up Peter, the district attorney's office will likely prosecute Bruce. Peter can also sue Bruce for money to compensate for the injuries and medical expenses he incurred. (To save victims the expense of bringing their own civil lawsuits against defendants, prosecutors often ask for restitution as part of the sentence. Restitution compensates a victim for losses—in other words, it's a substitute for at least a portion of the damages the victim would be able to sue for in civil court. However, whether restitution is available to compensate for less tangible damages such as pain and suffering varies from state to state and case to case. In general, though, pain-and-suffering damages are more readily available in civil lawsuits than through restitution orders.)

Related terms: convictions, consequences of; discovery; *mens rea;* civil compromise; restitution

clear and convincing evidence

See evidence.

C

commissioners

Judges appoint commissioners to carry out a variety of courtroom duties. These judicial officers receive a lower salary than judges, who typically can hire and fire them. By hiring commissioners rather than expanding the number of judges, counties gain personnel flexibility while operating courts at a lower cost.

In criminal cases, commissioners' duties may include presiding over bail hearings and arraignments, issuing search warrants, ruling on pretrial motions, and presiding over probation revocation hearings. Commissioners may also preside over trials, provided that the prosecutor and the defendant both consent.

Magistrates, also called magistrate judges, are the federal court equivalent to county court commissioners. They are appointed by a majority vote of the active district court judges in a federal judicial district.

Related term: magistrate.

common law

"Common law" refers to legal rules and principles created by judges through their decisions, as opposed to laws created by legislation. Common law is sometimes referred to as case law because it is based on the results of legal cases. Much of American law is derived from British common law—rules created by English judges.

competence to stand trial

To qualify as competent to stand trial, defendants must be able to understand what is happening in their cases and to participate intelligibly with their lawyers. Criminal cases cannot proceed unless defendants are competent to stand trial. Defendants who are incompetent can neither enter a plea nor be put on trial. Judges who doubt a defendant's competence (often based on information from defense counsel) have a duty to halt criminal proceedings and order a competency evaluation. (*Drope v. Missouri*, U.S. Sup. Ct. (1975).)

Determining a defendant's competency hinges on the defendant's ability to understand the proceedings. For example, a defendant who suffers from bipolar disorder—characterized by extreme mood swings and an inclination to act impulsively—is typically competent to stand trial even though the condition may trigger lapses in concentration. That's because the bipolar condition does not prevent the defendant from understanding the nature of the criminal proceedings.

Insanity vs. Incompetency. Competency to stand trial and the legal defense of insanity are separate issues. The legal tests for evaluating defendants' mental states are different and the evaluations consider mental state at different periods in time. For example, a defendant may have insane delusions at the time the crime is committed, yet still be competent at the time of trial. On the other hand, another defendant may have been "legally sane" at the time a crime is committed, yet after taking illegal mind-altering drugs for a month after the crime, be incompetent to stand trial.

Time Out … Time In. Criminal proceedings resume when (and if) defendants regain their competency to stand trial. In some circumstances judges can restore defendants to competency by ordering them to be given appropriate and prescribed medications. (*U.S. v. Sell*, U.S. Sup. Ct. (2003).)

 Real-Life Illustration

Jared Laughner was charged with federal and state capital crimes for killing six people and severely injuring Congresswoman Gabrielle Giffords in Tucson, Arizona. In May 2011, a federal judge in Tucson determined that Laughner was not competent to stand trial. The judge ordered Laughner to be committed to a mental hospital until such time as he became competent.

C

 Real-Life Illustration

Vincent "The Chin" Gigante was a Mafia crime boss who was charged with a variety of crimes in 1990. Gigante avoided trial for seven years by pretending that he was mentally incompetent. During this time, bodyguards dropped Gigante off at his mother's Greenwich Village apartment virtually every day. He would emerge in pajamas and a bathrobe and shuffle slowly around the neighborhood, stopping to rest in a park. A judge ruled that Gigante was competent to stand trial after a number of Gigante's henchmen turned on him and testified that they planned crimes with Gigante during these rest stops. Gigante was convicted of racketeering and died in prison in 2005.

Assessment Procedures. Psychiatrists or psychologists examine defendants whose competence to stand trial is uncertain. Examinations take place in private offices, locked facilities, or mental institutions, depending on a defendant's placement status. After examiners prepare reports, judges may hold hearings at which both parties can offer evidence and cross-examine adverse witnesses. Most states place on defendants the burden of proving incompetency by a preponderance of the evidence, a rule that is constitutional. (*Medina v. California*, U.S. Sup. Ct. (1992).)

 Legal Authority Examples

Alabama: A judge who doubts the sanity of a defendant charged with a felony suspends proceedings and impanels a jury to hear evidence and rule on the defendant's sanity. Defendants who are found insane are committed to a state hospital. Once they are restored to sanity, criminal proceedings resume.

Oregon: Judges determine whether defendants are competent to stand trial. A defendant deemed incompetent to stand trial may be released on supervision if a judge determines that care other than commitment to a state mental hospital would better serve the defendant and the community.

Related terms: arraignment; burdens of proof; defenses; insanity.

concurrent sentences

See sentencing (punishment options).

confession

See interrogation tactics.

Confrontation Clause

See confrontation of prosecution witnesses.

confrontation of prosecution witnesses

The hearsay rule—an evidence rule barring the introduction of certain out-of-court statements or documents—protects parties' right to cross-examine opposing witnesses in all cases, criminal and civil. But the hearsay rule is subject to many exceptions that often make hearsay admissible. In criminal cases, though, the Confrontation Clause of the Sixth Amendment strengthens the hearsay rule and limits these exceptions by requiring that a defendant have the opportunity for cross-examination (which can take place either before or during trial) in order for the prosecution to be able to offer testimonial hearsay into evidence. (*Crawford v. Washington*, U.S. Sup. Ct. (2004).)

For example, in a DUI prosecution, the prosecutor may seek to offer into evidence a lab technician's written report indicating that the defendant's blood alcohol level was 0.14, well above the state limit of 0.08. The report is hearsay, but in the absence of the Confrontation Clause would probably be admissible in evidence under an exception to the hearsay rule. Because of the Confrontation Clause, though, the report is not admissible unless the prosecution presents testimony from a lab technician who is subject to cross examination by the defendant. Depending on the circumstances, the prosecution's testifying lab technician can be an analyst who is knowledgeable about a lab's testing procedures rather than the technician who actually conducted the test and prepared the report. (*Williams v. Illinois*, U.S. Sup. Ct. (2012).)

The general impact of the Supreme Court's interpretation of the Confrontation Clause has been to make it more difficult for prosecutors to secure convictions, especially in domestic violence cases.

> **EXAMPLE:** Archie is charged with domestic violence for assaulting his former live-in girlfriend Veronica. Moments after Archie ran out of their flat following the alleged assault, Veronica gave a detailed account of the beating to a police officer. Apparently fearful of retribution from Archie if she testified against him, Veronica disappeared and could not be brought to court to testify. The domestic violence charges must be dismissed. The police officer cannot testify to Veronica's account of the abuse because the Confrontation Clause protects Archie's right to cross-examine Veronica. However, if Veronica described the assault and testified against Archie at a preliminary hearing and Archie was present at the preliminary hearing and had an opportunity to cross-examine Veronica, the prosecutor could offer Veronica's testimony from the preliminary hearing into evidence at trial—even if Veronica had disappeared at the time of trial—to prove that Archie is guilty of domestic violence.

Testimonial Hearsay. The Confrontation Clause bars only the use of testimonial hearsay against criminal defendants. Courts continue to refine the concept of "testimonial." Generally, hearsay is testimonial when it pertains to a completed crime and is generated by a government agent such as a police officer. Examples of testimonial hearsay include government reports, affidavits of victims and witnesses, depositions, and informal accounts of past crimes given by victims and witnesses to police officers. Nontestimonial statements include descriptions given by crime victims or witnesses to 911 operators during ongoing emergencies. Beyond these specific examples, testimonial hearsay generally consists of statements that victims and witnesses reasonably believe will be used at a trial. Here are two examples of admissible statements:

- **Nontestimonial eyewitness statement.** A badly wounded eyewitness to a liquor store armed robbery told another witness that "the guy who shot me had a scar on his right cheek, I saw it." Then the witness died. The witness's statement is likely to be admissible against the defendant at trial under the dying declaration exception to the hearsay rule. The eyewitness's statement was not testimonial because it was not generated by the government, nor was the eyewitness likely to have been thinking about a trial when the statement was made.

- **Nontestimonial victim statement.** While waiting for an ambulance to arrive, police officers ask a gunshot victim for information that might help them locate the shooter. The victim mentions the location where the shooting took place and then becomes unconscious. The Confrontation Clause does not bar the prosecution from offering the victim's statement into evidence at trial. The police officers were trying to resolve an ongoing emergency, not seeking evidence about a completed crime.

Forfeiture. Defendants' wrongful conduct can result in a forfeiture of their right to cross-examine an absent witness whose hearsay statement is offered into evidence. Forfeiture occurs when, with the intent to prevent a witness from testifying, a defendant procures (or collaborates in procuring) the witness's absence from a trial.

EXAMPLE: Archie is charged with domestic violence for assaulting his former live-in girlfriend Betty on March 1. Moments after Archie ran out of their flat following the alleged assault, Betty gave a detailed account of the beating to a police officer. On April 1, Archie returned to the flat and again attacked Betty. Betty then disappeared and could not be brought to court to testify to Archie's attack on March 1. Unless the prosecutor can prove that

Archie attacked Betty on April 1 with the intent of preventing her from testifying against him, and that the April 1 attack was the reason for Betty's absence from the trial, the domestic violence charges will probably be dismissed because Archie's April 1 attack does not result in a forfeiture of his right to cross-examine Betty concerning the March 1 assault.

Legal Authority Examples

Excerpt from the Sixth Amendment to the Constitution: "In all criminal prosecutions, the accused shall enjoy the right ... to be confronted with the witnesses against him."

Federal Rule of Evidence 804(b)(6): If a witness is unavailable to testify at trial, the witness's hearsay statement is admissible against a defendant who engaged or acquiesced in wrongdoing against the witness that was intended to and did procure the witness's absence.

Related terms: preliminary hearings; domestic violence.

consecutive sentences

See sentencing (punishment options).

consent searches

See warrantless searches.

conspiracy

Conspiracy is a crime that two or more people (often called coconspirators) agree to commit. So long as coconspirators take overt action toward carrying out a planned crime, they are guilty of conspiracy even if they fail to commit it. So, for example, making elaborate plans to rob a bank is not a crime if nothing is done to

C

carry out the robbery. But if the would-be bank robbers steal a getaway car, buy fright wigs, or take any other overt actions in furtherance of the robbery, they are guilty of conspiracy.

If they do commit the planned crime, coconspirators are guilty both of conspiracy and of the crime that they committed. So, for example, if robbers carry out their plan to commit a bank robbery, they can be convicted of both conspiracy to rob a bank and bank robbery. Their sentences will probably run concurrently, so the dual convictions probably will not lengthen their imprisonment.

Historical Antecedents. Conspiracies have been around since ancient times. In Act 2, Scene III, of Shakespeare's *Julius Caesar*, Artemidorus warns Caesar:

"[B]eware of Brutus; take heed of Cassius; come not near Casca; have an eye to Cinna; trust not Trebonius; mark well Metellus Cimber; Decius Brutus loves thee not; thou hast wronged Caius Ligarius. There is but one mind in all these men, and it is bent against Caesar. If thou beest not immortal, look about you. Security gives way to conspiracy." (Caesar apparently did not have his listening ears on when Artemidorus spoke.)

Boundaries. Unlike people who write wills and sign leases, coconspirators rarely draw up detailed agreements describing the scope of a conspiracy, its goals, and its members. Judges' rulings concerning the extent of a conspiracy often determine a defendant's guilt.

 Real-Life Illustration

In 1865, John Wilkes Booth assassinated President Abraham Lincoln, Lewis Powell attempted to assassinate Secretary of State William Seward, and George Atzerodt attempted to kill Vice President Andrew Johnson. If a judge ruled that each of these offenders was a coconspirator in a single conspiracy, then the government could try the coconspirators together and each coconspirator would be guilty of all of the crimes. Also, evidence and statements made by any coconspirator pertaining to any of the crimes would be admissible in evidence against all of them. On the other hand, if

C

a judge ruled that no overall conspiracy existed, each offender would have to be tried separately, each offender could be guilty only of the crime he committed, and only evidence and statements pertaining to that crime would be admissible in evidence.

Know Before You Go. Each coconspirator is legally responsible for the conspiracy-related actions of all other coconspirators. This rule applies to coconspirators who join an ongoing conspiracy unaware of decisions that were made before they joined.

EXAMPLE: A few days before a bank robbery, Thelma agrees to participate in a robbery by driving the getaway car. On the day of the robbery however, Thelma has a bad head cold so at Thelma's suggestion her friend Louise drives the getaway car. The gang pulls off the robbery but is captured when Louise stops at a red light so as not to accumulate more points on her driving record. Even though she didn't participate in the robbery, Thelma is guilty both of conspiracy to rob the bank and bank robbery because she was a coconspirator. If Thelma is unaware that before she joined the conspiracy, her coconspirators had decided to take a hostage out of the bank, she would still be guilty of conspiracy to commit bank robbery, bank robbery, conspiracy to kidnap, and kidnapping. That's because when she joined the conspiracy, Thelma became responsible for all of the conspirators' previous conspiracy-related decisions and actions.

 Legal Authority Examples

Nebraska: A criminal conspiracy exists when two or more people agree to commit a crime and commit an overt act in pursuance of the conspiracy, whether or not they know each other's identities. Multiple crimes constitute a single conspiracy so long as they are the object of the same agreement or continuous conspiratorial relationship. Conspiracy to commit a Class I felony is a Class II felony.

Oregon: A criminal conspiracy exists when two or more people agree to commit a crime punishable as a felony or a Class A misdemeanor. Conspiracy is a Class A felony if one of its objects is commission of murder, treason, or a Class A felony; it is a Class B felony if one of its objects is commission of a Class B felony; it is a Class C felony if one of its objects is commission of a Class C felony; and it is a Class A misdemeanor if one of its objects is commission of a Class A misdemeanor.

Related terms: sentencing (punishment options).

contempt of court

Contempt of court, which can be punishable by incarceration, occurs when a person violates a court order. An act constituting contempt of court can actually take place in court, as when an individual repeatedly disrupts court proceedings. Most contempts take place away from court, as when one former spouse disobeys a court order not to contact the other ex-spouse.

contraband

Property that a person cannot legally possess, such as unlawful drugs, counterfeit money, or a knife possessed by a prison inmate, is contraband. If contraband is seized in an illegal search, it will not be returned to its owner. For example, if a judge rules that a police officer violated the Fourth Amendment when seizing a defendant's coat containing an illegal drug stash, the defendant will get his coat back, but not the contraband stash.

convictions, consequences of

A conviction is a final judgment or verdict of guilt in a criminal case. A conviction may result from a guilty plea, a plea of *nolo contendere*, or a trial. The sections below describe common ancillary ramifications of convictions (other than direct consequences such as fines and imprisonment).

C

Future Shock. Perhaps the most common result of convictions is harsher punishment for future convictions. Statutes may require harsher punishment for offenders with a record of prior convictions. (Three strikes laws are a common example.) Statutory mandates aside, judges typically mete out harsher punishment to recidivists. Prior convictions can enhance punishment even if they have been expunged.

Impeachment. At trial, and typically subject to judges' discretion, adversaries can attack the credibility of opposing witnesses by offering evidence of prior convictions. Both felony and misdemeanor convictions are potentially admissible for impeachment, though the rules vary from one jurisdiction to another. For criminal defendants, the risk that prosecutors will offer their prior convictions into evidence if they testify is a primary reason why defendants often rely on their right to remain silent and refuse to testify.

> EXAMPLE: Al wants to testify that he was out of town when a robbery took place, but fears that if he does testify, the judge will allow the prosecutor to offer evidence that three years earlier, Al was convicted of failing to file an income tax return. Al may choose to remain silent rather than testify and enable the jury to find out that Al has a prior conviction.

Civil Cases. Many crimes are also civil wrongs for which victims can seek compensation by filing lawsuits against offenders in civil courts. Criminal convictions are often admissible in evidence in civil cases to prove that an offender committed an act giving rise to civil liability. So, for example, a victim of a car theft can use the thief's conviction in a civil lawsuit seeking compensation for the value of the car and other damages.

Licenses and Employment. Convictions can result in lost licenses for members of many professional groups. Also, convictions may disqualify offenders from certain types of employment, such as a job in law enforcement. Disqualification aside, employers often take convictions into account when making hiring decisions.

Sex Offender Registration. Increasingly, convictions for crimes of sexual violence or abuse require offenders to register with police agencies when they are released from confinement. Registration is an especially likely requirement when victims are minors. The names of registered sex offenders may be posted on community websites, and sex offenders may be limited as to where they can live and work.

Civil Disabilities. Felony convictions may have ripple effects that limit offenders' participation in public affairs—for example, in many states, convicted felons lose the right to vote, at least during the time period of their incarceration.

Parental Rights and Responsibilities. Custody of minor children may be taken away from incarcerated offenders for at least the period of their confinement. Incarcerated offenders with child support obligations may be required to contribute a percentage of inmate earnings toward child support. Making child support payments may also be a condition of probation that if ignored, results in revocation of probation.

Forfeiture of Property. Forfeiture occurs when conviction of a crime allows the government to seize items of property belonging to a convicted person that relate to or are derived from the activities that gave rise to the conviction. While many federal and state statutes authorize forfeiture, drug offenses are perhaps the most common type of conviction that lead to forfeiture. For example, the government may prosecute a defendant for selling illegal drugs, and, in addition to any other punishment, seek the forfeiture of the defendant's van if it was used to deliver the drugs.

 Legal Authority Examples

Massachusetts: A conviction for a first offense of stalking in violation of a restraining order is punishable by imprisonment from one to three years. A conviction for a second offense of stalking in violation of a restraining order requires a minimum term of incarceration of two years and is punishable by imprisonment for up to ten years.

C

Federal Rules of Evidence: Convictions for felony and misdemeanor offenses are automatically admissible to impeach witnesses if the crimes giving rise to the conviction involved dishonesty or false statement. Otherwise, felony convictions only are admissible to impeach witnesses if the judge determines that their probative value is greater than their prejudicial impact.

Federal Rules of Evidence: Felony convictions are admissible in civil cases to prove any fact essential to sustain the judgment. The pendency of an appeal may be shown but does not affect admissibility.

Federal Forfeiture Law: The Attorney General of the United States may seize all illegally manufactured or distributed substances as well as all conveyances, including aircraft, vehicles, or vessels, which are used, or are intended for use, to transport, possess, or conceal the illegal substances.

Related terms: character evidence; expungement of criminal records; sentencing (punishment options); three strikes laws.

cooking the books

See securities fraud.

cop a plea

Slang referring to a defendant's pleading guilty, often as a result of a plea bargaining agreement between the defendant's lawyer and prosecutors.

See plea bargaining.

corpus delicti

(Latin for "the body of the crime.") This phrase refers to proof that a crime took place. The term usually is used in connection with a murder, but applies to any crime. The concept's main import is that a defendant can't be convicted of a crime based only on the defendant's admission that he committed it. The prosecution has to offer independent proof that a crime took place before a defendant's confession is admissible in evidence. In a murder case, the prosecution does not have to find a dead body to satisfy the *corpus delicti* requirement, though that's obviously a helpful way of convincing a jury that the victim actually was killed.

counterfeiting

Counterfeiting, a type of forgery, is the crime of knowingly creating or passing off phony bills as lawful money and is generally punishable as a felony. Under intellectual property laws, counterfeiting refers to the act of making or selling look-alike goods or services bearing fake trademarks. For example, a business is guilty of counterfeiting if it deliberately duplicates the Coach trademark on handbags.

See forgery.

court-martial

A court-martial is a military trial convened over service-related offenses. For example, a soldier charged with refusing to obey a superior's lawful order will be tried by a court-martial. Soldiers who commit non-service-related crimes are tried by civilian rather than military authorities. For instance, a soldier who commits a burglary while on leave will be tried in a civilian criminal court. Courts-martial may involve different procedural rules than traditional courts.

crime

A crime is a violation of law that is punishable by a fine, incarceration, and/or other penalties. Acts constitute crimes only if they violate a federal or state statute or a local ordinance. Judges cannot deem conduct to be criminal just because they believe that a person acted immorally.

cross-examination

See trial phases (trial cycles); confrontation of prosecution witnesses.

cruel and unusual punishment

See sentencing (punishment options).

curfew

A curfew usually refers to a local municipal ordinance that forbids people (often minors) from being in a specific public area after a certain time. For example, following a disaster a locality might seek to prevent looting in the affected area by imposing a general 10 p.m. curfew. The term reflects the French roots of William the Conqueror's 1066 Norman invasion of England. The French term *covrefeu* meant "put out the fires," and in medieval times a *covrefeu* order protected villages against fires and the *noblesse* against nighttime peasant uprisings.

cyber-crimes

Cyber-crime is an umbrella term for a collection of crimes in which offenders use computers and the Internet to victimize individuals and organizations. Below are three of the most common variants.

- **Phishing.** Phishing is a form of fraud in which offenders mimic authentic websites to trick individuals into disclosing private personal information such as Social Security number and bank account and credit card numbers. Phishing is a popular method of committing the crime of "identity theft."

  EXAMPLE: Fisher creates a website that mimics that of a national retailer. Fisher sends out millions of spam email messages instructing consumers to log on to her website and enter their bank account and credit card numbers so that they can continue to receive notices of special Internet bargain prices. Consumers who follow Fisher's instructions visit her phony website, believing it is the retailer's website, and provide her with personal financial data that she uses to withdraw money, purchase goods, and take trips.

- **Cyber-Bullying**. Cyber-bullying consists of using electronic devices to threaten, harass, humiliate, or otherwise target victims. Cyber-bullies often use electronic mail, blogs, or social media websites to attack victims by disseminating false information or disclosing private information. Most cyber-bullies are teenagers, as are most victims of cyber-bullying. Laws making it illegal to threaten to harm others may not apply to cyber-bullying. Thus, many jurisdictions have enacted or are considering enacting laws specifically criminalizing cyber-bullying.

  > **EXAMPLE:** Thirteen-year-old Lois is furious at Megan for "stealing" Lois's boyfriend. Lois takes revenge on Megan by repeatedly posting false information about Megan's heritage, personality traits, and sexual history on social media sites that their school friends access constantly. Lois also uses a false identity to create a new social media account and uses the account to send phony messages to Megan that lead Megan to think that an older boy named Josh is in love with her. When "Josh" suddenly breaks up with her, Megan becomes so distraught that she attempts suicide. Lois's conduct constitutes cyber-bullying.

- **Hacking.** Hacking consists of using computers to gain unauthorized access to victims' computers. Offenders sometimes engage in hacking in order to commit crimes such as identity theft. They may instead want to spread computer viruses or gain access to and disseminate classified government information.

C

Real-Life Illustration

"Mafiaboy" was the pseudonym of a Canadian teenager who pleaded guilty in 2001 to 56 counts of hacking websites operated by numerous multi-national corporations. Mafiaboy spread a virus that paralyzed the websites, denying access to millions of computer users for five days.

Real-Life Illustration

In 2010, WikiLeaks electronically published thousands of previously classified U.S. government documents relating to military operations in Afghanistan covering the years 2004–2009. In 2013, Bradley Manning, a 25-year-old Army private who gave WikiLeaks thousands of such documents, was acquitted of aiding the enemy, but convicted of various other crimes, including espionage, theft, and computer fraud.

Legal Authority Examples

Federal CAN-SPAM Law: Registering and using information that materially falsifies the identity of an actual registrant for five or more online user accounts and intentionally transmitting multiple commercial electronic mail messages is a felony punishable by fine and imprisonment of up to five years.

Federal: 18 U.S.C. § 875 makes it illegal to use a means of interstate communication to threaten to kidnap or injure another person. The crime is a felony punishable by fine and imprisonment of up to five years.

Federal: 18 U.S.C. § 1030 makes it illegal to intentionally transmit a program, code, or command that causes damage to a protected computer. The crime is a felony punishable by fine and imprisonment of up to ten years.

Missouri: Knowingly making an electronic communication to frighten, intimidate, or cause emotional distress to another person, or to knowingly and repeatedly make unwanted communications to another person, is a misdemeanor. If an offender is over age 21 and the victim is age 17 or under, then the offense is a felony.

Related terms: fraud; invasion of privacy; terrorist threats (terroristic threats).

D

damages

See civil lawsuit.

date rape

See rape.

Daubert rule (aka the *Daubert* standard)

This rule of evidence, derived from a federal case (*Daubert v. Merrell Dow Pharmaceuticals, Inc.*, U.S. Sup. Ct. (1993)), sets the standard for admitting expert witness testimony in a federal legal proceeding. Basically, the rule establishes that judges are gatekeepers who should allow experts to testify only if their testimony is relevant, founded on reliable principles and methodologies that were applied in a reliable way to the facts of the case, and based upon sufficient facts or data. The *Daubert* rule replaced a previous and more conservative rule known as the *Frye* rule, which some states continue to use. The *Frye* rule provides that expert witness testimony is admissible only if it is based on scientific principles that a community of relevant experts deem reliable. Judges determine whether expert testimony is admissible, but in jury trials, juries ultimately determine the credibility of experts' testimony.

Related terms: expert witnesses.

deadly weapon

The use of a deadly weapon in the commission of a crime usually affects the crime that is charged and the severity of the punishment.

D

Whether an object constitutes a "deadly weapon" depends both on an object's inherent physical characteristics and the use to which an attacker puts it. For example, if an attacker hurls a brick at a victim, a judge or jury will almost surely conclude that the brick constitutes a deadly weapon. A brick's size, weight, and shape mean that it has the capacity to cause severe injuries. And the attacker used the brick in a way that created a likelihood of severe injury if it struck the victim. In a particular circumstance reasonable arguments on both sides may exist as to whether an object qualifies as a deadly weapon, and ultimately the issue is a factual one for a judge or jury to decide. For example, a pencil is not an object that one would ordinarily consider to be a deadly weapon. However, if a defendant carries out an attack by using a pencil in a way that risks serious injury, a judge or jury might reasonably convict the defendant of assault with a deadly weapon.

Related terms: assault with a deadly weapon; death penalty; self-defense.

death penalty

The federal government and 33 states currently provide for capital punishment (the imposition of death sentences). The number of states that authorize capital punishment and the number of executions actually carried out has diminished in recent years. Forty-three executions were carried out in 2012, the same number as in 2011. Texas carried out 15 of them, more than any other state.

The federal government also has the power to execute criminals and some of the notable federal executions include:

- Timothy McVeigh (2001), the Oklahoma City bomber
- Ethel and Julius Rosenberg (1953), the "atomic spies," convicted of espionage for passing secrets to the Soviet Union
- George Atzerodt, Mary Surratt, David Herold, and Lewis Powell (1865), conspiracy to assassinate President Lincoln.

The Eighth Amendment. The Eighth Amendment's ban on "cruel and unusual punishment" restricts the crimes for which a death sentence can be given. For example, the government cannot execute:

- defendants convicted of raping adults (*Coker v. Georgia*, U.S. Sup. Ct. (1977)) or children (*Kennedy v. Louisiana*, U.S. Sup. Ct. (2008))
- offenders who were less than 18 years old at the time they committed a crime subject to the death penalty (*Roper v. Simmons*, U.S. Sup. Ct. (2005)), or
- mentally retarded prisoners (*Atkins v. Virginia*, U.S. Sup. Ct. (2002)).

The Worst of the Worst. States that authorize the death penalty often have statutes that specify special circumstances that make a crime "death penalty eligible." These statutes signify that even among a deplorable group of murderers, some murders are so heinous that they merit the death penalty. Prosecutors, usually in teams, choose the eligible crimes for which they will seek death. Factors that influence prosecutors include an accused's background and rap sheet (criminal record) and the circumstances under which a killing took place. Political forces may also sway prosecutors in deciding whether to pursue the death penalty in a given case—for example, public outcry over the death of a vulnerable member of society such as a child can shape the decision.

Judges and Jurors. Defendants facing the death penalty typically opt for jury trials. Capital charges result in bifurcated trials in which jurors first decide whether a defendant is guilty of a capital crime. If so, the jurors reconvene for a "penalty phase," in which they hear evidence concerning the appropriateness of the death penalty. Family members of murder victims often testify during a penalty phase, describing the impact of a victim's death on their lives. If a jury recommends death, the judge has the power to ignore the recommendation and issue a lesser sentence. If a jury recommends a lesser sentence, the judge does not have the power to sentence a defendant to death.

D

 Real-Life Illustration

Nathan Leopold and Richard Loeb faced the death penalty when they went on trial in Chicago in 1924 for the so-called "thrill killing" of teenager Bobby Franks. They were both represented by Clarence Darrow, the famous defense lawyer. In one of the most dramatic tactical moves in U.S. courtroom history, Darrow changed his clients' plea to guilty after observing the jury's reaction to the prosecutor's opening statement. Darrow was convinced that the jury would return a death sentence. The guilty plea removed the jury and put the sentencing burden on the judge. Darrow's tactic succeeded. The judge sentenced Leopold and Loeb to life in prison. The 1957 film, *Compulsion*, starring Orson Welles, is a classic dramatization of the case. The film's climactic argument against the death penalty is taken directly from Darrow's courtroom speech.

Bounded Discretion. Death penalty statutes are constitutional only if they provide jurors with concrete "aggravating" and "mitigating" factors that they are to consider when deciding between life and death.

 Real-Life Illustration

Charles Manson was convicted of masterminding the Tate-La Bianca murders and sentenced to death in 1971. The death sentence was automatically and permanently reduced to life in prison because Manson was sentenced under a death penalty statute that was unconstitutional because it failed to set forth concrete parameters for the jury to consider.

During the penalty phase, the opposing parties offer evidence relevant to the aggravating and mitigating factors. A defense lawyer's failure to present adequate available evidence in mitigation can constitute ineffective assistance of counsel that results in reversal of a death sentence. In such cases, an appellate court would be likely to uphold the conviction but order a retrial of the penalty phase.

Future Directions. Public opinion polls suggest that popular support for the death penalty has eroded in recent years. One reason is that states now provide for LWOP (life without possibility of parole) sentences. Another factor is that death penalty cases are far more costly than noncapital cases. If current trends continue, the next decade may see the near-extinction of the death penalty in the United States.

 Legal Authority Examples

Federal Law: Crimes for which offenders may be executed include killing the president, a member of the Cabinet, a member of Congress, or a member of the Supreme Court, espionage, torture resulting in death, sexual abuse resulting in death, and causing death by using an explosive or a chemical weapon.

New York: First degree murder is subject to the death penalty and includes intentional killings of police officers or correctional facilities officers, killings by prisoners serving life sentences, killings committed in the course of specified serious felonies, killings by defendants previously convicted of murder, and killings that are carried out in an especially cruel and heinous manner.

Related terms: sentencing (punishment options); first degree murder (Murder One); second degree murder (Murder Two); manslaughter.

defendant

The person charged with a crime.

defense counsel (defense attorney)

Defense counsel refers to all lawyers representing defendants charged with crimes (including indigent defendants whose lawyers are court-appointed and paid by the government). The sections below explain the role and organization of criminal defense lawyers.

"How Can You Represent Those Criminals?" Many nonlawyers lump criminal defense lawyers together with the defendants themselves and deem the lawyers to be disreputable. In reality, defense lawyers are independent agents who promote the efficiency and fairness of the criminal justice system. A commitment to zealous representation protects the rights of the guilty and the innocent, and everyone in between. For example, a defense attorney's investigation may uncover information that provides the jurors with a more complete version of events and results in a client's conviction of a lesser crime that more accurately reflects the client's moral responsibility. Moreover, defense lawyers' role extends well beyond trying to "get guilty people off scot free." Defense lawyers often try to achieve an outcome that maximizes clients' chances of being successful in the future, no matter what they've done in the past. For example, an attorney representing a client charged with driving under the influence of alcohol may counsel the client to see the arrest and charge as an opportunity to get help for a serious substance abuse problem and negotiate an acceptable sentence that is contingent on the client's completion of a rigorous rehab program.

When Judges Appoint Counsel. If conviction of a crime results in imprisonment, indigent defendants (those who cannot afford to hire a lawyer) are entitled to be represented by a government-paid lawyer. This right does not extend to crimes punishable by fines or nonjail consequences. So, for example, an indigent person who commits a traffic infraction that is punishable only by a small fine is not entitled to (and the judge will not appoint) a government-paid lawyer. If the case involves a crime that may or may not involve imprisonment, judges typically preserve their ability to impose a jail sentence by appointing government-paid lawyers for all indigent defendants.

To provide indigent defendants with government-paid lawyers, many states and counties have established public defender offices. Judges appoint attorneys from these offices to represent indigent defendants at trial and on appeal. Other states or counties rely on panel attorneys who are "on call" for appointments after they are vetted by local judges. Whatever the system, many programs are so severely underfunded and indigent defense lawyer caseloads so high that judges in some states have declared them invalid.

Public Defenders. Many states and counties believe that the most cost-effective method of providing criminal legal defense services for indigents is to establish public defender offices. Offices normally consist of a chief public defender ("P.D."), assistant P.D.s, investigators, and other personnel. P.D.s are assigned to courtrooms and judges appoint them for defendants who want but cannot afford to hire a lawyer. P.D.s are licensed attorneys who typically receive excellent training and quickly build up local courtroom knowledge and experience.

Disenchantment With Public Defenders. Politicians rarely score political points by bragging about the expansion of P.D. services they've helped bring about. As a result, and especially in urban areas, P.D.s are typically burdened with large caseloads that may give clients the impression of "assembly line justice." This in turn creates disenchantment among defendants saddled with a public defender perceived to be overworked and unfocused. However, a right to representation does not mean a right to the lawyer of choice. Because indigent defendants cannot handpick their lawyers (or choose friends who are not lawyers), a judge may, at most, appoint a different lawyer to represent a dissatisfied defendant.

Indigent Panels. Panel attorneys are lawyers in private practice who survive a selection process and agree to represent indigent defendants at fees set by a state, county, or federal system. Panel attorneys typically serve at the pleasure of local judges and so may be reluctant to use strategies that, while proper, may discomfort some judges. A locality may set up a panel attorney system in lieu of P.D. offices. But many localities with P.D. offices also maintain indigent panels for defendants whom the P.D. cannot ethically represent. For example, codefendants charged with armed robbery have conflicting legal interests, and a public defender could ethically represent only one of them. A judge would have to appoint a separate lawyer, in many localities a panel attorney, to represent the other defendant.

Private Defense Lawyers. Defendants with financial means often choose to be represented by lawyers in private practice. Private lawyers sometimes charge an hourly rate that varies according to locality, the lawyer's experience, and the severity of criminal charges. Private lawyers may charge a set fee for routine types of cases. Ethical rules forbid private criminal defense attorneys from charging "contingent fees" in which the amount of the fee depends on the outcome of a case. Many private criminal defense lawyers spend years as a prosecutor before turning to criminal defense work. A defendant has the right to substitute one privately retained lawyer for another so long as the delay involved in doing so does not unfairly affect the prosecution's case.

Self-Representation. Criminal defendants who are capable of understanding and participating in trial proceedings also have a right to represent themselves (referred to as "pro per" or "pro se" representation). (*Faretta v. California*, U.S. Sup. Ct. (1975).) Judges can appoint legal advisors, but they cannot force legal representation on competent defendants who insist on representing themselves.

Real-Life Illustration

Colin Ferguson, nicknamed the Long Island Railroad Killer, was tried for murdering six commuters in 1995. Ferguson faced imprisonment for life with no possibility of parole if he was convicted, and testifying survivors would undoubtedly suffer stress and anxiety when Ferguson cross-examined them in court. Nevertheless, the judge had no basis for refusing Ferguson's demand to represent himself. Though Ferguson was legally competent, his defense was inept and he was convicted of all six murders.

Timing. The right to counsel often begins when a defendant is formally charged with a crime and first appears in court for a bail hearing or arraignment. However, important earlier stages of criminal investigations can trigger an indigent suspect's right to representation by a government-paid lawyer. For example, a suspect who is interrogated and then put into a lineup has the right to counsel during these proceedings. The right to counsel continues through the first appeal of a conviction. In the event of further appeals and other postconviction petitions for relief (often called *collateral attacks* on a conviction), judges may appoint lawyers for indigent offenders but typically need not do so.

> **EXAMPLE:** Taylor is in prison, serving a sentence of 25-years-to-life. Though the conviction that resulted in the lengthy sentence was minor, it triggered the state's three strikes law. After serving ten years, and long after the appeals process concluded, Taylor submits a petition for *habeas corpus* to the court, arguing that his sentence is unconstitutional because it imposed cruel and unusual punishment. Taylor has no right to representation by a government-paid lawyer, though the state can appoint a lawyer for Taylor if it chooses to do so.

Effective Assistance. To assure that trials are fair, defendants have a constitutional right to *effective* legal representation. (*Strickland v. Washington*, U.S. Sup. Ct. (1984).) A conviction is set aside if an attorney's deficient representation caused prejudice to a defendant. Prejudice results if a reasonable probability exists that competent counsel would have achieved a better outcome. Here are three examples of how that rule works:

- **Overwhelming Evidence of Guilt.** When a defendant is convicted of a crime based on overwhelming evidence of guilt, it is difficult to set aside a conviction based on ineffective counsel. This may be true, for example, even if the defendant's government-paid lawyer dozed off at trial or neglected to object to the admission of improper evidence.
- **Failure to Mitigate Death Sentencing.** If a reasonable probability exists that ineffective counsel resulted in a death sentence instead of life imprisonment, the death sentence will be set aside and a new sentencing hearing will take place. For example, this might occur if a defendant's lawyer neglected to present mitigating evidence about physical and sexual abuse endured by the defendant throughout his childhood.
- **The Fool for a Client.** Ineffective self-representation rarely results in setting aside a conviction. A conviction will stand so long as

the trial judge had an adequate basis for concluding that the defendant was capable of participating in the trial. Defendants who attempt to set aside convictions on the basis of their own poor performance should remember the aphorism, "He who represents himself has a fool for a client."

 Legal Authority Examples

Sixth Amendment: "In all criminal prosecutions, the accused shall enjoy the right to ... have the assistance of counsel for his defense."

Utah: Legal counsel shall be assigned to represent each indigent and the indigent shall also be provided access to defense resources necessary for an effective defense, if there is a substantial probability that the penalty to be imposed is confinement in either jail or prison if the indigent requests counsel or defense resources or if the court on its own orders counsel, defense resources, or both and the defendant does not reject the opportunity to be represented and provided defense resources.

Virginia: To determine whether defendants are indigent, judges orally question them and consider other evidence of their financial condition. Defendants are entitled to be represented by counsel at state expense if their available funds are equal to or below 125% of the federal poverty income guidelines prescribed for the size of the household of the accused by the federal Department of Health and Human Services.

Except in jurisdictions having a public defender, judges appoint counsel for indigent defendants according to a fair system of rotation among lawyers whose names are on a list maintained by the Indigent Defense Commission.

Georgia: A county may use a public defender system, legal aid and defender society, agency for indigent defense, a panel of private attorneys, or other means to provide adequate legal defense for indigents accused of felonies. Appointments of private attorneys shall be made on an impartial and equitable basis. More difficult or complex cases shall be assigned to attorneys with sufficient levels of experience and competence to afford adequate representation.

Related terms: arraignment; bail; death penalty; eyewitness identification; *Miranda* rights; three strikes laws; writ of *habeas corpus*; attorney-client privilege.

defense of property

See self-defense.

defenses

See affirmative defenses; alibi; duress; entrapment; impossibility; insanity; necessity; failure of proof; self-defense; statute of limitations.

deportation

Aliens who commit crimes while in the United States may be deported (or "removed") as well as fined and imprisoned. Though the federal government determines deportation rules, commission of either a federal or a state crime can result in an alien's deportation.

Convictions of Non-Immigration-Related Offenses. Title 8, Section 1227 of the United States Code identifies a host of non-immigration-related criminal offenses that can result in an alien's deportation. For example, crimes involving "moral turpitude," a category that includes virtually all felonies, can lead to deportation if a crime is committed within five years of an alien's admission to the country. (Crimes that are minor infractions will not trigger deportation—for example speeding tickets or shoplifting violations.) Aliens convicted of drug offenses, domestic violence, or child abuse at any time after admission are also subject to deportation—so, for example, an alien who has been in the U.S. for decades may be deported after a conviction for domestic violence or misdemeanor possession of marijuana.

Convictions of Immigration-Related Offenses. Convictions for violating federal immigration laws are a common basis of deportation orders. Virtually all of the activities that support illegal immigration constitute felonies and are punishable by fines, imprisonment, and

D

deportation. So, for example, a U.S. citizen who pays to have laborers smuggled into the U.S may be fined and imprisoned for felony trafficking. A U.S. citizen who participates in a sham marriage with a foreign national may be fined and imprisoned, and the foreign national may be deported.

No Conviction Needed. Even if aliens are neither charged with nor convicted of crimes, they may be deported for committing criminal offenses. This may be the case with foreign citizens who stay in the U.S. after a visa expires or if the U.S. government learns that a foreign national was part of an illegal criminal enterprise in the national's home country.

Guilty Pleas. In roughly 95% of all criminal cases, prosecutors obtain convictions by securing guilty pleas from defendants. Before defendants plead guilty, defense lawyers are responsible for advising them of a conviction's likely consequences. In situations in which noncitizens are charged with crimes, defense lawyers' responsibility extends to advising them that a conviction may result in deportation. (*Padilla v. Kentucky*, U.S. Sup. Ct. (2010).)

> **EXAMPLE:** Kane is a resident alien who has been in the U.S. legally for about six years. He is charged with felony drug trafficking. The offense is punishable by imprisonment of up to ten years. Kane's lawyer informs Kane that as a result of his willingness to inform on other members of the drug trafficking ring, if Kane pleads guilty the prosecutor will reduce the charge to a misdemeanor and recommend to the judge that Kane be imprisoned for no longer than six months. Before Kane pleads guilty, Kane's lawyer has to advise him that the conviction means that Kane is deportable. Note, a conviction for drug trafficking would not only result in Kane's deportation, but would also render him permanently ineligible to apply for readmission to the U.S. at a future time. The question of whether criminal defense lawyers are responsible for advising defendants of this consequence before they plead guilty was not addressed by the case of *Padilla v. Kentucky* and is unknown.

Due Process Limitations. U.S. immigration agencies do not have to extend the same due process rights to aliens facing deportation that the criminal justice system extends to individuals charged with crimes. Many aliens are eligible for a hearing before an immigration judge at which they may seek relief from a deportation order. At these hearings, aliens are entitled to be represented by counsel (at their own expense), to present evidence, and to cross-examine government witnesses. However, aliens who are repeat immigration law violators or who have committed serious crimes are subject to *summary removal*. With summary removal, no hearings take place and agents of the Department of Homeland Security rather than immigration judges decide whether to deport aliens. Federal judges do not generally review deportation orders.

That's a Relief. Immigration authorities have discretion to grant a deportable alien's request to remain in the U.S. An alien's status in the U.S. can affect deportation. For example, all else being equal, an immigration judge is more likely to exercise discretion in favor of a lawful permanent resident than an alien who is in the U.S. on a temporary visa. So long as they have not committed serious crimes, deportable aliens may be able to prevent deportation by showing that they are of good moral character. The U.S. Attorney General has the power to allow even deportable aliens who have been convicted of serious crimes to remain in the country. And deportable aliens may be able to remain in the U.S. if they can prove that they are likely to face persecution and torture if they are deported.

 Real-Life Illustration

Chinese national Kang was a member of a Chinese human rights group that provided food and shelter to Korean refugees. Kang fled to the U.S. to avoid arrest by Chinese authorities. Seeking to avoid deportation back to China, Kang demonstrated that Chinese authorities had arrested other members of the group and subjected them to various forms of torture, including beatings, suffocation, electric shocks, and sleep deprivation. Nevertheless,

D

the U.S. Board of Immigration Appeals ordered her deportation. But in 2010, a federal appellate court overturned the decision and allowed Kang to remain in the U.S. on the ground that Chinese authorities would torture her if she were deported.

 Legal Authority Examples

United States Code, Title 8: A noncitizen who enters the United States illegally is guilty of a misdemeanor punishable by a fine, incarceration for up to six months, and deportation. Repeat violations constitute a felony.

United States Code, Title 8: Any alien who (prior to the date of entry, at the time of any entry, or within five years of the date of any entry) knowingly has encouraged, induced, assisted, abetted, or aided any other alien to enter or to try to enter the United States in violation of law is deportable. The Attorney General may, in his discretion for humanitarian purposes, to assure family unity, or when it is otherwise in the public interest, waive deportation in the case of any alien lawfully admitted for permanent residence if the alien has encouraged, induced, assisted, abetted, or aided only an individual who at the time of the offense was the alien's spouse, parent, son, or daughter (and no other individual) to enter the United States in violation of law.

Related terms: plea bargaining; sentencing (punishment options).

determinate sentences

See sentencing (punishment options).

diminished capacity

Diminished capacity is a partial defense to a criminal charge that some states allow and others do not. A diminished capacity defense consists of a claim that a perpetrator of a crime may be legally sane yet have a mental disease or impairment that makes the offense in some sense unintentional. A successful diminished capacity defense

D

typically results in a conviction of a less serious crime, such as manslaughter instead of murder.

> **EXAMPLE:** In 1979, former San Francisco city supervisor Dan White fatally shot Mayor George Moscone and Supervisor Harvey Milk. White planned the killings: He carried extra bullets and climbed into City Hall through a window to avoid metal detectors. The jury accepted White's defense of diminished capacity based on evidence that his habit of eating junk food had created a chemical imbalance in his brain that left him legally incapable of premeditating his actions. White was convicted of voluntary manslaughter rather than murder. He served five years in prison and committed suicide two years after his release. The public anger over the success of the so-called "Twinkie defense" resulted in California voters approving a 1982 proposition that outlawed the diminished capacity defense.

 Legal Authority Examples

Section 5K2.13, United States Sentencing Guidelines: A judge may reduce the sentence of a defendant who committed a nonviolent offense while suffering from a significantly reduced mental capacity that contributed substantially to the commission of the offense. A judge cannot reduce a sentence however if the significantly reduced mental capacity was caused by the voluntary use of drugs or if a defendant's criminal history indicates that the defendant is dangerous.

Related terms: insanity.

direct examination

See trial phases (trial cycles).

D

discovery

Discovery is a pretrial process through which parties to lawsuits disclose information to each other prior to trial. One goal of discovery is to promote fair trial outcomes by reducing lawyers' opportunities to ambush adversaries at trial with surprise evidence. Discovery also promotes plea bargaining, as it allows prosecutors and defendants to evaluate the strengths and weaknesses of each other's evidence.

Civil vs. Criminal Discovery. Discovery methods such as depositions (oral questioning) and interrogatories (written questions) feature prominently in civil litigation. Moreover, parties to civil litigation control the discovery process, deciding what information to seek and when and how to seek it. Civil discovery is akin to the children's card game Go Fish in which a player can obtain certain cards only by asking for them. By contrast, the methods of civil discovery are largely unavailable in criminal cases, and rules, rather than prosecutors and defendants, control the discovery process. "Compelled disclosure" is probably a more accurate term than discovery for the pretrial exchanges of information in criminal cases.

To get an idea of the difference in discovery process between a civil and criminal case, consider a driver who struck and killed a pedestrian. If the driver is charged with the crime of vehicular manslaughter, the driver's investigator could attempt to interview witnesses that the prosecutor is likely to call to testify, but the witnesses do not have to speak to the investigator. The driver probably will be unable to depose the witnesses, and cannot send them written interrogatories. Nor can the prosecutor depose the driver or any defense witnesses. If the victim's family pursues the driver in a civil wrongful death suit, however, the driver and the victim's family can depose each other, and each can submit written interrogatories that the other must answer under oath.

Exculpatory Evidence. Prosecutors have a constitutional duty to turn over to defendants any material information they come across that might conceivably be exculpatory. (*Brady v. Maryland*, U.S.

Sup. Ct. (1963).) Exculpatory evidence is material if a reasonable probability exists that its disclosure would have changed a trial's outcome. (*Smith v. Cain*, U.S. Sup. Ct. (2012).) The duty to turn over exculpatory information exists even if defendants neglect to ask for it. This is true even if the prosecutor doubts the credibility of such evidence—for example a drunk witness who told a police officer that the defendant wasn't the perpetrator and then passed out, or a witness who makes conflicting statements.

> **EXAMPLE:** Murray is charged with residential burglary. The prosecutor turns over to Murray's attorney a written statement by prosecution witness Joan that she saw Murray enter the residence through an open window. Earlier, Joan had told a police officer that Murray had broken a window in order to get into the residence. The prosecutor has to disclose Joan's conflicting oral statement to the police officer to the defense, as it bears on Joan's credibility as a witness. If Joan has a previous criminal record, the prosecutor would have to disclose that information to Murray as well.

Open Wide. Prosecutors' broad duty of disclosure is such that they have to more or less open their files to defendants. Information that prosecutors routinely turn over to defendants includes:

- any statements defendants made to police officers
- police reports
- records of pretrial identification procedures such as lineups
- witness statements and contact information, including transcripts of grand jury testimony
- the results of forensic lab testing
- defendants' rap sheets.

Prosecutors do not have to disclose confidential information or information that might place witnesses in danger. For example, prosecutors typically do not have to disclose information that would enable defendants to learn the identity of undercover police informants. Nor do prosecutors have to turn over "strategy memos" that indicate their trial strategy.

D

Save Some for Me. Forensic testing has become a standard part of criminal prosecutions. For example, police lab tests indicate whether substances are illegal drugs, the alcohol content of a driver's blood, and whether the DNA of semen found at a crime scene closely resembles a suspect's DNA. Prosecutors not only have to turn over a record of the testing procedures and the results to defendants, but also, if at all possible, they have to preserve the sample so that defendants can conduct independent tests.

Defendants' Physical Characteristics. The Fifth Amendment states that defendants in criminal cases cannot be compelled to be witnesses against themselves. Nevertheless, discovery rules can constitutionally compel defendants to submit to reasonable physical and medical inspections of their bodies. The Fifth Amendment is not violated because these requirements are not the equivalent of testimony. For example, prosecutors can compel defendants to participate in lineups, and in appropriate cases to provide samples of their blood, hair, handwriting, and voice.

Affirmative Defenses. Discovery rules can also constitutionally compel defendants to disclose and turn over information related to affirmative defenses. For example:

- **Alibi Defense.** Defendants who plan to offer alibi evidence or claim that they acted in self-defense have to notify prosecutors of their plan, provide prosecutors with contact information of defense witnesses, and provide prosecutors with summaries of those witnesses' expected testimony.
- **Insanity Defense.** Defendants who intend to rely on an insanity defense have to notify prosecutors of their intent and have to make themselves available for examination by prosecutors' mental health experts.

These compelled defense disclosures do not violate the Fifth Amendment because discovery rules merely advance the time at which defendants must provide information from the time of trial to a time prior to trial. (*Williams v. Florida*, U.S. Sup. Ct. (1970).) Reciprocal discovery laws justify these disclosures. When defendants demand information from prosecutors, the theory goes, discovery should be a two-way street. Reciprocal discovery rules are the legal equivalent of the old saying, "I showed you mine, so you have to show me yours." So, for example, if a defendant refuses to turn over any information to the prosecutor concerning his intended alibi defense, the judge is likely to rule that the defendant is barred from offering alibi evidence at trial. However, a judge might also allow the defendant to present alibi evidence and then recess the trial so as to give the prosecutor a chance to prepare a response to the alibi evidence.

 Legal Authority Examples

Indiana: A defendant who intends to offer an alibi defense must notify the prosecutor of that intention in writing before trial. The notice must include specific information concerning the exact place where the defendant claims to have been on the date stated in the indictment or information. If a defendant fails to provide the required notice, and cannot show good cause for the failure to do so, the court shall exclude evidence offered by the defendant to establish an alibi.

Federal Rule of Criminal Procedure 15: A judge may grant a party's request to depose a witness prior to trial if exceptional circumstances exist.

Federal Rule of Criminal Procedure 16: Information that prosecutors have to disclose or provide to defendants includes a summary of any oral statements made to police officers; all written statements made by them in the government's possession; a copy of their criminal record; any tangible objects or photos that the government plans to use at trial; reports of any physical or mental examinations or scientific tests; and a written summary of any expert testimony the government intends to use at trial. Defendants are not entitled to internal government documents relating to the investigation or prosecution of a case.

Related terms: alibi; self-defense; insanity; eyewitness identification.

disorderly conduct

Disorderly conduct encompasses a variety of ways in which people can create a public disturbance. Activities constituting disorderly conduct vary from one state to another. Some states gather together these offenses under the phrase "breach of the peace" or public order laws. Disorderly conduct can constitute either an infraction or a misdemeanor, usually punishable at most by a small fine and a short jail sentence.

Status Offenses; Loitering and Vagrancy. Disorderly conduct laws are the permissible descendants of centuries-old and sometimes colorful laws that allowed police to arrest people based on their disfavored status. For example, older and now-obsolete laws allowed police officers to arrest people for being a vagabond, a vagrant, a rogue, a common drunk, a drug addict, or a common loafer. Such laws constitute cruel and unusual punishment prohibited by the Eighth Amendment because they punish people for who they are rather than what they did. (*Powell v. Texas*, U.S. Sup. Ct. (1968).) Vagrancy laws are also unconstitutional under the Due Process of Law clause of the Fourteenth Amendment because their vagueness fails to provide people with fair notice of improper behavior—for example, a law that prohibits loitering (remaining in a public place for a lengthy period of time without apparent purpose). At the same time, more modern laws that have tried to make it illegal to be a gang member are also unconstitutional because they punish people for their status rather than for their conduct. (That said, the punishment for a crime can constitutionally be increased if the offender committed it to benefit a street gang.)

Drunk in Public. This offense (aka "drunk and disorderly" and "public intoxication") consists of being in a public place while willfully under the influence of alcohol, drugs, or both to such an extent as to be unable to care for oneself, or others, or while obstructing a public sidewalk or road. The language of this law is sufficiently clear to provide people with notice of prohibited behavior. Involuntary intoxication, where someone was forced to drink alcohol or was drugged, will not result in a drunk and disorderly conviction.

Disturbing the Peace. This offense encompasses such activities as fighting in public, making an unreasonably loud amount of noise to disrupt a public activity or provoke another person to violence, and directing belligerent words at another person that are likely to provoke an immediate and violent response. In other words, disturbing the peace covers the type of behavior expected from hooligans, ne'er-do-wells, and drunks.

Bargaining Chips. Prosecutors frequently use disorderly conduct offenses as bargaining chips. They may dismiss charges of more serious misdemeanors in return for defendants pleading guilty (or *nolo contendere*) to a charge of disorderly conduct.

> EXAMPLE: Bo is charged with assault relating to a drunken altercation with a man outside a bar. Bo has no previous arrests. It's clear that he was acting aggressively, but he can make a viable argument that he was merely defending himself during the altercation. After negotiations between Bo's attorney and the prosecutor, the prosecutor agrees to dismiss the assault charge if Bo pleads guilty to disturbing the peace and furnishes proof that he has completed a court-approved alcohol education program (such as attending a certain number of AA meetings).

 Legal Authority Examples

Texas: Using abusive, indecent, profane, or vulgar language in a public place that tends to incite an immediate breach of the peace is a class C misdemeanor.

California: Intentionally engaging in a fight with another person in a public place is a misdemeanor punishable by a fine of not more than $400 and/or incarceration for not more than 90 days.

Related terms: plea bargaining; elements of a crime; intoxication defense.

district attorney (D.A.)

See prosecutors.

diversion

See sentencing (punishment options).

DNA analysis

DNA—deoxyribonucleic acid—is a molecule that determines genetic makeup. Each human being has a unique DNA structure. DNA's uniqueness makes it possible for experts to testify to the likelihood that a defendant committed a charged crime. DNA samples are usually obtained from traces of hair, blood, saliva, or semen found at a crime scene. Sometimes experts may find evidence of a victim's DNA on a suspect. Judges began to admit DNA evidence in criminal cases in the mid-1980s, approximately 30 years after DNA was initially decoded. An English geneticist named Alec Jeffreys (later Sir Alec Jeffreys) was the first to use DNA analysis to identify a criminal suspect—a baker with the odd name of Colin Pitchfork, who was convicted as the 1986 killer of two teenage girls in Leicestershire.

Strike Up the Band. Forensic DNA experts use a gel electrophoresis process to produce pictures of DNA fragments in the form of bands. These bands show up at different heights in a picture. Experts estimate match probabilities when the band patterns in different samples are sufficiently similar.

When making comparisons, a forensic DNA expert typically displays two pictures of band patterns, one known to depict a defendant's DNA and the other taken from a specimen found at a crime scene. Though the bands may not match up exactly, the expert can estimate the probabilities of a match if the differences are within tolerances established by the FBI's "match window."

Probabilities. Even if DNA samples appear to match, forensic experts usually cannot say with certainty that they came from the same person. The reason is that two different people can have the same genotype—that is, they may have a similar genetic constitution or pattern. Thus, forensic experts usually testify to the probability that any randomly selected person's DNA would also produce a match. For example, a forensic expert may testify, "The likelihood that any randomly selected person's DNA would match the defendant's DNA is one in 59 million." In other cases, the expert's opinion relies on a rough estimate rather than on a numerical estimate of probability. For example, the expert might state, "DNA analysis leads to an overwhelming likelihood that the defendant was the source of the DNA that was extracted from the rape victim's vaginal swab."

DNA for Two. Typically, police agencies collect physical evidence and conduct DNA analyses. The government's duty is to preserve evidence whenever possible so that defendants can conduct their own DNA analyses.

> **EXAMPLE:** In the process of extracting DNA from a tiny bone fragment that the police found at a crime scene, forensic expert Sam necessarily destroys the fragment. Though the defense has no opportunity to conduct its own DNA analysis of the fragment, the results of Sam's analysis are likely to be admissible so long as the prosecution turns over to the defense copies of the records pertaining to the fragment's collection and testing.

A Forensic Gold Standard. Both the principles underlying DNA analysis and the methods for extracting and profiling DNA samples are universally accepted. When DNA analysis excludes suspects, police look elsewhere to solve crimes and judges overturn convictions that postconviction DNA testing proved wrong. When DNA analysis implicates suspects, they almost always plead guilty. Of course, no human process is completely infallible. For example, lab testing errors can occur. A previously unknown identical twin

D

can turn out to be "the real killer," but this is more the stuff of daytime soap operas than reality. In general, DNA analysis is far more conclusive than any other type of evidence in the criminal justice system. For example, a 2009 report of a study conducted by the National Academy of Sciences entitled *Strengthening Forensic Sciences in the United States* sharply criticized the standards and functioning of government forensic laboratories, but excepted DNA testing from its criticism.

Prisoners and DNA. Over a period of approximately 20 years, DNA analysis obtained through court orders obtained by attorneys associated with The Innocence Project has led to the release of around 250 wrongly convicted prisoners. Many of these prisoners served years in prison and some were on Death Row. In *District Attorney's Office v. Osborne* (2009), the U.S. Supreme Court ruled that prisoners do not have a constitutional right to demand DNA testing of evidence. However, statutes in most states give courts the power to order postconviction DNA testing.

All in the Family. A process known as Familial DNA Testing helps forensic experts by tracking similar but not identical DNA patterns. These patterns are then compared with the patterns of other family members to determine if there is a likely match. Currently, only a handful of states allow Familial DNA Testing—for example, California permits the practice in the case of violent crimes.

 Real-Life Illustration

Familial DNA Testing was used to arrest Lonnie Franklin, Jr., in 2010 for murdering at least ten women over a period of approximately two decades. The case was cracked when Franklin's son was arrested for an unrelated crime. Police collected a DNA sample and realized that Franklin's son's DNA was similar to DNA collected from the sites where the murders had occurred. The similarity led police to suspect that Franklin might be the killer. They extracted a sample of Franklin's DNA from a piece of pizza that he had discarded, and arrested him after analysis showed that his DNA matched that collected from the crime scenes.

Brr—It's Cold in Here. DNA analysis has enabled police officers to solve many "cold" cases (crimes that have remained unsolved for years). So long as biological evidence pertaining to the crime still exists, police officers may subject it to DNA analysis in an attempt to identify the wrongdoer.

 Real-Life Illustration

Los Angeles newlywed Sherri Rasmussen was shot to death in 1986. Partly due to sloppy work by LAPD homicide investigators, the crime remained unsolved until LAPD officer Stephanie Lazarus was charged in 2009 with Rasmussen's murder. Rasmussen had bitten her killer, and a swab of the bite mark tissue that had been made shortly after the murder had remained in a freezer in the coroner's office ever since. When an LAPD Cold Case unit identified Lazarus as the possible killer, plainclothes police officers surreptitiously trailed her as she ran errands. When Lazarus threw out the cup and straw that she'd been drinking from, the officers grabbed the items from the trash and subjected them to DNA analysis. When the DNA matched the DNA on the bite mark swab that had remained frozen for 23 years, Lazarus was charged with Rasmussen's murder. (Lazarus was the spurned former girlfriend of Rasmussen's husband.)

 Legal Authority Examples

Federal Rule of Evidence 702: Pursuant to *Daubert v. Merrell Dow* (U.S. Sup. Ct. (1993)): Qualified forensic experts can testify to the results of DNA analysis because the testimony is the product of reliable principles and methods, so long as the expert has sufficient data to support the analysis and has applied the principles and methods reliably to the facts of the case.

California: Following convictions, the government is to preserve evidence that is reasonably likely to contain biological information for as long as a prisoner is incarcerated. Upon motion by prisoners, courts can order postconviction DNA testing of evidence if the offender's identity was a significant issue in dispute and if a reasonable probability exists that testing would alter the verdict or reduce the sentence. A court can order DNA testing of evidence that was not tested previously, or that was tested but a reasonable probability exists that additional DNA testing will produce a result that favors a prisoner.

Related terms: expert witnesses; forensic science.

D.O.A.

Dead on arrival, usually at a hospital.

domestic violence

Domestic violence statutes punish physical abuse of intimate partners or former intimate partners, and in some jurisdictions, threats to inflict abuse as well. While definitions vary, an intimate partner or former partner for the purposes of domestic violence statutes often includes a spouse or ex-spouse, a cohabitant, a child, or even a person in a current or past dating relationship. The relationship may be hetero- or homosexual. Domestic violence is an umbrella term that encompasses a variety of specific crimes such as spouse abuse, child abuse, child sexual abuse, child neglect, and elder abuse. Some states also criminalize emotional abuse of children and intimate partners, and parental abuse. Crimes of domestic violence can be either misdemeanors or felonies depending on the severity of the abusive acts.

Reasons for Domestic Violence Statutes. Many domestic violence crimes could also be prosecuted under more general statutes that criminalize stalking, assault, and rape (see separate entries). But because domestic violence is a breach of intimate trust as well as an act of violence, its penalties are often more severe. For example, conviction of a crime of domestic violence may entail a mandatory jail sentence and a "no contact with victim" order. Also, since an abuser's relationship with a victim may be a continuing one, identifying a crime as one of domestic violence allows judges to order abusers to participate in therapeutic counseling. Finally, keeping track of the number and types of domestic violence convictions helps researchers and lawmakers develop programs to try to stem the frequency of these all-too-common crimes.

Police Response to Domestic Violence Assaults. Probably the most common form of domestic violence involves a man physically assaulting a female intimate partner. In such cases, police officers were for many years criticized for not taking domestic violence seriously. Instead of arresting alleged abusers, police officers often told them, "Walk around the block a few times and cool off, and don't do it again." Stung by the criticism, many police departments have responded with "zero tolerance" policies requiring the arrest of domestic violence suspects, even when the target of abuse tells the police, "I don't want him arrested." However, assaults against intimate partners continue to be a major social problem, and whether toughened responses by police officers have in any way diminished cycles of abuse is uncertain.

The Confrontation Clause and Domestic Violence Assault Prosecutions. A common scenario in domestic violence cases occurs when female victims refuse to cooperate with police officers and prosecutors after their attackers are charged with crimes. Victims often recant their stories, ask prosecutors to drop the charges, and decline to testify in court or even go into hiding until after the case is over.

Until the U.S. Supreme Court's ruling in the case of *Crawford v. Washington* (2004), prosecutors were often able to convict domestic abusers even without a victim's testimony. Prosecutors would rely on testimony by a police officer, who would typically testify to a victim's physical injuries following an attack and to the description of the attack and the attacker that the victim gave soon after the attack occurred. But the Court ruled in *Crawford* that police officers could no longer testify to an absent victim's account of an attack. The Court ruled that the officer's testimony was inadmissible hearsay that violated the Sixth Amendment's Confrontation Clause by denying the defendant an opportunity to confront and cross-examine the victim personally. The Court recognized that its ruling

D

might result in a "windfall" to domestic violence defendants, but decided that upholding what it considered to be valid constitutional principles outweighed the risk of letting guilty abusers go free. *Crawford* and its progeny have put a major crimp in prosecutors' efforts to convict domestic abusers.

See confrontation of prosecution witnesses.

Domestic Abusers Can't Own Guns. Believing that many domestic abusers are recidivists, and hoping to reduce the injuries that they might inflict, Congress passed a law making it a federal crime for people convicted of domestic violence to own a gun. (18 U.S.C. § 922(g)(9).) The U.S. Supreme Court upheld the law in the case of *United States v. Hayes* (2009), ruling that it applied to any conviction based on an act of domestic violence, even if a defendant was not convicted of a crime falling under the "domestic violence" classification.

 Real-Life Illustration

On October 21, 2012, Radcliffe Haughton, a 45-year-old man with a history of spousal abuse, entered a spa in a Milwaukee mall and opened fire. He killed his wife (very likely his primary target) and two additional victims, and injured four other women before killing himself. Haughton had purchased the gun he used the day before the shootings. Despite Haughton's history of domestic violence, Wisconsin state law did not require a background check because the seller was a private individual rather than a gun dealer.

 Legal Authority Examples

Wisconsin defines domestic violence as an offense committed by an adult against another adult that he or she lives with, has lived with, or shares a child with involving intentional infliction of pain, illness, or injury, or intentional impairment of physical ability, or any type of sexual assault, or a physical act that would cause a reasonable person to fear for his or her safety.

Minnesota: Child abuse crimes include the following types of physical abuse:

- acts resulting in nonaccidental injuries to a child including patterns of unexplained injuries and injuries that appear to have been caused in a manner inconsistent with an explanation of how the injuries occurred.

- unreasonably restraining a child with tying, caging, or chaining and excessive or unreasonably forceful discipline that leaves injuries or marks on a child.

- assaultive behavior not usually associated with discipline such as shaking, kicking, cutting, and burning.

 RESOURCE
For information on how each state defines and punishes domestic violence, go to www.nolo.com/domesticviolence.

double jeopardy

The Fifth Amendment protects people against being tried or punished more than once for the same offense. In general, a defendant is "in jeopardy" for purposes of the Fifth Amendment once a jury is empanelled or (in a nonjury trial) when the first witness testifies. So, for example, if a judge dismisses a case after the jurors are sworn in, the defendant cannot be put on trial again for that crime (even if he goes on television and brags about getting away with it).

When Prosecutors Can Try and Try Again. Successive trials of the same person for the same charges can take place in a variety of circumstances despite the Fifth Amendment's prohibition of double jeopardy. Midtrial illness that renders a necessary party such as the trial judge too ill to continue on the case might result in a mistrial and a second trial before a new judge and jury. When jurors cannot agree on a unanimous verdict, a hung jury results and the prosecution may choose to refile the same charges. Defendants who appeal and convince an appellate court to reverse their conviction

D

usually can be tried again. For example, consider a defendant who is found not guilty of first and second degree murder, but is convicted of the less serious crime of voluntary manslaughter. If the defendant appeals and the conviction is reversed because improper evidence was admitted at the trial, the government can retry the defendant on the charge of voluntary manslaughter. Double jeopardy principles prevent the government from retrying the defendant for first or second degree murder because the defendant has already been acquitted of those charges.

When the same conduct violates both state and federal laws, each jurisdiction can charge the same person with a crime without violating the prohibition against double jeopardy. Unless exceptional circumstances exist, however, either a state or the federal government will typically prosecute a defendant, but not both.

EXAMPLE: Sears is charged with the murder of Roe. Because the alleged murder took place in a post office (U.S. property), both the state and the federal government have the right to try Sears for murder. The federal government defers to the state, which files murder charges against Sears. Sears is acquitted. Ordinarily, the federal government would not prosecute Sears a second time. But, if the jurors in the state trial had been bribed to acquit Sears, the federal government could try him for murder without violating the double jeopardy clause of the Fifth Amendment.

 Real-Life Illustration

After a series of gruesome California murders drew worldwide attention, Charles Manson was convicted of conspiracy to commit murder in 1971 and was sentenced to death. Shortly afterwards, the U.S. Supreme Court ruled that California's death penalty statute was unconstitutional because it gave unfettered discretion to jurors. As a result of the ruling, Manson's sentence was reduced to life in prison. The double jeopardy clause of the Fifth Amendment prevented reinstatement of the death penalty against

Manson, even after California enacted a constitutionally valid death penalty statute.

Lesser-Included Offenses. The same unlawful conduct can violate a gaggle of different laws. The prohibition against double jeopardy means that states get one bite at the illegal apple. They cannot file successive, separate charges under each law that criminalizes the same conduct. Consider a defendant who is charged with assault with intent to murder. Other less serious crimes may also apply to the defendant's alleged misconduct, including assault with a deadly weapon, simple assault, battery, and trespass. These separate crimes constitute a single crime for purposes of the double jeopardy clause. So, if the state prosecutes the defendant for assault with intent to commit murder, whether the defendant is convicted or acquitted, the defendant cannot separately be tried for any of the other crimes.

Multiple Crimes, One Punishment. The double jeopardy clause also means that defendants can only be punished once for the same misconduct, no matter how many separate rules that conduct violates. For example, if an attack on a single victim results in convictions for assault with a deadly weapon, assault with intent to kill, and attempted murder, the defendant can only receive a single punishment. However, each victim can be the subject of a separate crime for double jeopardy purposes. For example, someone who robs two people at gunpoint has committed two separate crimes for purposes of double jeopardy and may be convicted and punished for each crime. The judge has discretion to run the sentences concurrently (at the same time) or consecutively (one after the other).

 Legal Authority Examples

Double Jeopardy Clause of the Fifth Amendment: "Nor shall any person be subject for the same offense to be twice put in jeopardy of life or limb."

California: A crime that is punishable in different ways by different laws shall be punished under the provision that provides for the longest potential term of imprisonment; the crime cannot be punished under more than one provision. An acquittal or conviction and sentence for one crime bars a separate prosecution for the same conduct.

Related terms: sentencing (punishment options).

drug offenses

Drug offenses refer to state and federal laws that criminalize virtually every aspect of the country's flourishing illegal drug industry—from importation, manufacture, and cultivation of illegal drugs, through distribution ("trafficking"), and eventually to the sale of drugs to individuals and the possession and use of the drugs by those individuals. Criminal statutes typically restrict or prohibit:

- commonly used illegal drugs such as marijuana, cocaine, heroin, ecstasy, and methamphetamine
- inhalants, hallucinogens, and synthetic "club drugs," and
- abusive use of prescription drugs, furnishing alcohol to minors, and being under the influence of drugs or alcohol.

Many drug offenses are felonies. However, possession of a small quantity of a drug for personal use is often a misdemeanor and can even constitute only an infraction.

Search and Seizure. Most legal disputes in a drug crime prosecution concern the legality of a police officer's search for (and seizure of) contraband. Typically, a judge's ruling that a search violated the Fourth Amendment terminates a prosecution. For example, a prosecutor has no case if the evidence was obtained by an officer who, acting on a hunch, climbed through the open window of a residence and found bags of illegal drugs hidden in a closet. The illegality of the search means that the drugs are not admissible in evidence.

For-Sale Signs. The penalty for selling illegal drugs or possessing them for sale is typically far more severe than the penalty for possessing them for personal use. Thus, another critical issue in many drug cases is whether a wrongdoer intended to use or sell drugs. Factors that typically determine the outcome of the "sale or use" issue include drug quantity and the presence or absence of packaging materials and weapons. For example, if a legal search pursuant to an arrest warrant reveals numerous baggies containing methamphetamine in a backpack, the quantity of meth makes it much more likely that it is for sale; an individual user would not be likely to consume that quantity.

Paraphernalia. Drug use commonly entails the use of devices. For example, methamphetamine and opium users may use small pipes, heroin users may use hypodermic needles, and cocaine users may use spoons. Suspects may be charged with a crime for possessing such paraphernalia even if they are not in possession of illegal drugs.

Prescription Drugs. Prescription drugs often serve as the basis of criminal charges. The doctors who overprescribe them and the patients and patients' associates who abuse them may all be guilty of drug law violations.

 Real-Life Illustration

Anna Nicole Smith was a celebrity model who died of an accidental drug overdose in 2007. An autopsy revealed that she had about ten different prescription drugs in her system when she died. Smith's ex-boyfriend, Howard K. Stern, and two doctors, Sandeep Kapoor and Khristine Eroshevich, were tried in Los Angeles in 2010 for conspiring to provide excessive prescription drugs to Smith even though they knew she was an addict.

Under the Influence. Appearing in public or driving while under the influence of a drug, whether legal or illegal, is itself a crime.

 RESOURCE
For information on how each state defines and punishes driving under the influence of marijuana, go to www.nolo.com/marijuanadui.

Diversion. Many states have created diversion programs to try to help drug users get clean and stay sober. In a typical diversion

D

program, criminal charges are dismissed for offenders who complete an authorized treatment program and avoid further arrests for a program's duration (often one to two years). Diversion typically is available only to first-time offenders who are charged with possession of an illegal drug.

> EXAMPLE: Though she has used heroin for many years, Val is arrested for possession of a small baggie of powder cocaine for the first time after a police officer pulls her car over for running a stop sign. Val may be eligible for diversion because, although she is a long-term user, she is a first-time offender. However, if the police officer opens the trunk of Val's car and finds it filled with boxes of powder cocaine (and Val is charged with transportation of cocaine), she is not eligible for diversion.

Policy Debates. The criminal justice system is the battleground on which much of the country's decades-long war on drugs has been fought. Among the specific battles:

- The amount of money and resources to devote to arresting, prosecuting, and incarcerating nonviolent drug offenders.
- The disparate racial impact of drug laws. For example, for many years, under federal law the punishment for possession of crack cocaine (a drug of choice primarily for black users) was 100 times more severe than the punishment for possession of the same amount of powder cocaine (a drug of choice primarily for Caucasian users). In 2010, Congress voted to reduce the sentencing disparity to 18 to 1.
- The arguable incoherency of drug vs. alcohol laws. Alcohol is at least as harmful and addicting as many drugs that cannot be legally possessed or used at all, yet generally legal.

 Legal Authority Examples

Federal: A first offense of trafficking in up to 5,000 grams of cocaine is a felony punishable by imprisonment for not less than five nor more than 40 years.

Arizona: The following activities are felonies of different degrees: knowingly possessing or using a narcotic drug, possessing a narcotic drug for sale, possessing equipment or chemicals for the purpose of manufacturing a narcotic drug, manufacturing a narcotic drug, administering a narcotic drug to another person, obtaining a narcotic drug by fraud, deceit, misrepresentation, or subterfuge, and transporting for sale or offering to transport for sale or selling, transferring, or offering to sell or transfer a narcotic drug.

Ohio: Possession or use of drug abuse instruments by anyone other than licensed health professions is a misdemeanor of the second degree; a repeat offense is a misdemeanor of the first degree. The penalty for a violation includes suspension of an offender's driver's license for not less than six months nor more than five years. Possession of a small amount of illegal drugs is a misdemeanor of the first degree.

RESOURCE

For information on how each state defines and punishes drug possession offenses, go to www.nolo.com/drugs.

Related terms: entrapment; intoxication defense; marijuana offenses; sentencing (punishment options); search and seizure.

drunk driving (DUI or DWI)

Drivers typically commit the crime popularly called drunk driving in one of two ways.

- Drive Drunk. One way is to exhibit impaired driving (e.g., driving too fast or too slow, or weaving in and out of lanes) while displaying symptoms of excessive use of alcohol or drugs (e.g., an unsteady gait, slurred speech, bloodshot eyes).
- High BAC. The second way that drivers commit the crime is to drive with a blood alcohol content (BAC) of 0.08% or higher, regardless of whether alcohol use impaired driving or

D

affected a driver's physical condition. In rare cases a high BAC reading may be caused by circumstances not related to the consumption of alcohol and in those situations may not serve as the basis for a DUI conviction.

EXAMPLE: A highway patrol officer finds Daniel Jackson asleep behind the wheel of his car with the keys in the ignition on the shoulder of a rural highway. The officer rouses Jackson and asks him to get out of the car. The officer then carries out a field sobriety test and later administers a Breathalyzer test. The test shows that Jackson's BAC is 0.13%. Jackson is guilty of drunk driving even in the absence of evidence of impaired driving.

However, if Jackson denies ingesting alcohol or drugs and produces an expert witness to testify that the BAC reading was erroneous and caused by the specialized experimental diet program that he had recently begun, there is a basis to conclude that Jackson is not guilty.

 Legal Authority Examples

California: Driving under the influence of alcohol or drugs, or with a blood alcohol level of 0.08 or higher, is a misdemeanor. A first offense is punishable by incarceration of up to a year, probation, driver's license revocation or restriction, and completion of an alcohol education program. Judges might also order offenders to fit their cars with an ignition interlock device (preventing the car from starting without an alcohol-free breath sample from the driver).

See intoxication defense.

due process

Due process refers to the concept derived from the Constitution that there should be fairness in all legal matters, both civil and criminal. To guarantee due process, all legal procedures set by statute and court practice must be followed in the same manner for each individual so that no prejudicial or unequal treatment will result. While somewhat indefinite, the term due process can be gauged by its aim to safeguard both private and public rights against unfairness. Due process provisions are located in the Fifth and Fourteenth amendments to the U.S. Constitution. The primary difference between them is that the Fifth Amendment binds the federal government and the Fourteenth Amendment binds state governments.

See writ of *habeas corpus*; presumed innocent; interrogation tactics.

DUI (driving under the influence of alcohol or drugs)

See drunk driving (DUI or DWI).

duress

Duress refers to a genuine threat of immediate and serious physical harm. Offenders can escape criminal liability if they commit crimes under duress—for example, someone holds a gun to a perpetrator's head and demands that the perpetrator commit a robbery.

No "I for an Eye." Most states do not permit a duress defense in murder cases. In the horrible and hopefully rare situation in which an individual is threatened with immediate death unless he or she slays another, the law threatens those who decide not to sacrifice their lives for the lives of others with murder charges. However, a few states reduce the crime to manslaughter when a defendant kills under duress.

Immediate and Serious. A valid duress defense requires threatened bodily harm to be both immediate and serious. So, threats regarding property—"I'm going to huff and puff your house to the ground"—or threats about actions in the future—"I'm going to come back after I finish viewing the Impressionists exhibit at the art museum and beat you up"—will not qualify. Similarly, the threatened harm must be specific and serious, so euphemisms such as "I'm going to

D

kick your ass" or "I'm going to open a can on you," also would not likely trigger a duress defense.

Battered Woman Syndrome. Women who have been subjected to a pattern of violent abuse by their partners may commit a crime (or assist their partners to commit one) out of a learned fear that their partners will otherwise subject them to additional abuse. In such situations, courts may allow a duress defense even though an abuser does not directly threaten immediate and serious harm.

 Legal Authority Examples

Washington State: Duress is a defense if a defendant is compelled to participate in a crime by another's threat or use of force that creates a reasonable apprehension in the defendant's mind that refusal will result in immediate death or grievous bodily harm. The defense of duress is not available if the crime charged is murder or manslaughter, or if the defendant intentionally or recklessly placed himself or herself in a situation in which duress was probable. The defense of duress is not established solely by a showing that a married person acted on the command of his or her spouse.

Related terms: expert witnesses; syndrome evidence; abuse excuse.

DWI (driving while intoxicated)

See drunk driving (DUI or DWI).

electronic surveillance

Electronic surveillance occurs when police officers track people's locations and movements by monitoring the signals emitted by mobile phones, global positioning systems (GPSs), and similar electronic devices. Because the signals are in the public space, police officers can keep tabs on people without physically observing them.

Legislators and judges have not yet developed broadly accepted guidelines for evaluating when government officials' monitoring of electronic signals constitutes a Fourth Amendment search requiring a search warrant. As electronic signals go through public airways, people cannot reasonably expect complete privacy. Nevertheless, courts will almost certainly not allow police officers to monitor people randomly for weeks at a time, hoping to eventually uncover evidence of criminal activity. On the other hand, if police officers receive credible information that a specific crime is about to occur or is unfolding, they probably won't need to obtain a search warrant in order to electronically monitor the locations and movements of the suspects.

Related terms: search and seizure.

elements of a crime

When the government charges a defendant with a crime, the charge consists of separate components called *elements*. For example, the crime of first degree murder has five elements: The defendant (1) killed (2) another human being (3) unlawfully (4) with premeditation and (5) malice aforethought. So, if an indictment for murder fails to state that the alleged victim was a human being, the indictment is defective and must be dismissed. (Because the

E

indictment's filing does not place the defendant in legal jeopardy, the prosecutor can reinstate the charge by obtaining and filing an amended indictment.)

Similarly, the crime of robbery consists of two elements: The defendant (1) took property (2) by means of force or fear. So if a defendant is accused of robbing a jewelry store and the jurors are unable to conclude beyond a reasonable doubt that the defendant accomplished the theft by means of force or fear, the defendant is not guilty of robbery.

Sentencing Enhancements. Many criminal statutes provide for harsher sentences when specified circumstances exist. These circumstances are the equivalent of elements that prosecutors have to include in charges and prove beyond a reasonable doubt when they want judges to impose harsher sentences. (*Apprendi v. New Jersey*, U.S. Sup. Ct. (2001).) So, if a statute provides for longer prison terms for offenders who use weapons, the prosecutor can charge the defendant with use of a weapon and the jury must make a finding as to whether a weapon was used. Absent such actions, a judge cannot impose a longer prison term based on the defendant's use of a weapon.

Clarity. A basic criminal law tenet is that rules should provide people with adequate notice of what it is that the law forbids them to do. Laws can include abstract elements that judges and jurors have to interpret in the context of concrete events. But excessively vague legal elements that give police officers and judges unfettered discretion to make arrests and impose punishment render a rule invalid. For example, the term "reckless" is sufficiently precise so as to advise drivers of what kind of driving is punishable as reckless driving. But that would not be the case for a statute that made it a crime to "hang around on a public street without a good reason." This statute is invalid because a person has no way of knowing what a police officer, a judge, or a jury might consider to be a "good reason."

"Switcheroo—The Burden's on You." Rules can impose on defendants the burden of proving affirmative defenses such as entrapment and insanity. However, rule makers cannot switch the burden of proving elements of crimes away from prosecutors and onto defendants by redefining them as affirmative defenses. So, for example, a new criminal statute would be invalid if it provided, "Robbery is the taking of property, unless a defendant proves by a preponderance of the evidence that the defendant did not use means of force or fear." Such a statute would improperly shift the burden of proof of an element to defendants.

 Legal Authority Examples

The Due Process clauses of the Fifth and Fourteenth Amendments. Prosecutors are required to prove every fact necessary to constitute a charged crime beyond a reasonable doubt. (*In re Winship*, U.S. Sup. Ct. (1970).)

California: Jury instruction 2.90 instructs jurors that the prosecution has to prove each element of a charge beyond a reasonable doubt.

Related terms: burdens of proof; defenses: alibi; defenses: insanity; double jeopardy; first degree murder; robbery.

embezzlement

Embezzlement is a form of theft in which the owner has willingly given the thief access to, or possession of, the property that is stolen. Embezzlement is a form of "white-collar crime" because the thieves are often ordinary employees or professionals who abuse a property owner's trust rather than use physical violence. An example is a clerk in a convenience store regularly taking $50 from the till. People are guilty of embezzlement even if they have created (or implemented) a detailed plan to repay the embezzled sums. Embezzlement can be either a misdemeanor or a felony depending on the value of the property involved, but virtually all embezzlers steal property of sufficient value to qualify as felons. "Misappropriation" is another common term for embezzlement.

Nine-Tenths of the Law. Another form of embezzlement takes place when the thief keeps property that was given to the thief to give to another person, or to apply for the benefit of another person or cause. Typical examples include money that is collected for a cause and then siphoned off by the embezzler, and funds that are intended to be part of an estate plan and are embezzled by the trustee, attorney, or executor. (Note: the "rule" that you may have heard—possession is nine-tenths of the law—is not true.)

Punishment. Punishment for embezzlement can include a monetary fine, imprisonment followed by a term of probation, community service, and restitution. Restitution is money that the thief pays to the victim, compared to a fine that the thief pays to the state. When determining restitution a judge will typically include these factors:

- the amount of money stolen from the company or person
- the direct cost to the victim of fixing problems caused by the embezzlement, and
- the legal costs triggered by the embezzlement.

 Legal Authority Examples

Texas: Embezzlement occurs when one takes another's money and property through abuse of an official job or position of trust. Embezzlement of $15,000–$25,000 is punishable by imprisonment for up to 12 years.

New York: Embezzlement is the fraudulent appropriation of funds or property entrusted to a person's care but actually owned by someone else. Embezzlement of more than $3,000 but less than $25,000 is a felony punishable by imprisonment from 18 months to 20 years.

 RESOURCE
For information on how each state defines and punishes embezzlement, go to www.nolo.com/embezzlement.

Related terms: robbery; restitution.

entrapment

Entrapment is an affirmative defense that arises when government agents use overbearing tactics to induce people to commit a crime.

Opportunity Knocking. Government agents do not entrap defendants simply by offering them an *opportunity* to commit a crime. The justice system expects individuals to resist ordinary temptations to violate the law. An entrapment defense arises when government agents resort to repugnant behavior such as the use of threats, harassment, fraud, or even flattery to induce defendants to commit crimes. Here are three examples of how the entrapment defense works:

- **No Entrapment; the Lying Police Officer:** Berry is charged with selling illegal drugs to an undercover police officer. Berry testifies that the drugs were for her personal use, and explains that the reason she sold some to the officer is that at a party, the officer falsely said that she wanted some drugs for her mom, who was in a lot of pain. According to Berry, the officer even assured Berry that she wasn't a cop and wasn't setting Berry up. The police officer's actions probably do not amount to entrapment. Police officers are allowed to tell lies. The officer gave Berry an opportunity to break the law, but the officer did not engage in extreme or overbearing behavior.

- **Entrapment; the Lying Police Officer 2:** Berry is charged with selling illegal drugs to an undercover police officer. Berry testifies, "The drugs were for my personal use. For nearly two weeks, the undercover officer stopped by my apartment and pleaded with me to sell her some of my stash because her mom was extremely sick and needed the drugs for pain relief. I kept refusing. When the officer told me that her mom only had a few days left to live and that the drugs would allow her mom to be comfortable for the few days she had left, I broke down and sold her some drugs. She immediately arrested me." The undercover agent's repeated entreaties and lies are likely to be considered sufficiently extreme to constitute entrapment and result in a not-guilty verdict.

E

- **Entrapment; the Flattering, Forceful Police Officer:** Posing as a prostitute, an undercover officer walks over to John, who is seated in a parked car. The officer asks John if he's interested in a little fun, and John says no. The officer tells John that he is sexy, and promises him that she'll be the best he's ever had. John reaches for the ignition, but the officer grabs John's hand and prevents him from pushing the car's starter button. The officer tells John that he seems lonely, and that for only $100 he can have the time of his life. When John finally says "Okay" and hands over money, the officer arrests him for soliciting a prostitute. The officer entrapped John by verbally and physically bullying him into paying for sex.

Subjective and Objective Standards. States employ either an *objective* or a *subjective* standard to determine whether entrapment occurred. Under an objective standard, when defendants offer entrapment evidence jurors decide whether a police officer's actions would have induced a normally law-abiding person to commit a crime. Entrapment defenses are less likely to succeed under a subjective standard. The reason is that under a subjective standard, when defendants offer entrapment evidence jurors decide whether the specific defendant's predisposition to commit a crime means that the defendant is responsible for his or her actions despite a government agent's inducements.

> **EXAMPLE:** Jim is charged with serving as a lookout during a liquor store robbery carried out by a street gang. Jim claims that Snitch, a neighborhood friend who turned out to be an undercover police officer, entrapped him by telling him that he had to participate in the robbery or Snitch would be unable to protect him from gang retribution. In a state that employs an objective test for entrapment, a jury decides whether Snitch's actions would have induced a normally law-abiding person to participate in the robbery. In a state that uses a subjective test for entrapment, the prosecutor can offer evidence of Jim's predisposition to commit the crime, including that Jim had a

lengthy rap sheet and that he was anxious to join the street gang and wanted to prove his mettle by participating in a violent crime. A jury would then decide whether Jim participated in the robbery because of his own willingness to do so regardless of Snitch's actions.

Only Government Agents Can Entrap. Entrapment law is a leash intended to curb outrageous conduct by police officers and other public officials. An entrapment defense does not arise if private individuals induce defendants to commit crimes.

Burdens of Proof. Because entrapment is an affirmative defense, defendants have the burden of convincing jurors by a preponderance of the evidence that government agents' actions constitute entrapment. In a state that employs an objective test of entrapment, a conclusion that entrapment took place results in a not-guilty verdict. In a state that employs a subjective test of entrapment, a conclusion that entrapment took place results in the burden of proof shifting back to the prosecution to prove beyond a reasonable doubt that a defendant is guilty because the defendant's predisposition to commit the crime—rather than the government agent's actions—resulted in the defendant committing the crime.

 Legal Authority Examples

California (objective standard state): Entrapment is a defense if conduct by law enforcement agents that would likely induce a normally law-abiding person to commit a crime induced the defendant to commit a charged crime. The defendant has the burden of proving entrapment by a preponderance of the evidence. Law enforcement agents are allowed to provide opportunity for the commission of a crime, but they cannot induce people to commit crimes by engaging in overbearing conduct such as badgering, coaxing or cajoling, importuning, or other acts likely to induce a normally law-abiding person to commit a crime.

E

Florida (subjective standard state): Defendants who allege entrapment have the burden of proving by a preponderance of the evidence that a government agent induced them to commit a charged crime. Defendants also have to offer evidence that they were not predisposed to commit the crime. If a defendant offers evidence of lack of predisposition, the burden of proof shifts to the prosecution to prove beyond a reasonable doubt that the defendant was predisposed to commit the crime.

Related terms: affirmative defense; burdens of proof.

evidence

In popular parlance, the term "evidence" can refer to any information that relates to criminal activity. But the term has a narrower meaning inside courtrooms, where evidence consists only of the information that prosecutors and defendants seek to present to judges or juries, and that judges deem admissible under the rules of evidence. So for example, if a prosecutor decides not to offer a victim's diary into the trial record, or if the judge refuses to permit the diary's admission, the diary would not constitute evidence for purposes of the criminal justice system.

Testimonial and Tangible Evidence. Virtually all evidence at trial is either "testimonial" or "tangible." Testimonial evidence is oral. Witnesses typically provide testimonial evidence by coming into court and answering questions. However, there are other ways to create testimonial evidence. For example, a prosecutor may read a transcript of an unavailable witness's preliminary hearing testimony into the record at a trial. The preliminary hearing testimony is testimonial evidence even though the prosecutor read it into the record from a printed transcript

Tangible evidence consists of weapons, contraband, documents, and other physical items that judges receive in evidence. Inside a courtroom, tangible items offered into evidence are called "exhibits."

EXAMPLE: To prove that a defendant operated an illegal Ponzi scheme, the prosecutor offers into evidence numerous printouts of email messages from the defendant to various investors that assure the investors that their nonexistent investments were in great shape. The email messages are tangible evidence. Depending on the number of messages, their subject matter, and the judge's preference, each message may constitute an exhibit, or each exhibit may encompass several messages.

Real and Demonstrative Evidence. Real evidence consists of the instrumentalities by which crimes are committed. For example, in a prosecution for selling illegal drugs, the drugs would constitute real evidence. Similarly, in a murder trial, a gun found lying on the street next to the murder victim is real evidence.

Demonstrative evidence is illustrative; such evidence typically enhances attorneys' presentations by providing a visual counterpart to oral testimony. Judges usually allow jurors to have real evidence in the jury room while they deliberate. Demonstrative evidence generally remains in the courtroom, although judges may allow jurors to examine it upon request. A typical example of demonstrative evidence is a photograph that depicts the victim at the crime scene.

Direct and Circumstantial Evidence. Direct evidence proves an element of a crime without the aid of an inference. An example of direct evidence in a murder case would be an eyewitness's testimony that she saw the defendant point a gun at and shoot the victim. However, the credibility of this evidence rests on inferences about such matters as the witness's ability to perceive the incident, as well as the witness's memory and truthfulness.

Circumstantial evidence requires judges and jurors to make an inference to link evidence to a crime element. An example, in the same murder case, is an expert witness testifying that scientific testing established that the defendant had gunshot residue on his hands that came from the gun that was used to shoot the victim. Movie and TV lawyers routinely ridicule adversaries' proof as "nothing but a bunch of circumstantial evidence." In reality, neither form of evidence is entitled to greater weight than the other. At the end of the day, the distinction is largely meaningless because the credibility of direct evidence rests on an inference as to its accuracy.

E

Foundational Evidence. In order to convince judges to admit evidence, attorneys often must justify the admission under evidence rules. This is referred to as "creating (or laying) a foundation." Foundations differ according to the evidence that parties seek to admit. When calling lay witnesses (nonexperts) to testify, a foundation must be established that the witness has personal knowledge of the event—for example, by asking, "Did you personally observe the robbery?" When calling expert witnesses, a foundation must be created that the expert is qualified and that the subject matter is within the witness's expertise—for example a fingerprint expert would have to establish her background, training, and experience.

Evidence Admission Process. The most common way to introduce evidence in court is by asking questions of witnesses. Sometimes lawyers question "sponsoring witnesses"—witnesses who testify as to the source, identification, and reliability of tangible pieces of evidence—in order to establish a foundation for admitting those items of evidence.

> EXAMPLE: A prosecutor wants a judge to receive into evidence a gun that Officer Moriarity found at a murder scene. The prosecutor marks the item as Exhibit 1, and identifies it as "a gun." (If the prosecutor seeks to offer more than one gun into evidence, more detailed distinguishing characteristics will be needed.) The prosecutor then hands Exhibit 1 to the sponsoring witness, Officer Moriarity, and asks Moriarity to identify it. After Moriarity explains how he can identify the gun and ties the gun to the crime scene, the prosecutor asks the judge to receive the gun into evidence.

 Legal Authority Examples

Federal Rule of Evidence 104: Preliminary questions concerning the qualification of a person to be a witness or the admissibility of evidence shall be determined by the court.

Federal Rule of Evidence 602: A witness may not testify to a matter unless evidence is introduced sufficient to support a finding that the witness has personal knowledge of the matter. Evidence to prove personal knowledge may, but need not, consist of the witness's own testimony.

California Jury Instruction No. 223: Facts may be proved by direct or circumstantial evidence or by a combination of both. *Direct evidence* can prove a fact by itself. *Circumstantial evidence* is evidence of another fact or group of facts from which you may logically and reasonably conclude the truth of the fact in question. Both direct and circumstantial evidence are acceptable types of evidence to prove or disprove the elements of a charge, and neither is necessarily more reliable than the other. Neither is entitled to any greater weight than the other. You must decide whether a fact in issue has been proved based on all the evidence.

Related Terms: best evidence rule; chain of custody; elements of a crime; expert witnesses; fingerprint analysis; forensic science; trial by jury (jury trial).

ex parte

(Latin for "by one party.") An *ex parte* action is taken by one party to a lawsuit in the absence of the opposing party. *Ex parte* actions are generally improper in criminal cases. For example, one party to a lawsuit should not seek to have *ex parte* contact with the trial judge. *Ex parte* actions are occasionally necessary, as when an alleged emergency exists and one party has no time to notify the adverse party before seeking a court order. In such situations, a judge may issue the order and arrange for a hearing as quickly as possible at which both parties can be present.

ex post facto law

(Latin for "after the action.") An *ex post facto* law seeks to criminalize activity that took place before the law was enacted. Such laws violate Article 1, Section 9, of the U.S. Constitution (which states, "No *ex post facto* law shall be passed"). A law also violates this provision if it increases the punishment for a crime that was committed before the punishment was increased. For example, if an illegal act was a misdemeanor at the time that a defendant violated the law, and subsequently becomes punishable as a felony, the defendant can be punished only for committing a misdemeanor.

exclusionary rule

See search and seizure.

exculpatory evidence

See discovery.

exhibit

See evidence.

expert witnesses

The usual role of expert witnesses is to draw inferences from circumstantial evidence when judges and jurors lack the experience to recognize its true significance. Expert testimony will not be admitted unless it is established that the subject matter is such that an expert is required or at least of help to a jury. For example, most jurors would lack the experience to appreciate the terminology used by urban gangs. Thus, a police officer with years of experience with urban gangs may testify as an expert witness regarding a gang member's statements that a major drug sale was about to take place.

> EXAMPLE: In the classic courtroom comedy *My Cousin Vinny*, automotive expert witness Mona Lisa Vito testified that the defendant's car did not leave the skid marks on the street in front of the scene of a murder. Mona Lisa drew this inference based on evidence that the skidmarks were made by a car that had positraction and that the defendant's car was not equipped

with positraction. Mona Lisa's testimony is admissible because most jurors lack the experience to connect the skidmarks to positraction.

Admissibility of Expert Testimony. As a result of the United States Supreme Court decisions in *Daubert v. Merrell Dow Pharmaceuticals, Inc.* (1993) and *Kumho Tire v. Carmichael* (2000), testimony from expert witnesses is admissible in evidence only if a judge rules that the expert is qualified in a field of expertise that is reliable. An inquiry into whether a field is recognized as a reliable science may be necessary. For example, an expert on astrology would not be allowed to testify, no matter how extensive his qualifications, because courts do not recognize astrology as a reliable science.

Qualifications. Proposed experts can testify only if the party calling them convinces a judge of their qualifications to provide an opinion. Experts may be qualified by dint of education, training, or experience. For example, in the previous example from the movie *My Cousin Vinny*, Mona Lisa Vito can qualify as an expert in automotive mechanics based on the training she received from family members who are mechanics and her own experience as a mechanic.

EXAMPLE: The prosecutor in an aggravated assault case seeks to call Dr. Scruvillo as an expert witness. The prosecutor asks Dr. Scruvillo to testify to an opinion that the defendant was the source of the teeth marks that were on the victim's arm following an attack. Dr. Scruvillo arrived at this opinion after comparing the teeth marks to a plaster cast of the defendant's teeth. Dr. Scruvillo testifies that he is a dentist in general practice. However, Dr. Scruvillo admits that he has no formal training in bite mark analysis, that he has never previously compared bite marks to a set of teeth, and that he has never previously qualified as an expert in bite marks. The judge rules that Dr. Scruvillo is not qualified to testify to this opinion.

Case-Specific Personal Knowledge. Like experts, lay (nonexpert) witnesses can testify to opinions. The difference is that lay witnesses are limited to giving opinions about matters that they have actually observed. Experts, by contrast, can give opinions based on information that has been furnished to them but which they have not personally observed. For example, consider the following: the prosecutor in a drunk driving case asks a witness to "assume that a 120-pound woman was in a tavern for 45 minutes, during which she consumed four martinis and had nothing to eat. What is your opinion as to whether the woman was likely to have been under the influence of alcohol when she left the tavern?" A lay witness could not answer this question, but a properly qualified expert witness could.

The Ultimate Issue. Expert witnesses are not allowed to provide an opinion that a defendant is guilty or not guilty. This is an issue that is solely in the province of judges and jurors. For example, a defense psychiatrist cannot testify, "In my opinion, the defendant was unable to distinguish right from wrong." This is the legal definition of insanity and it is a judgment that only the judge and jurors can make. However, experts' conclusions may of course provide the bases for verdicts. For example, a defense psychiatrist can describe a defendant's mental illness. Based on that description, a jury may conclude that the defendant could not distinguish right from wrong.

Legal Authority Examples

Federal Rule of Evidence 701: A witness who does not qualify as an expert can testify only to opinions or inferences that are rationally based on the witness's perception.

Federal Rule of Evidence 702: A witness qualified as an expert by knowledge, skill, experience, training, or education, may testify if (1) the testimony is based upon sufficient facts or data, (2) the testimony is the product of reliable principles and methods, and (3) the witness has applied the principles and methods reliably to the facts of the case.

Federal Rule of Evidence 704: Expert testimony is not objectionable because it embraces an ultimate issue, but in criminal cases expert witnesses may not state an opinion or inference as to whether a defendant did or did not have the mental state or condition constituting an element of the crime charged or of a defense thereto. Such ultimate issues are for the trier of fact alone.

Related terms: forensic science; evidence.

expungement of criminal records

Expungement refers to the process of sealing arrest and conviction records. Virtually every state has enacted laws that allow people to expunge arrests and convictions from their records. Though the details can vary from one state to the next, most states' laws provide that once an arrest or conviction has been expunged, it need not be disclosed, including to potential employers or landlords. That said, the conviction usually won't be removed from the court's records and can be used to increase the punishment for subsequent crimes (depending on the offense) by the defendant. And the conviction may be available if the defendant applies for certain jobs (such as law enforcement or working with children or vulnerable adults).

In many jurisdictions, people who have been arrested or convicted for drug crimes and juvenile offenders may have an easier path to expungement. For example, many people arrested for first-time drug offenses are eligible for diversion programs. These programs typically provide for the expungement of records following the satisfactory completion of a program.

Related terms: sentencing (punishment options).

extortion

Extortion consists of the use of threats to obtain property or favorable public actions. Blackmail is a form of extortion that generally no longer exists as an independent crime. Bribery is another common form of extortion, and it continues to exist as an independent crime in many states. Corruption is a form of extortion engaged in by public officials.

Extortion by Public Officials. Public officials can be the instigators as well as the targets of extortion.

Real-Life Illustration

Rod Blagojevich was the governor of Illinois when then-Illinois Senator Barack Obama was elected president of the United States. in 2008. As governor, Blagojevich had the authority to appoint Obama's successor to the Senate. Based on recordings indicating that (among other things) Blagojevich offered the Senate seat to several people in exchange for a payoff of several hundred thousand dollars, Blagojevich was impeached and removed from office in 2009. In April 2009, a federal grand jury indicted Blagojevich on 19 counts, including extortion, attempted extortion, and racketeering. He was eventually convicted and sentenced to prison.

Information Extortion. Another form of extortion, colloquially know as blackmail, consists of threatening to reveal private information unless the target of the extortion agrees to a demand. For example it would constitute extortion in most states to threaten someone with an email message stating, "If you don't pay what you owe me, I'll tell your employer that you lied about your employment history on your job application." Even though the recipient may legitimately owe the money to the extorting party, and even though the recipient may have misstated his employment history, the threat still amounts to extortion. Perhaps paradoxically, no crime would be committed if the emailer simply contacted the employer and accurately revealed the misstated employment history.

Legal Authority Examples

Pennsylvania: Extortion consists of obtaining or withholding another's property by threatening to commit a criminal offense, accusing someone of a criminal offense, exposing a secret tending to subject a person to hatred, contempt, or ridicule, taking or withholding action as an official or causing an official to take or withhold action, bringing about or continuing a strike, boycott, or other collective unofficial action if property is not demanded or received for the benefit of the group in whose interest the offender purports to act, testifying or providing information or withholding testimony or information pertaining to another person's legal claim, or inflicting any other harm that would not benefit the offender. Alleged extortion does not exist if the property obtained by threat of accusation, exposure, lawsuit, or other invocation of official action was honestly claimed as restitution or indemnification for harm done in the circumstances to which such accusation, exposure, lawsuit, or other official action relates, or as compensation for property or lawful services.

Texas: A railroad commits extortion if it charges or demands a greater rate or compensation than that fixed by law for the transportation of passengers or freight or for any other service. Extortion under this statute is punishable by a fine of up to $5,000.

extradition

Extradition is the process by which one state or country returns a fugitive to another state or country. A fugitive is a person who has fled from the custody or control of a jurisdiction—for example, a defendant who has skipped bail or a person accused of a crime who leaves the state or even the country.

Interstate extradition in the U.S. is established by the Extradition of Fugitives Clause in the Constitution, which requires one state, when requested by another, to deliver anyone who's committed a "treason, felony or other crime." All states are signatories to the Uniform Criminal Extradition Act. The Act establishes procedures that allow states to demand the return of fugitives for prosecution. Usually the demand-and-return process occurs within 30 to 90 days of the arrest of the defendant in the foreign state or country.

> EXAMPLE: Bill is indicted for murder in South Carolina and is on the run. After receiving tips that Bill is in Maine, South

Carolina officials ask Maine authorities to arrest Bill and extradite him to South Carolina. The South Carolina officials support the request by emailing electronic versions of the indictment and arrest warrant to the Maine authorities. After Maine police officers arrest Bill, a Maine court conducts a hearing at which Bill can contest South Carolina's jurisdiction. After the judge concludes that South Carolina has submitted the proper documents and has jurisdiction to prosecute Bill, Maine turns over custody of Bill to South Carolina officials, who return him to South Carolina for prosecution.

International extradition is based upon treaties between the arresting country and the country seeking extradition. Extradition can also occur absent a treaty and is based on reciprocal arrangements between the two countries.

 Legal Authority Examples

Idaho: The governor has an obligation to arrest and deliver up to the executive authority of any other state of the United States any person charged in that state with treason, felony, or other crime, who has fled from justice and is found in this state.

eyewitness identification

Eyewitness identification is evidence from a witness to the identity of the perpetrator. Typically, eyewitness identification is associated with the moment in countless courtroom films in which the music builds and a witness dramatically points to a defendant and says, "That's the person I saw holding the gun."

Despite the media attention on forensic scientists who use state-of-the-art technology to identify perpetrators (the so-called "CSI factor"), prosecutors more routinely rely on eyewitnesses for identifications and convictions. One reason is that forensic evidence is often either unavailable or unnecessary. Another is that judges and juries are often impressed with witnesses who come into court and say things like, "I'll never forget that face as long as I live."

But, like all of us, eyewitnesses are fallible. Most of the prisoners who have been exonerated through DNA testing (that was unavailable at the time of their convictions) have been victims of mistaken eyewitness testimony. The fallibility of eyewitness identification was demonstrated most famously by Earl Rogers, a Los Angeles criminal defense attorney in the early 1900s. Rogers had his client, seated at counsel table, switch places with a courtroom spectator while Rogers cross-examined a prosecution eyewitness. Rogers concluded his questioning by asking the witness to once again, point to the culprit. The witness pointed to the man seated at counsel table. When Rogers asked his client to stand up in the back of the courtroom, the case was dismissed. The stunt was memorialized in the pilot episode of the great TV lawyer show *The Defenders*.

Pretrial Identification. Out-of-court identifications precede most in-court identifications. Victims and witnesses may identify defendants during "show-ups" (in which police officers bring suspects to crime scenes), while looking through mug shots, and when picking them out of lineups. At trial, witnesses can testify to both in-court and any out-of-court identifications. The latter tend to bolster eyewitnesses' credibility, since out-of-court identifications are made closer in time to crimes. So, for example, a prosecution witness in an armed robbery trial can testify that he picked the defendant out of the lineup that took place five days after the robbery.

Fairness of Pretrial Identifications. Judges often scrutinize pretrial identification procedures in an effort to ensure that identifications are the product of eyewitnesses' observations rather than police officer suggestiveness. Unfair procedures may result in a judge ruling that an eyewitness cannot testify to a pretrial identification, or in cases of extreme suggestiveness, that an eyewitness cannot even provide an in-court identification.

Suspects have the right to have counsel present if a lineup takes place after charges have been filed. Lineup arrays must be photographed, so that judges can make sure that the suspect was not

E

presented as the only participant who could possibly have been the culprit. Witnesses must view lineup arrays one at a time so that they do not influence each other. And police officers must avoid suggesting the identification of a particular suspect and, even statements such as, "We're pretty positive that the robber is one of the guys in the lineup." Such comments are likely to overcome any reservations an eyewitness may have about whom the suspect is and whether that person is even in the lineup.

Sequential Lineups. Reports of convictions based on mistaken eyewitness identifications have led some localities to use sequential lineups rather than the usual "six-pack." In a sequential lineup, witnesses view one lineup participant at a time, and must decline to identify one participant before seeing the next one. Sequential lineups are thought to prevent identifications based on a guess as to which of the six lineup participants looks most like the culprit.

Eyewitness Identification Experts. Cognitive psychologists often testify as experts to factors that in research experiments have been associated with mistaken identifications. The scope of their expertise does not allow these experts to testify to the accuracy of a particular witness's identification—for example, they cannot say, "I think there's less than a 50% chance that the prosecution eyewitness is accurate." However, they can educate jurors and help them evaluate the credibility of eyewitnesses. Research findings that cognitive psychological experts often provide to juries include the following:

- Stress reduces the likelihood of accuracy.
- Eyewitnesses who express great confidence in their identifications are no more likely to be accurate than those who are less confident.
- Cross-racial identifications are less likely to be accurate for members of all racial groups.
- The presence of weapons reduces the likelihood of accuracy because witnesses focus on the weapons rather than the perpetrators.

Legal Authority Examples

Federal Rules of Evidence: A testifying witness's pretrial identification is admissible so long as the witness is available for cross-examination at trial.

California Jury Instruction: When deciding whether an eyewitness gave truthful and accurate testimony, jurors should consider whether the witness knew or had contact with the defendant before the event; how well the witness could see the perpetrator; physical circumstances such as lighting, weather conditions, obstructions, and distance; how closely the witness was paying attention; whether the witness was under stress; whether the witness gave a description and how that description compares to the defendant; how much time passed between the event and the identification; whether the witness picked the perpetrator out of a group; whether the witness ever failed to identify the defendant; whether the witness ever changed his or her mind about the identification; how certain a witness was of the identification's accuracy; and whether the witness and the defendant are different races.

Related terms: expert witnesses; evidence.

E

failure of proof

The Constitution requires prosecutors to prove criminal defendants guilty beyond a reasonable doubt. (*In re Winship*, U.S. Sup. Ct. (1972).) This is the highest burden of proof that the legal system can impose on a party to a court case. At the same time, criminal defendants have a right to remain silent. Prosecutors cannot call defendants as witnesses, nor are defendants obligated to testify on their own behalves. A prosecutor's high burden of proof and a defendant's right to remain silent combine to make a "failure of proof" argument the most common criminal defense strategy.

Beyond a Reasonable Doubt. When instructing jurors, judges often describe reasonable doubt as requiring "near certainty" or "moral certainty." Ultimately, the phrase has only the meaning that judges and juries choose to give it in concrete cases. However, lawyers cannot give misleading definitions when they explain reasonable doubt to jurors. For example, a defense lawyer cannot state, "Reasonable doubt requires you to be 100% convinced that the prosecution witness's testimony was accurate. If there's any chance at all that the witness made a mistake, you must find the defendant not guilty." (The law does not require absolute certainty. Virtually every aspect of human activity is subject to an element of doubt, and prosecutors do not have to eliminate every possibility of innocence in order to convict.)

The Human Scales of Justice. Defense lawyers sometimes imitate the scales of justice to explain the meaning of "beyond a reasonable doubt." With arms outstretched at shoulder level, defense lawyers tilt their bodies ever so slightly to demonstrate the "preponderance of the evidence" standard of proof that plaintiffs have in civil cases. They then tilt dramatically further so that one arm is nearly pointing straight down and the other arm is nearly pointing to the ceiling to emphasize the far higher burden of proof that prosecutors have in criminal cases. (Defense lawyers who practice yoga can probably give more convincing demonstrations.)

Defense Stories Without Burdens. Normally, defendants do not have to convince jurors that defense evidence is accurate; the burden of proof, after all, is on the prosecution. Thus, defense lawyers often argue that the jurors need not believe all of the defense evidence in order to acquit.

> EXAMPLE: Humphrey is charged with killing Holt. He testifies that he was prospecting for gold with his friend Walter at the time Holt was killed. Walter testifies in support of Humphrey's alibi. Humphrey's lawyer will probably argue that the alibi story is correct. But the lawyer will emphasize that Humphrey does not have the burden of proving that the alibi story is correct, and that Humphrey is not guilty unless the prosecution's evidence proves his guilt beyond a reasonable doubt.

Burdening Defendants. Though prosecutors always have the burden of proving that defendants are guilty, rules can require defendants to carry the burden of proving affirmative defenses. While rules vary from one state to another, defendants who rely on affirmative defenses such as insanity, duress, and entrapment typically have the burden of proof with respect to those defenses. The defendant's burden of proof is either "preponderance of the evidence" or "clear and convincing evidence." Both of these burdens are less demanding than the prosecution's burden of "beyond a reasonable doubt."

Inferring Guilt From Silence. Defendants cannot be penalized for exercising a constitutional right. When defendants remain silent at trial, judges instruct jurors that the burden of proof is on the prosecution, and that they may not infer guilt from silence. Judges have only a limited power to enforce this jury instruction—for example, after a jury has rendered its verdict, a judge cannot set it aside if it is learned that one of the jurors stated that she thought that the defendant had something to hide by remaining silent.

Blowing Smoke. Defendants relying on a failure-of-proof defense often claim that the crime they are charged with was actually committed by a third party. This is sometimes called a "blowing smoke" defense because often the purpose is to confuse a jury by clouding a prosecutor's case. (Another common term for this defense is "SODDI"—"Some Other Dude Did It.") Judges often thwart "blowing smoke" defenses by ruling that evidence of a third party's motive to commit a crime is not by itself adequate to cast suspicion on that party. All that said, there are cases in which SODDI explains what really happened—for example, instances of mistaken identity.

> **EXAMPLE:** In an episode of the TV comedy/drama *Boston Legal*, defense attorney Alan Shore's client Paul Stewart is charged with murder. During closing argument, Shore tells the jurors that the prosecution failed to prove Stewart's guilt beyond a reasonable doubt. Shore then suggests that the murderer could have been Stewart's wife, or his mother, or his next-door neighbor, or his priest, because they all had motives to want the victim dead. Because Shore had no evidence besides motive to prove that any of these people committed the murder, Shore's argument was improper and the prosecutor should have objected and asked the judge to instruct the jurors to disregard it.

 Legal Authority Examples

Illinois: In criminal cases the burden is on the prosecution to prove guilt beyond a reasonable doubt, which means proof of each essential element beyond a reasonable doubt.

Illinois: A defendant who enters a plea of not guilty by reason of insanity has the burden of proving insanity by clear and convincing evidence.

Related terms: burdens of proof; evidence; affirmative defense.

F

false imprisonment

False imprisonment arises when a culprit restrains or confines a victim against the victim's will. For example, a robber commits the crime of false imprisonment by tying a homeowner to a chair while carrying out a residential robbery. Even a verbal threat can give rise to false imprisonment, as when a holdup man dramatically tells a convenience store customer, "Lie face down on the floor until I leave, or else." False imprisonment can constitute either a misdemeanor or a felony depending on such factors as the duration of the imprisonment and whether a victim is physically injured.

Related Terms: kidnapping.

felony

See hierarchy of criminal offenses.

felony murder rule

The felony murder rule provides that a victim's death during the commission or attempted commission of a specified felony constitutes murder. The crime can be punishable as either first degree or second degree murder, depending on the jurisdiction and the dangerousness of the felony. Most but not all states have enacted a felony murder rule.

Strict Liability. Traditionally, the felony murder rule is a rule of strict liability. This means that a victim's death is punishable as a murder regardless of an offender's intent or knowledge. In effect, the felony murder rule substitutes commission of the crime for malice aforethought, the usual *mens rea* element of murder. For example, even if an arsonist believes that a house is empty, and he does not intend to kill anyone, he can be convicted of felony murder if he commits arson and someone (such as a resident, a firefighter, or even a coconspirator) dies from the commission of this inherently dangerous felony. The same would be true if during an armed robbery, a gun drops to the ground, accidentally discharges, and kills someone.

Any Felony? The felony murder rule has been traditionally applied to all felonies, regardless of their severity. Either through statutes or judicial decisions, many states have limited the scope of the felony murder rule to deaths that occur during the commission of dangerous felonies.

> EXAMPLE: Lisa grabs cosmetics off of a store shelf and runs out the door without paying for them. Just outside the door, Lisa accidentally collides with a woman who is about to enter the store. The collision knocks the woman into the path of a car, which strikes and kills her. Lisa has a previous conviction for petty theft, and the law in her state provides that a second petty theft can be prosecuted as a felony. A strict application of the felony murder rule would therefore make Lisa guilty of murder, since the woman's death occurred in the course of a felony. (Lisa's attempt to escape is part of the commission of the crime.) But as "petty theft with a prior" is not an inherently dangerous felony, most states would not apply the felony murder rule in this situation. Lisa would at most be guilty of involuntary manslaughter for causing the woman's death.

First or Second Degree Murder. Felony murder statutes typically indicate whether a death that occurs in the course of a felony is punishable as first degree murder or second degree murder. Typically, violent crimes such as armed robbery trigger first degree murder charges. On the other hand, a death that results from ingesting unintentionally tainted illegal drugs may trigger punishment of the drugs' supplier as second degree murder.

 Legal Authority Examples

Pennsylvania: A criminal homicide constitutes murder of the second degree when it is committed while the defendant was engaged as a principal or an accomplice in the perpetration of a felony.

Alabama: A person who causes the death of another human being in the course of committing or attempting to commit first degree arson, first or second degree burglary, first degree escape, first degree rape, robbery of any degree, first degree sodomy, or any other felony that is clearly dangerous to human life is guilty of murder.

Florida: A person who kills another human being during the commission or attempted commission of arson, robbery, sexual battery, burglary, escape, kidnapping, aggravated child abuse, carjacking, aggravated elder or disabled person abuse, aircraft piracy, aggravated stalking, and violent resistance to a police officer is guilty of first degree murder and is subject to the death penalty.

Related terms: manslaughter; *mens rea*; first degree murder (Murder One); second degree murder (Murder Two); shoplifting.

fence

Slang for an offender who buys and resells stolen goods.

Fifth Amendment right against self-incrimination

See privilege against self-incrimination.

fingerprint analysis

Fingerprint analysis consists of comparing prints—typically fingertips, or hand or palm prints—found at crime scenes with those of known individuals. Experts decide whether matches exist by comparing the points at which ridges branch or terminate. Traditionally, fingerprint experts declare matches when they find at least 12 points in common between two fingerprints, though this number is not an absolute requirement.

Historical Antecedents. Relying on an authority that trumps even the U.S. Supreme Court, one of the early court opinions admitting fingerprint evidence referred to "God's finger print language, the voiceless speech, and the indelible writing on the fingers, hand palms, and foot soles of humanity, by the All Wise Creator for some good and useful purpose, namely the ultimate elimination of crime by unquestionable evidence of identity in all cases." (*State v. Kuhl,* Nevada (1918).)

A Subjective Science. Influenced by movies and TV shows, many people assume that computers are the real fingerprint experts, flashing "Match" or "No Match" when two fingerprints are fed into them. In reality, fingerprint analysis rests on the subjective judgment of forensic experts. They have to consider not only points of similarity, but also such factors as the clarity, condition, and extent of prints left at a crime scene when deciding whether matches between two prints exist.

> EXAMPLE: Forensic fingerprint expert Prince compares a fingerprint found on the windowsill of a burgled house to a print known to be that of Red. Though the print in the house was only a partial one, Prince declares a match based on finding ten points in common because the print was exceptionally clear and Prince has many years of experience. Prince also testifies that, at his request, a second expert examined the same prints and confirmed Prince's conclusion without knowing of that conclusion ahead of time. (If Red argues that "my identical twin brother Wright is equally likely as me to have left the print that was found on the windowsill," that argument is irrelevant; even identical twins have different fingerprints.)

All or Nothing at All. Fingerprint experts do not estimate the likelihood of matches. If fingerprint experts cannot declare with absolute certainty that two prints do or do not match, they refuse to provide an opinion.

> EXAMPLE: In the previous scenario, fingerprint expert Prince finds only eight points in common between the two prints. Moreover, the disrepair of the windowsill affected the quality of the crime scene print. Prince believes that there is a substantial likelihood that Red left the crime scene print, but because he is

F

not absolutely certain of this fact, he will offer no opinion on the question of whether the windowsill print is that of Red.

No Dating. Fingerprint experts cannot usually determine the age of fingerprints. Thus, suspects whose prints are found at crime scenes may be able to offer reasonable and innocent explanations for their prints. So, for example, a fingerprint expert would not be able to disprove a defendant's claim that he left the print when performing some legitimate task, such as working as a handyman.

Admissibility of Fingerprint Testimony. Judges in all states regard fingerprint analysis as reliable for purposes of *Daubert v. Merrell Dow Pharmaceuticals, Inc.* (U.S. Sup. Ct. (1993).) Thus, in their role as gatekeepers judges routinely admit fingerprint testimony from properly qualified expert witnesses. Nevertheless, critics argue that a major principle on which fingerprint analysis rests, that no two people can have the same fingerprints, has never been scientifically proven. However, no two people have ever been found to have identical prints.

Related terms: expert witnesses; forensic science; evidence.

first degree murder (Murder One)

Most states have established two degrees of murder. First degree murder (sometimes referred to as "murder one"), is an unlawful and premeditated killing of a human being with malice aforethought. These elements of first degree murder signify the most vicious, cold-blooded homicides. Intentional killings that do not constitute first degree murder are second degree murder (or "murder two"), or voluntary manslaughter. First degree murder is a felony punishable by life in prison, often without possibility of parole. In the states that provide for capital punishment, offenders convicted of first degree murder can be executed.

Historical Antecedents. Pennsylvania in 1794 was the first state to separate murder into two degrees. In an essay entitled "Criminal Law Reform: Historical Development in the United States," legal historians Kahan and McClain argue, "The division of murder into two degrees proved to be Pennsylvania's most lasting contribution to the general criminal jurisprudence of the United States." But while these items may have nothing to do with criminal jurisprudence, let's also give Pennsylvania credit for soft pretzels and cheesesteaks.

Malice Aforethought. First degree murder's element of "malice aforethought" sounds like impressive legal mumbo-jumbo, but it translates simply as "intent to kill." Malice aforethought does not require evidence that a murderer harbored an evil motive toward a victim. For example, a gang member who intentionally shoots and kills a randomly selected victim as part of a street gang initiation has malice aforethought.

Premeditation. Premeditation generally distinguishes first degree murder from second degree. Premeditation consists of evidence of advance planning. However, planning and preparation need not be extensive for premeditation to exist. It exists even if a killer decides to commit a murder just moments before carrying out the crime. For example, a fistfight that escalates into a stabbing that results in a death is not likely to be considered premeditated. However, if the fistfight ends and then one party returns moments later with a knife and stabs the other fighter in the back and kills him, premeditation occurred.

Victim's Status. Though justice is supposedly blind, it sometimes takes a peek at a murder victim's position or status. If a murder victim occupies a status that the government is especially anxious to protect, an intentional killing constitutes first degree murder.

> EXAMPLE: Archie and George are involved in a fistfight that escalates into murder when Archie stabs George in the back. The murder takes place in a state with a statute providing that an intentional killing constitutes first degree murder when a victim is a police officer, a judge, or a correctional officer. If Archie knew prior to the stabbing that George was a police officer, the killing constitutes first degree murder under this statute regardless of the absence of premeditation. But if Archie

was unaware that George was a police officer, in all likelihood the killing constitutes second degree murder.

Felony Murder Rule. Commission of an inherently dangerous felony can serve as a stand-in for malice aforethought and premeditation in most states. In other words, if a specified violent crime results in a victim's death, the perpetrator can be convicted of first degree murder even if the perpetrator did not premeditate and did not intend for anyone to die.

Capital Murder. At the time of U.S. independence from England, all murders were a capital crime—that is, they triggered the death penalty. The term "capital" reflects the legal system's love for Latin (*capitalis* means "head") and the traditional execution method of chopping off a murderer's head. Evolving standards of justice plus the occasional difficulty of convincing jurors to convict a murderer for whom the death penalty seemed too harsh led to the development of the noncapital crime of second degree murder. Today, most states retain the death penalty—they identify types of murders that qualify defendants for execution. Statutes in those states aim to identify the "worst of the worst" by establishing circumstances that make a defendant death-penalty eligible. There is, however, a recent gradual trend of states abolishing the death penalty.

 Legal Authority Examples

New York: First degree murder is an intentional killing of another person if the killer is over age 18 and knew or should have known that the victim was a police officer performing his official duties, or if the victim was a correctional officer performing his official duties, or if the killer was already serving a life sentence when the killing took place, or if the victim was a witness or family member of a witness and the purpose of the killing was to prevent the witness from testifying, or if the killer was a hired killer, or if a killing occurred in the course of the killer's committing a specified violent felony, or if the killer had previously been convicted of murder, or if the killer's method of killing the victim was especially cruel and inhumane, or if the victim was a judge, or if the killing was an act of terrorism, or if the killer killed two or more victims within a two-year period pursuant to a common scheme or plan. First degree murder is punishable by death and by life in prison without possibility of parole.

California: Murder is the unlawful killing of a human being with malice aforethought. Malice may be express or implied. It is express when there is manifested a deliberate intention unlawfully to take away the life of a fellow creature. It is implied when no considerable provocation appears, or when the circumstances attending the killing show an abandoned and malignant heart. Murder is first-degree murder if it is perpetrated by means of a destructive device or explosive, or the killer knowingly uses ammunition designed primarily to penetrate metal or armor, or poison, or lies in wait, or tortures the victim, or if the killing is premeditated, or if a killing is committed in the course of certain specified dangerous felonies. First degree murder is punishable by death, imprisonment in the state prison for life without the possibility of parole, or imprisonment in the state prison for a term of 25 years to life.

Related terms: death penalty; elements of a crime; forensic science; felony murder rule; second degree murder (murder two); manslaughter.

forensic science

Forensic science is the application of scientific principles and methodologies to legal issues. As technology and scientific understanding advance, the criminal justice system increasingly relies on forensic science and the experts who can explain the scientific significance of circumstantial evidence. (As some forensic experts might say, "As science advances and the world becomes more complex, I know more and more about less and less.") For example:

- A blood analyst may compare a suspect's DNA to DNA found at a crime scene to exonerate or implicate the suspect.

- An expert in sound spectography may explain the characteristics of two voice samples that lead the expert to believe that a suspect made a recorded bomb threat.
- A coroner may explain how the condition of a murder victim's remains allow the coroner to establish the cause and approximate time of a victim's death.

Reliability. In *Daubert v. Merrell Dow Pharmaceuticals, Inc.* (1993), the U.S. Supreme Court decided that experts' scientific testimony is admissible if a judge concludes that the principles and methods underlying the testimony are valid and reliable. By turning judges into "gatekeepers" who have the power to decide whether expert testimony is based on reliable principles and methods, *Daubert* overturned a decades-old rule that scientific testimony was admissible only if the principles and methods on which it was based were generally accepted by scientists themselves. The current, conservative approach sprang from judges' often-expressed fear that smooth-talking charlatans would sell crackpot theories to gullible jurors. However, the previous test (known as the "*Frye* test" based on the 1923 New York court opinion that developed it) also made life easier for judges, as they could decide admissibility issues by counting noses in scientific communities rather than by resolving complex issues of science. The *Frye* test was of little comfort to innovative scientists—for example, the general acceptance test would have prevented Galileo, the extraordinary 16th century Italian scientist, from testifying to his theory that the world was round, because scientists of his era did not generally accept this theory. The newer approach under *Daubert* would permit Galileo to testify so long as a judge is convinced that his theory is valid.

In general, however, the change from the "general acceptance" to the "reliability" test has not greatly affected the admissibility of forensic science in criminal cases. For example, under the general acceptance standard, judges uniformly rejected evidence of polygraph (lie detector) tests because the relevant scientific community did not accept its validity. Judges continue to exclude polygraph test results as unreliable under the *Daubert* standard, though evidence rules in some states admit polygraph test results if both prosecutor and defense attorneys agree to their admission.

One Standard Fits All. In *Kumho Tire Co. v. Carmichael* (2000) and other cases following *Daubert*, the U.S. Supreme Court ruled that the reliability standard applies not only to scientific evidence, but to all forensic testimony based on specialized knowledge.

> **EXAMPLE:** Defendant Hy testifies that he was harvesting rutabaga at the time of a murder. To bolster his defense, Hy calls Ruth as a witness to testify that the rutabaga was ripe and ready for harvesting on the date of the murder. Ruth bases this opinion on her 30 years of experience as a grower and seller of rutabaga. Under *Daubert*, the judge must decide whether the principles and methods that form the bases for Ruth's opinion are reliable.

Promises and Reality. Forensic science promises to reduce the miscarriages of justice that occur when guilty people go free and innocent people are convicted. However, forensic evidence is irrelevant to many criminal charges. Even when it is relevant, forensic testing can promote justice only if it is performed correctly and interpreted correctly by judges and jurors.

A good example of the value in forensic evidence is The Innocence Project, which has used DNA testing to exonerate approximately 250 wrongly convicted prisoners. Some of these prisoners were on Death Row. In 75% of the cases, the convictions were based largely on eyewitness identification testimony that proved to be wrong.

Forensic Lab Failures. In 2009, a report issued by the National Academy of Sciences identified severe problems confronting the police crime labs that often are the source of forensic evidence in criminal cases. Among the study's conclusions:
- standardized testing protocols often don't exist
- many lab technicians lack adequate training, and
- audits of crime labs to determine the propensity for errors rarely occur.

F

The CSI Effect. Many prosecutors claim that a phenomenon they call "The CSI Effect" unfairly makes it harder for them to obtain convictions. "CSI," or "Crime Scene Investigation," is the title of a popular group of television shows that glorify the work of forensic scientists using cutting-edge scientific technology to solve crimes. Many prosecutors claim that jurors who watch "CSI" are reluctant to convict in the absence of testimony from forensic scientists, even when that testimony would be irrelevant.

 Legal Authority Examples

Federal Rule of Evidence 702: If scientific, technical, or other specialized knowledge will assist the trier of fact to understand the evidence or to determine a fact in issue, a witness qualified as an expert by knowledge, skill, experience, training, or education, may testify thereto in the form of an opinion or otherwise, if (1) the testimony is based upon sufficient facts or data, (2) the testimony is the product of reliable principles and methods, and (3) the witness has applied the principles and methods reliably to the facts of the case.

Related terms: DNA evidence; expert witnesses; eyewitness identification; fingerprint analysis; polygraph machines (lie detectors).

forfeiture of property

A forfeiture is a court order transferring ownership of property from a convicted defendant to the government. Forfeiture typically is in addition to other forms of punishment such as a fine and imprisonment. Statutes can prescribe forfeiture of property that a defendant used as a means of committing a crime. For example, the government can ask a judge to order forfeiture of the vehicle that a defendant used to smuggle illegal drugs into the country.

Related terms: sentencing.

forfeiture of right to cross-examine

See confrontation of prosecution witnesses.

forgery

Forgery is a form of theft that consists of creating or altering a document for the purpose of deceiving or injuring a victim.

The Big Bounce. A typical forgery would be writing a check on someone else's account and faking the signature. However, not all bad checks are forgeries; some may be noncriminal (you thought you had sufficient funds but didn't), while some may be theft (you knew you didn't have the funds but wrote the check anyway). If you wrote the check knowing that the account or bank did not exist, that would be forgery.

Prove It. Laws criminalizing forgery go back at least to the days of the Roman Empire. For most of recorded history, forged documents were usually handwritten, and proof of forgery ordinarily rested on testimony from a handwriting expert or a nonexpert who was familiar with a forger's or a victim's handwriting or signature. In an electronic age, proof of forgery may require testimony from a forensic computer expert—for example, to document an unauthorized payment from PayPal.

The Forgers' Art. Many jurisdictions have enacted specific statutes that punish offenders for passing off phony art objects as originals.

> EXAMPLE: Gus creates and engraves Rodin's name onto a bronze sculpture that looks nearly identical to the famous Rodin sculpture, *The Burghers of Calais.* Gus sells his copy to a gullible but wealthy collector who is convinced by Gus that it is a Rodin original. Gus is guilty of forgery.

Counterfeiting. Counterfeiting, the crime of knowingly creating or passing off phony currency as lawful money, is a form of forgery, generally punishable as a felony. Another form of counterfeiting is the act of making or selling look-alike goods or services bearing fake trademarks. An example is a business deliberately duplicating the

Adidas trademark on athletic gear or placing the Nolo logo on an inferior criminal law desk reference.

 Legal Authority Examples

California: Signing the name of a different or fictitious person without permission and with the intent to defraud to a check, money order, promissory note, contract, lottery ticket, power of attorney, certificate of title, stock certificate, or various other types of documents constitutes forgery.

Pennsylvania: A person who with intent to defraud makes or alters an object so that it appears to have value because of antiquity, rarity, source, or authorship that it does not possess is guilty of a misdemeanor of the first degree.

Related terms: robbery.

foundational evidence

See evidence.

Fourth Amendment

See search and seizure.

fraud

Fraud is a label for a variety of theft crimes in which thieves deceive victims into giving up possession of or title to property. Most crimes of fraud involve misrepresentations that wrongdoers know are false—for example, in a foreclosure scam, the scammer lies about the transfer of title. However, fraud convictions can also result from offenders making assertions without knowing whether the assertions are accurate. It can also occur when offenders don't disclose important information—for example, a used car salesperson deliberately failing to tell a customer that a car lacks state-mandated safety equipment. Fraudulent behavior is punishable as a felony or a misdemeanor depending on the value of stolen property.

The Pigeon Drop. A classic fraud scheme involves a scammer telling a victim (the pigeon) that the scammer has won a huge sum of money in a contest. However, the scammer needs to prove to the game's operators that the scammer had the ability to pay the entry fee if the scammer lost. The scammer promises the pigeon that in return for the pigeon lending the scammer the necessary amount of money, the scammer will split the winnings with the pigeon. After the pigeon lends the money, the scammer disappears.

Mail Fraud. Article I, Section 8 of the Constitution gives Congress the power "to regulate commerce among the several states." One way that Congress has exercised this power is by enacting mail fraud statutes that give the federal government the power to prosecute illegal schemes that use the postal system and other tools of interstate commerce.

> **EXAMPLE:** In the film *Trial and Error* (1996), a scammer runs ads selling portraits of President Abraham Lincoln for $1.00 each. Customers who order a portrait receive a penny by return mail. The scammer's failure to describe the portrait accurately constitutes mail fraud.

Ponzi Schemes. Ponzi schemes (named for a 1920s-era Italian thief) take advantage of the common desire to make easy money. Scammers attract investors by promising large and safe returns. As new investors join in, scammers pocket part of their investments and use the rest to satisfy earlier investors. Ponzi schemes are doomed to fail because the investments either are of poor quality or non-existent. Scammers have to attract an ever-expanding number of new investors to continue to satisfy earlier investors and thereby exacerbate the losses.

Real-Life Illustration

Bernard Madoff was a former stock exchange president who for many years operated the largest Ponzi scheme in history. Madoff cheated investors out of approximately $65 billion. In 2009, Madoff pleaded guilty to numerous federal offenses, including securities fraud, wire fraud, and mail fraud. He was sentenced to 150 years in prison.

Puffing. Gullible people cannot necessarily count on fraud statutes to protect them from making poor choices with their money. Sellers are allowed to "puff," meaning that they can make exaggerated general claims that reasonable people would realize are more expressions of opinion than statements of fact. An example is telling a car purchaser that "everyone will admire you when they see you tooling along in this hot little number."

 Legal Authority Examples

Connecticut: A person who issues a bad check or order on a nonexistent account is guilty of a misdemeanor if the amount of the check is less than $1,000 and is guilty of a felony if the amount of the check is over $1,000.

Colorado: Knowingly issuing a false financial statement in order to obtain a loan is a Class 2 misdemeanor.

Arizona: Taking the identity of another person or entity or knowingly accepting the identity of another person is a class 4 felony.

Related terms: embezzlement; forgery; larceny.

fruit of the poisonous tree

See search and seizure.

gambling

Gambling consists of betting on the outcomes of games of chance or sporting events in the hope of winning money or other prizes. Many common gambling law violations constitute misdemeanors rather than felonies.

Historical Antecedents. Lotteries were well established in England by the time of the American Revolution. According to an 18th century Virginian, lotteries were the "reall and substantial food by which Virginia hath been nourished." By the time of the U.S. Civil War, state-run lotteries had disappeared. They began to reappear after New Hampshire adopted a sweepstakes in 1964.

Justifying Punishment. Legal forms of gambling include day trading in stocks, horse racing, church-sponsored bingo, lotteries and betting offices licensed or operated by governments, and gaming casinos on land and rivers. Happy to collect the taxes that so much legitimate gambling produces, states no longer justify punishment by claiming that gambling is immoral. Instead, justifications for outlawing non-state-sanctioned gambling include the government's inability to assure players of consistent or fair payouts, the influence of organized crime, and the violence that tends to occur when gamblers are unable to make good on their losses to nonsanctioned game operators.

Bookmaking. Bookmaking is a long-established form of illegal gambling. Bookies collect bets on a wide range of sporting and other types of events. Bookies often establish odds that attract bets on conflicting outcomes. Even if they pay winners with the equivalent sums of money bet by losers, bookies may profit by keeping a percentage of the wagered amounts. For example, a bookmaker may permit bettors to place wagers and receive betting slips in return. The bookmaker's payouts reflect amounts that the "house" retains to cover expenses and earn profits.

Card Games. In some states, rarely enforced laws prohibit all gambling activities, including friendly card games involving betting. Other states prohibit only card games in which game operators collect fees from players. Generally, in the absence of statutory permission, card-game businesses in which players pay to play and dealers retain a percentage of the money in each pot are illegal.

Paraphernalia. Many forms of illegal gambling rely on devices such as slot machines, roulette wheels and tables, and craps tables. Gambling laws generally make it illegal to possess or distribute devices such as these—so, for example, the sale of used slot machines from licensed casinos to illegal gambling businesses is illegal.

Internet Gambling. Legions of Internet gaming sites allow bettors to establish accounts and place wagers over their computers, mobile phones, and other electronic devices. These sites cannot operate legally inside U.S. borders. However, the U.S. has no jurisdiction to punish operators who maintain offices and site operations in other countries. And U.S. laws do not punish Internet gamblers.

> **EXAMPLE:** Harvey is a Kansas resident who has an account and bets online with cantlosegaming.com. Harvey's gambling activity is not illegal. Later, deciding that the grass is greener on the other side of the bet, Harvey establishes his own Internet gaming site. Harvey's new business violates U.S. laws.

 Legal Authority Examples

Federal: The Unlawful Internet Gambling Enforcement Act prohibits operators of online gaming websites from accepting bets. The act does not prohibit participation by bettors.

Idaho: Anyone who gambles or permits others to gamble in owned or leased property is guilty of a misdemeanor.

South Carolina: Betting on the outcome of an election is a misdemeanor punishable by a fine of up to $500 and incarceration for up to a month.

California: Possession of slot machines is not prohibited so long as a machine is more than 25 years old and is not used for gambling.

Related Items: sentencing (punishment options).

gang-related crime

Although membership in a street gang is not itself illegal, gang-related criminal activity has been targeted with special laws in every jurisdiction.

The principle that membership in a gang is not punishable is based on the fact that people cannot be punished for who they are, only for what they do. (*Robinson v. California*, U.S. Sup. Ct. (1962).) So, for example, an individual can't be convicted for being a member of a gang that has committed crimes. However, if a gang member recruits other members into the gang, then he has taken action on behalf of the gang and can be convicted of a crime.

Definition. Street gangs do not create mission statements or set out their purposes in formal documents along the lines of articles of incorporation. As a result, statutes define groups as gangs based on the unlawful actions of their members. For example, under some state laws, a group qualifies as a gang only if at least two members in concert have committed at least two specified serious felonies on behalf of the gang within a particular period of time. If an alleged gang member steals a car by himself, the member cannot be charged with committing a gang-related offense because only one member of the group has committed a crime. The crime can become a gang-related offense if the prosecutor can prove that the car was stolen with the intent to further a gang-related purpose, such as serving as the getaway car for a robbery that two or more gang members plan to commit.

Sentence Enhancements. The criminal justice system relies largely on sentence enhancements to combat gang-related criminal activity. Sentence enhancement laws authorize judges to mete out harsher punishment for offenders who commit an illegal act in furtherance of a gang's aims. An enhancement cannot be imposed if, for example, there is no evidence that the member committed the crime on behalf of or in association with the gang (or with the intention of benefitting the gang). However, if there is evidence that the crime is gang-related—for example, as part of a gang initiation rite—the judge can impose a harsher sentence.

Injunctions. Many states have tried to reduce the impact of gang activities by authorizing judges to issue injunctions that forbid gang members from activities such as congregating together. Gang injunction court proceedings are civil, but gang members who violate injunctions can be incarcerated for contempt of court. The constitutionality of gang injunctions is debatable, as they forbid people to engage in otherwise lawful conduct. The U.S. Supreme Court has ruled that overbroad injunctions are invalid. (*Chicago v. Morales*, U.S. Sup. Ct. (1999).) However, judges have upheld the legality of injunctions that identify specific gang members and forbidden activities, and that have precise geographical boundaries. For example, a judge may prohibit specific gang members from congregating in a two- or three-block area that is known for gang activity.

 Legal Authority Examples

Idaho: An offender who knowingly commits a misdemeanor for the benefit or at the direction of, or in association with, any criminal gang or criminal gang member shall be punished by an additional term of imprisonment in the county jail for not more than one year. In the same circumstances, a conviction of a felony results in an extended term of not more than two years in prison. In the same circumstances, if an offense is committed on school grounds when the school is open for classes or school-related programs, the extended term shall be not less than one year and not more than four years.

California: An offender who commits a gang-related felony that is punishable by imprisonment for life has to serve a minimum of 15 years before the offender is eligible for parole.

Related terms: burdens of proof; disorderly conduct; sentencing (punishment options).

general intent crimes

See *mens rea*.

Gerstein Hearing

In a *Gerstein* hearing, a judge or magistrate determines whether probable cause for an arrest existed. The name has its origin in the 1975 case of *Gerstein v. Pugh*, in which the U.S. Supreme Court ruled that before a defendant can be detained prior to trial, a court must make a timely court determination of probable cause.

Related terms: arraignment.

Good Samaritan laws

These are laws that protect those who try to aid crime victims and others in distress. Typically, Good Samaritan laws provide that rescuers are not liable for harms they cause in the course of rendering reasonable assistance. Of course, Good Samaritans are not protected if they act unreasonably: "Looks like a bad gash on your forearm, I've always wanted to try treating a wound like this with Diet Coke." Laws generally do not *require* onlookers to try to prevent crimes from occurring or going to the aid of crime victims.

Related terms: *actus reus*.

grand juries

Grand juries determine whether prosecutors have enough evidence to file criminal charges. Grand juries theoretically serve as a protective intermediary between individuals and the criminal justice system and are distinct from "petit" juries—the trial juries that typically decide whether defendants are guilty.

Grand Juries and Preliminary Hearings. Under the Fifth Amendment to the U.S. Constitution, federal prosecutors who seek to file felony charges against individuals have to obtain indictments from grand juries. That is, federal prosecutors cannot directly charge individuals with committing federal felonies. Rather, they have to present their evidence to grand juries made up of citizens, and grand juries decide whether the evidence justifies the filing of criminal charges. Many states also require prosecutors to secure grand jury indictments in order to file charges. However, the grand jury clause of the Fifth Amendment is not binding on the states. In some states, prosecutors file charges and conduct preliminary hearings at which a judge rather than a grand jury decides whether the evidence justifies criminal charges. These prosecutors often have a choice between using a grand jury and going the preliminary hearing route.

Grand Jury Procedures. In a marked departure from the usual adversarial hearing with all parties present, grand jury proceedings are totally one-sided. Suspects are not present when prosecutors present evidence. Judges aren't even there. In fact, suspects may not even know that a prosecutor is seeking to indict them, receiving the bad news only after they are indicted and arrested.

Prosecutors present evidence in support of the charges they believe are warranted, including testimony from witnesses, to grand juries. Federal grand juries are larger than petit juries, consisting of 16–23 grand jurors. In the case of federal grand juries, if at least 12 of the jurors agree that probable cause exists to believe that a suspect committed a crime, then prosecutors can go forward with criminal charges. The one-sided aspect of grand jury proceedings results in claims that grand juries serve as rubber stamps for prosecutors rather than as true intermediaries that protect individuals against excessive or ill-founded charges.

Big and Little Fish. Witnesses subpoenaed to testify before a grand jury are sometimes themselves the targets of a criminal investigation. The Fifth Amendment right not to incriminate oneself applies to grand jury proceedings, and individuals who believe that they may be indicted can refuse to testify before a grand jury on the ground that the answers may incriminate them. Alternatively, targets who are the "small fish" in a larger illegal scheme often use their testimony as a bargaining chip. Prosecutors may grant a small fish immunity from prosecution, either completely or as to the most serious charges, in exchange for testimony inculpating a criminal scheme's big fish.

> EXAMPLE: Sam is an electronics retailer. At various times he purchased for sale in his shop electronic items from an organization that stole the products. Sam is subpoenaed to testify before a grand jury about his role in the crimes. Because he faces possible indictment, Sam's lawyer might contact the prosecutor who issued the subpoena and seek to exchange Sam's testimony for a grant of immunity from prosecution. If the prosecutor refuses, and refuses even to agree not to use Sam's grand jury testimony against him in the event Sam is charged with a crime, Sam may respond to all questions with the statement, "I refuse to answer under the Fifth Amendment on the grounds that the answer may incriminate me."

Grand Juries and Double Jeopardy. A suspect is not "in jeopardy" when prosecutors seek grand jury indictments. If a grand jury refuses to return an indictment against a suspect, a prosecutor can go before the grand jury again with additional evidence and perhaps obtain an indictment the second or even the third time around.

Legal Authority Examples

Excerpt from the Fifth Amendment to the U.S. Constitution: "No person shall be held to answer for a capital, or otherwise infamous crime, unless on a presentment or indictment of a Grand Jury, except in cases arising in the land or naval forces, or in the Militia, when in actual service in time of War or public danger."

Excerpts from the *Illinois Grand Juror Handbook*: Initial charges may be brought by indictment following a grand jury hearing or after a preliminary hearing takes place .... A grand jury determines that a person should be charged or prosecuted for a criminal act when it finds there is probable cause to believe the person has committed an offense .... A grand jury is composed of 16 citizens who serve until they are ordered discharged by the Court ... at least 12 members must be present at each session .... The Court selects a foreperson who presides over all sessions. The Prosecutor is the officer charged by law with the prosecution of crime in the county. However, the grand jury possesses broad powers of its own to inquire into crime and corruption .... Ordinarily only witnesses for the State will be called to testify .... However, the grand jury itself has the right to subpoena and question any person against whom the Prosecutor is seeking a Bill of Indictment, or any other person, and to obtain and examine any documents or transcripts relevant to the matter being presented by the Prosecutor .... Witnesses may have legal counsel present in the grand jury room to advise them of their rights but counsel may not participate during the proceedings in any other way.

Related terms: preliminary hearings; trial by jury (jury trials); double jeopardy; self-incrimination.

grand theft vs. petty theft

See shoplifting.

gun laws

An array of federal and state criminal laws regulate the ownership, transfer, possession, and use of guns despite the fact that the Second Amendment provides individuals with a right to own them. (*Heller v. District of Columbia*, U.S. Sup. Ct. (2008).)

Illegal Possessors. Laws in all jurisdictions identify background factors that make it illegal for individuals to possess a gun. While specific factors vary from one jurisdiction to another, common disqualifying factors include felony convictions, convictions of misdemeanors involving violence—for example, a conviction for misdemeanor domestic violence—and substance abuse.

Assault Weapons. The usual legitimate uses of firearms consist of hunting, target shooting, and self-defense. Individuals cannot legally own or possess assault weapons and semiautomatic weapons because of the risk that those who own or possess them will use them to commit crimes. Definitions of prohibited weapons vary widely among jurisdictions, and may include assault weapons—for example, .50-caliber BMG rifles—and bullets that pose more than the usual risk of serious harm.

Concealed Weapons. Carrying a concealed weapon on one's person, or concealing it in a place that is near at hand, is illegal in nearly all states. However, virtually all states allow individuals to apply for permits to carry concealed weapons. While requirements for obtaining licenses vary, individuals seeking a license to have a concealed weapon may have to demonstrate a legitimate need for the gun. Weapons are concealed for purposes of these laws if they are hidden from view yet easily accessible—for example, a handgun tucked under a car seat. In some states concealed weapons permits are granted routinely to individuals over 21 with no previous criminal record. There are also exceptions to concealment laws. For example, in some states, a store owner may be permitted to store a loaded handgun in a drawer near the cash register.

Prohibited Areas. Gun laws make it illegal to carry guns into statutorily protected areas such as schools, courthouses, airports, and other types of public buildings. For example, a state's law may make it illegal to have a weapon within 500 feet of a public school.

Obliterating Serial Numbers. Obliterating serial numbers on guns is illegal because the likely reason for destroying the numbers is to make guns harder to connect to offenders who use them to commit other crimes.

Gun Enhancements. Many statutes provide for harsher punishment, called gun enhancements, when offenders use guns in the commission of crimes. In jury trials, judges can impose gun enhancements only if a jury concludes beyond a reasonable doubt that a convicted defendant used a gun to commit a charged crime. (*Apprendi v. New Jersey*, U.S. Sup. Ct. (2000).)

> EXAMPLE: A jury convicts Lars of robbery of a jewelry store. The store clerk and three customers all testified that Lars threatened all of them with a gun while holding up the store. Nevertheless, the judge cannot impose a gun enhancement unless the prosecutor explicitly charged and the jury found true beyond a reasonable doubt that Lars used a gun during the commission of the robbery.

 Legal Authority Examples

Second Amendment: "A well-regulated militia being necessary to the security of a free state, the right of the people to keep and bear arms shall not be infringed."

Connecticut: First degree kidnapping is a felony. A kidnapper who uses a gun must be incarcerated for at least one year.

Missouri: It is a misdemeanor to possess an unloaded gun while intoxicated, and a felony to possess a loaded gun while intoxicated. Among other places, it is illegal to carry a concealed gun into a polling place on election day, or into bars and lounges, airports, sports arenas, places of worship, or hospitals.

Real-Life Illustration

Adam Lanza, age 20, shot and killed his mother, then went to nearby Sandy Hook Elementary School and fatally shot 29 first grade children and six adult members of the school's staff. When police officers arrived, Lanza shot and killed himself. Lanza destroyed his computer's hard drive and left no messages describing his plans, so the motives for his actions are unknown. The tragedy led to renewed (but failed) efforts to enact gun control laws.

G

RESOURCE

For information on how each state defines and punishes concealed weapons offenses, go to www.nolo.com/concealed.

For information on gun possession and use laws by state, go to www.nolo.com/gunlaws.

Related terms: chain of custody; convictions, consequences of; domestic violence; elements of a crime; hierarchy of criminal offenses; kidnapping; search and seizure.

habeas corpus

See writ of *habeas corpus*.

hate crimes

Hate crimes are those in which a culprit is motivated by bias against a victim because that victim has a characteristic (real or imagined) identified by a hate crime law. The characteristics that typical hate crime statutes identify are race, color, national origin, religion, and sexual orientation. In some states, the reach of hate crime laws extends to crimes motivated by a victim's age or disability. When bias based on a specified characteristic is a substantial motivation for commission of either a misdemeanor or a felony, the effect of a hate crime law is to enhance the offender's punishment.

 Real-Life Illustration

The widely publicized and gruesome murder of Matthew Shepard by Aaron McKinney and Russell Henderson in 1998 prompted many states to extend existing hate crime legislation to bias against homosexuals. McKinney and Henderson targeted Shepard because he was gay. They robbed and beat him and left him to die, tied to a fence in a remote area of Wyoming. Both defendants pleaded guilty and were sentenced to life in prison without possibility of parole.

At the same time, not all crimes committed against minorities or other protected classes constitute hate crimes. For example, in a state where an offense motivated by animosity against elderly people qualifies as a hate crime, a nurse who regularly steals from older patients would probably not be charged with a hate crime. Unless the prosecution can identify concrete evidence proving that ill will toward the elderly motivated her conduct, the prosecution would probably conclude that the nurse was just a thief motivated by a desire for ill-gotten gains.

Conflicting Attitudes Toward Hate Crimes Legislation. A principal justification for adding to the punishment of offenders whose crimes are motivated by bias against protected classes of people is that the impact of hate crimes often reaches beyond the victims personally to the communities that share the same characteristics. That is, an attack based on a victim's skin color, ethnicity, or religious beliefs is likely to instill fear and a sense of loss in other members of the victim's community. A second and perhaps more abstract justification is that hate crimes diminish society as a whole because they violate widely shared norms of equality and pluralism.

A primary criticism of hate crimes laws is that they punish thoughts rather than acts. As a general rule, criminal law doctrine ignores the underlying reasons for criminal acts. Robbery is equally illegal whether the robber is motivated by greed or revenge. By enhancing punishment because of an offender's motive, hate crimes laws are an exception to this underlying policy.

In the 1992 case of *Wisconsin v. Mitchell*, the U.S. Supreme Court upheld a state law that provided enhanced penalties for hate crimes. That decision put an end to the wrangling over the legality of hate crimes laws.

Proving a Hate Crime Motive. A prosecutor who seeks enhanced punishment under a hate crime law must prove beyond a reasonable doubt that a bias identified in a hate crime law was a substantial factor that motivated the charged crime. The illegal bias need not be the sole reason for the crime for a hate crime law to apply. For example, a mugger may guilty of a hate crime if a substantial factor in choosing victims is their ethnic background.

Hate Crimes Data. The FBI keeps track of hate crime incidents. In 2011 U.S. law enforcement agencies reported 6,222 hate crime incidents, of which 46.9% were due to race, 20.8% were motivated by sexual orientation bias, 19.8% were inspired by religious prejudice, 11.6% resulted from animosity on the basis of ethnicity or national origin, and 0.9% were caused by disability bias. These crimes encompassed offenses against both people and property. (www.fbi.gov/about-us/cjis/ucr/hate-crime/2011.)

 Legal Authority Examples

California: Vandalism that is otherwise punishable as a misdemeanor can be charged as a felony if the crime was motivated by a victim's race, religion, sexual orientation, color, ancestry, disability, or national origin.

Texas: In the case of a Class A misdemeanor motivated by bias or prejudice, the minimum term of confinement increases to 180 days. For most other types of convictions, a hate crime finding increases the punishment to the term prescribed for the next higher category of offense. For example, a second degree felony is punishable by imprisonment for a term of not less than two years or more than 20 years. But a second degree felony that is a hate crime is punished as a first degree felony, in which case the punishment is life in prison, or a term of not less than five years or more than 99 years.

hearsay

Hearsay is a verbal or written statement by someone to a witness who, while testifying in court, repeats the statement. The statement is hearsay only if it is offered for the truth of its contents. For example, if a friend tells you about a robbery and the prosecutor calls you as a witness to repeat your friend's statements at trial in order to prove how the robbery took place, your friend's statements constitute hearsay.

The hearsay rule protects a party's right to cross-examine opposing witnesses, a fundamental aspect of the U.S. adversarial system of trial.

Historical Antecedents. Sir Walter Raleigh was the English adventurer, historian, and tobacco grower who laid his cloak across a puddle for Queen Elizabeth I. Raleigh was convicted of treason in 1603 and ultimately beheaded for plotting against King James I's succession to the English throne. The main evidence against Raleigh, apart from his refusal to support James's right to be the king, was a Portuguese fisherman's hearsay statement that "Raleigh is in on the plot." Raleigh demanded without success that his prosecutors produce the fisherman for cross-examination. The controversy over using hearsay to convict and behead a national hero eventually crystallized into the hearsay rule.

The Exceptions. The hearsay rule has so many exceptions that cynics suggest that the rule ought to read, "Hearsay is admissible unless a lawyer is too dumb to think of an exception." This entry illustrates a few common hearsay exceptions in the context of criminal cases.

- **Party Admissions (Opposing Party Statements).** Prosecutors can offer into evidence statements made by defendants that are relevant to prove their guilt. When two or more people are coconspirators, a statement made by any conspirator constitutes a party admission of all the conspirators.

EXAMPLE: When Officer Columbo arrests Hans for shoplifting, Hans immediately blurts out, "You got me, I did it." The prosecutor can offer Hans's statement into evidence as a party admission. The statement is admissible even though it was not preceded by *Miranda* warnings, because Columbo did not interrogate Hans.

EXAMPLE: Daffy and Dizzy jointly engage in identity theft. In Daffy's separate trial for identity theft, the prosecutor can offer evidence that Dizzy told a victim, "Before I give you your prize, I need to see your Social Security number to verify your identity."

- **Dying Declarations.** Statements describing the cause and circumstances of what a person believes to be immediately impending death are admissible at trial under the dying declarations exception. Traditionally, dying declarations are considered reliable because few people want to "meet their Maker with a lie on their lips."

EXAMPLE: Moments after a car runs down a pedestrian and speeds off, the fatally injured pedestrian says to Bob, a bystander, before dying, "Won't make it … red car hit me … driver was bald." If the driver is prosecuted for murder, the pedestrian's statement constitutes a dying declaration to which Bob could testify to link the defendant to the death.

- **Pretrial Identifications.** This exception typically allows prosecutors to bolster testifying witnesses' in-court identifications of defendants by offering into evidence their pretrial hearsay statements of identification. This exception recognizes that identifications made closer in time to crimes are more likely to be reliable than identifications that may be made in court weeks or even months after a crime. (The existence of the exception also illustrates that prosecutors have more political power than defendants.)

EXAMPLE: In a robbery trial, prosecution eyewitness Ida identifies Joe as the robber. Ida then testifies that she told the police that Joe was the robber when she observed Joe in a lineup a few days after the robbery.

- **Beliefs and Intentions.** The "state of mind" hearsay exception is important in criminal cases because criminal laws so often require prosecutors to prove what defendants intended, knew, or believed to be true. These same factors may also be relevant to a defendant's alleged motive for committing a charged crime. The exception works the other way, too. Defendants can offer exculpatory state-of-mind hearsay. The exception recognizes that people's mental states are unobservable, and that often their statements are the best available evidence of their intention, knowledge, and belief.

EXAMPLE: Hillman is charged with murdering his romantic rival Walters while they the two men were camping at Crooked Creek. Hillman claims that he shot Walters in self-defense when Walters suddenly pulled a gun on him. A tweet that Hillman wrote saying, "I've had it with Walters going after my woman" is admissible to prove that Hillman intentionally shot Walters. Likewise, Walters's tweet that "Hillman is in the camping group, but I plan to stay clear of him" is admissible to prove that Walters did not instigate an attack on Hillman.

- **Excited Utterances.** Statements describing startling events or conditions are admissible to prove how those events or conditions took place. Excited utterances are deemed reliable because people who speak while under stress or when they are startled do not usually have time to make up lies. Unfortunately, studies suggest that stress also tends to reduce observers' accuracy. But why let reality intrude on a hearsay exception with such a lengthy pedigree?

EXAMPLE: Laurel is charged with attempted murder. To prove that Hardy was the shooter, Laurel offers evidence that just before the shooting took place, an onlooker cried out, "Oh my God, Hardy just pulled out a gun." (Those who hope that their statements will qualify as excited utterances may find it helpful to preface whatever they say with the words "oh my God.")

Confrontation Clause. The Sixth Amendment's Confrontation Clause—the clause that protects defendants' right to cross-examine prosecution witnesses—outranks the hearsay rule. The Confrontation Clause often prevents prosecutors from offering into evidence testimonial statements even if they qualify under a hearsay exception.

See confrontation of prosecution witnesses.

Legal Authority Examples

Federal Rule of Evidence 801(c): Hearsay is a statement, other than one made by the declarant while testifying at a trial or hearing, offered to prove the truth of the matter asserted.

Federal Rule of Evidence 801(d): Hearsay is admissible if it constitutes a pretrial identification made by a witness who testifies at trial and is subject to cross examination.

Federal Rule of Evidence Rule 802: Hearsay is not admissible unless evidence rules provide otherwise.

Federal Rule of Evidence 803(2): The hearsay rule does not exclude statements relating to a startling event or condition made while the declarant was under the stress of excitement caused by the event or condition.

Federal Rule of Evidence 803(3): The hearsay rule does not exclude statements of a declarant's presently existing state of mind, emotion, sensation, or physical condition (such as intent, plan, motive, design, mental feeling, pain, and bodily health).

Federal Rule of Evidence 804(b)(2): In homicide prosecutions, the hearsay rule does not exclude statements made by declarants who believe that death is imminent that concern the cause or circumstances of what they believe to be impending death.

Related terms: Confrontation Clause; conspiracy; eyewitness identification.

hierarchy of criminal offenses

Criminal offenses are organized in a hierarchy based on the seriousness of the crime and the severity of the punishment. Usually the hierarchy is expressed as three groups of crimes: infractions, misdemeanors, and felonies (the most serious crimes). As you might expect, capital murder ranks highest amongst felonies and has the severest penalties.

Infractions. Infractions (sometimes called violations) are petty offenses that are often punishable by small fines only. Because infractions cannot result in a jail sentence or even probation, defendants charged with them do not have a right to a jury trial. Traffic offenses—for example, running a red light or speeding—are the most common form of infraction.

Defendants accused of infractions can be represented by lawyers, but because there is no chance of jail time, the government does not have a constitutional duty to appoint a government-paid attorney for defendants charged with infractions. Often, prosecutors do not appear on behalf of the government in infraction matters. Evidence of infractions usually cannot be admitted into civil trials. So, for example, a conviction for speeding cannot be used in a civil lawsuit over a fender-bender.

Misdemeanors. Misdemeanors are criminal offenses that are punishable by up to a year in jail. Punishment for misdemeanors can also include payment of a fine, probation, community service, and restitution. Defendants charged with misdemeanors are entitled to a jury trial. Indigent defendants charged with misdemeanors are entitled to legal representation at government expense. Some states subdivide misdemeanors by "class" or by "degree," or define more serious misdemeanor offenses as "gross misdemeanors." These classifications affect the severity of punishment, so for example, a Class C misdemeanor such as furnishing cigarettes to a minor may carry only a maximum penalty of a fine of up to $100.

Municipalities may also create misdemeanors for offenses committed within their municipal limits. For example, a city may enact an ordinance that is effective only within the city limits that provides that the use of leaf blowers within the city constitutes a misdemeanor.

Felonies. Felonies typically involve serious physical harm (or threat of harm) to victims, and are the most serious type of criminal offense. Felony offenses can also include white-collar crimes and fraud schemes. Some offenses that otherwise are misdemeanors can be elevated to felonies for second-time offenders. Punishment for felonies ranges from imprisonment in prison for one year or longer to death. As with misdemeanors, states may also subdivide felonies by class or by degree.

Wobblers. Wobblers are offenses that may be prosecuted either as a felony or as a misdemeanor. An offense that was prosecuted as a felony may also be downgraded to a misdemeanor at the time of sentencing. This occurs when statutes authorize judges to punish offenders as either misdemeanants or felons.

> **EXAMPLE:** Randy threw a bottle at another patron in a tavern and missed his intended target. Randy is convicted of assault with a deadly weapon. State law provides that the offense is punishable by up to one year in jail (a misdemeanor) or up to five years in prison (a felony). The judge sentences Randy to a misdemeanor punishment—four months in jail, three years of probation, and 200 hours of community service.

 Legal Authority Examples

Rhode Island: Criminal offenses punishable by imprisonment for longer than a year or by a fine of more than $1,000 are felonies. Criminal offenses punishable by imprisonment for a term not exceeding one year or by a fine of not more than $1,000 or both are misdemeanors. Criminal offenses punishable by imprisonment for a term not exceeding six months or by a fine of not more than $500 or both are petty misdemeanors. Offenses punishable only by a fine of not more than $500 are violations.

Oregon: For sentencing purposes, felonies are classified as Class A, Class B, Class C, and unclassified felonies. Felony offenses not defined as Class A, B, or C felonies are unclassified felonies.

When a crime that is punishable as a felony is also punishable by imprisonment for a maximum term of one year or by a fine, the crime shall be classed as a misdemeanor if the court imposes a punishment other than imprisonment.

Santa Monica, California: Allowing an animal to bark for more than five minutes in any one-hour period is a misdemeanor punishable by a fine of up to $500 and incarceration for up to six months, or both.

 RESOURCE

For information on how each state classifies and penalizes misdemeanors and felonies, go to www.nolo.com/hierarchy.

Related terms: death penalty; sentencing (punishment options).

homicide

Homicide refers to the killing of a human being by another human being. The criminal law metes out punishment for homicides that are not excused nor otherwise justified. Criminal law statutes create categories of criminal homicide that recognize killers' different levels of moral responsibility for their actions. Common categories of criminal homicide, which this reference book addresses in more detail under separate headings, are as follows.

- **First Degree Murder.** A person who kills intentionally and with premeditation may be convicted of first degree murder.
- **Second Degree Murder.** A person who kills intentionally or by extreme recklessness but without premeditation may be convicted of second degree murder.
- **Voluntary Manslaughter.** A person who kills intentionally but under circumstances that reduce the person's moral culpability may be convicted of voluntary manslaughter—for example, a "heat of passion" killing that is suddenly provoked by a victim's behavior.
- **Involuntary Manslaughter.** When a death is the result of a person's reckless but unintentional behavior, the person may be convicted of involuntary manslaughter. Involuntary manslaughter may also arise when a death is the unintentional result of an illegal act. For example, if a liquor store salesman

knowingly sells alcohol to a minor who dies as a result of drinking the alcohol, the salesman might be convicted of involuntary manslaughter.

- **Vehicular Homicide.** Some states have created a separate category of criminal responsibility akin to involuntary manslaughter for deaths that result from negligent driving of a car (or other vehicle, such as a boat).

When Is a Fetus a Living "Human Being?" State laws (known as fetal homicide laws), often differ as to when a fetus is considered living for purposes of homicide rules. In at least 15 states, a fetus is considered to be "living" at the time of conception.

> **EXAMPLE:** Ezra hires a contract killer to kill his ex-wife Bonnie. Bonnie survives the killer's attempt to kill her, but the attack results in the death of the eight-week-old fetus that Bonnie was carrying at the time of the attack. State law provides that a fetus more than seven weeks old shall be treated as a human being for purposes of homicide. Ezra and the contract killer may be charged with murder for the death of the fetus.

Noncriminal Homicide. Noncriminal homicide refers to the killing of a human being that is legally excused or justified. Below are common types of noncriminal homicides, some of which have separate entries in this desk reference.

- **Self-Defense.** People have the right to defend themselves. A person who kills an assailant in the course of defending against the assailant's use of deadly force commits a noncriminal homicide.
- **Insanity Defense.** The criminal law punishes only people who are morally responsible for their actions. People who are adjudged to have been legally insane at the time of a killing are not morally responsible for their actions and therefore do not violate the criminal laws.
- **Official Duties.** The state cannot punish a person for carrying out a killing that it has authorized the person to perform. For

example, an executioner is not legally responsible for carrying out a lawfully imposed death penalty. Similarly, police officers who kill suspects in the legitimate carrying out of their official duties commit noncriminal homicides.

- **Wartime Combat.** Killings that soldiers commit on the field of battle are noncriminal homicides.
- **Duress Defense.** A duress defense arises when a person kills due to such overwhelming coercion exerted over the killer by another individual that the killing is a noncriminal homicide. The duress offense rarely applies to homicides, though.
- **Infancy.** Killings committed by children whom the law deems too young to realize the moral implication of their actions are noncriminal homicides. At common law, children under the age of seven were immune from criminal prosecution for their actions, including killing. Statutes in some states diverge from this common law rule.
- **Intoxication.** A person who kills as a result of being under the influence of alcohol or drugs that the person ingested involuntarily commits a noncriminal homicide—for example, a person kills after being unknowingly fed a powerful psychedelic drug. By contrast, voluntary intoxication is rarely a defense to criminal charges.
- **Necessity.** In situations that are extremely unlikely to arise, a killing may be a noncriminal homicide because the killing is necessary to prevent even more people from dying.
- **Abortion.** The destruction of a fetus by a qualified medical professional in the first trimester of pregnancy constitutes a noncriminal homicide; during this period a pregnant woman's right to determine her future outweighs other possible moral claims.

 Legal Authority Examples

California: Penal Code Section 189 defines first degree murder as follows:

All murder which is perpetrated by means of a destructive device or explosive, a weapon of mass destruction, knowing use of ammunition designed primarily to penetrate metal or armor, poison, lying in wait, torture, or by any other kind of willful, deliberate, and premeditated killing, or which is committed in the perpetration of, or attempt to perpetrate, arson, rape, carjacking, robbery, burglary, mayhem, kidnapping, train wrecking, or any act punishable under Section 206, 286, 288, 288a, or 289, or any murder which is perpetrated by means of discharging a firearm from a motor vehicle, intentionally at another person outside of the vehicle with the intent to inflict death, is murder of the first degree. All other kinds of murders are of the second degree.

New York: Article 125.25 of the New York Penal Laws defines second degree murder as follows: A person is guilty of murder in the second degree when:

1. With intent to cause the death of another person, he causes the death of such person or of a third person; except that in any prosecution under this subdivision, it is an affirmative defense that:

   (a) The defendant acted under the influence of extreme emotional disturbance for which there was a reasonable explanation or excuse, the reasonableness of which is to be determined from the viewpoint of a person in the defendant's situation under the circumstances as the defendant believed them to be. Nothing contained in this paragraph shall constitute a defense to a prosecution for, or preclude a conviction of, manslaughter in the first degree or any other crime; or

   (b) The defendant's conduct consisted of causing or aiding, without the use of duress or deception, another person to commit suicide. Nothing contained in this paragraph shall constitute a defense to a prosecution for, or preclude a conviction of, manslaughter in the second degree or any other crime; or

2. Under circumstances evincing a depraved indifference to human life, he recklessly engages in conduct which creates a grave risk of death to another person, and thereby causes the death of another person; or

3. Acting either alone or with one or more other persons, he commits or attempts to commit robbery, burglary, kidnapping, arson, rape in the first degree, criminal sexual act in the first degree, sexual

abuse in the first degree, aggravated sexual abuse, escape in the first degree, or escape in the second degree, and, in the course of and in furtherance of such crime or of immediate flight therefrom, he, or another participant, if there be any, causes the death of a person other than one of the participants; except that in any prosecution under this subdivision, in which the defendant was not the only participant in the underlying crime, it is an affirmative defense that the defendant.

(a) Did not commit the homicidal act or in any way solicit, request, command, importune, cause or aid the commission thereof; and

(b) Was not armed with a deadly weapon, or any instrument, article or substance readily capable of causing death or serious physical injury and of a sort not ordinarily carried in public places by law-abiding persons; and

(c) Had no reasonable ground to believe that any other participant was armed with such a weapon, instrument, article or substance; and

(d) Had no reasonable ground to believe that any other participant intended to engage in conduct likely to result in death or serious physical injury; or

4. Under circumstances evincing a depraved indifference to human life, and being eighteen years old or more the defendant recklessly engages in conduct which creates a grave risk of serious physical injury or death to another person less than eleven years old and thereby causes the death of such person; or

5. Being eighteen years old or more, while in the course of committing rape in the first, second or third degree, criminal sexual act in the first, second or third degree, sexual abuse in the first degree, aggravated sexual abuse in the first, second, third or fourth degree, or incest in the first, second or third degree, against a person less than fourteen years old, he or she intentionally causes the death of such person.

Related terms: deadly weapon; first degree murder (Murder One), second degree murder (Murder Two); manslaughter; felony murder rule.

hostile witness

A "hostile witness" is a witness whom the judge determines to be hostile (or "adverse") to the position of the party who calls the witness to testify. On direct examination, parties are allowed to ask leading questions of hostile witnesses. (Normally attorneys may ask leading questions only during cross-examination.) Judges may also declare a "turncoat witness"—a witness who was expected to be friendly, but who becomes hostile during the course of the trial—to be hostile, allowing the party that called the witness to ask leading questions.

Related terms: trial by jury (jury trial); trial phases (trial cycles); confrontation of prosecution witnesses; evidence.

identity theft

Identity theft is a form of fraud in which a thief impersonates a victim in order to acquire goods or property. Modern, up-to-date thieves typically use electronic methods to commit identity theft, such as gaining electronic access to a victim's credit card information and then using the information to make purchases online.

RESOURCE
For information on how each state defines and punishes identity theft, go to www.nolo.com/idtheft.

Related terms: cyber-crimes; fraud.

immunity

See privilege against self-incrimination.

impeach

See character evidence.

impossibility

Depending on the circumstances, a crime may be impossible to commit. Some crimes are legally impossible, while others are factually impossible. When people intend to violate the law but engage in actions that aren't actually illegal, the crimes they have attempted to commit are legally impossible. Conversely, a crime is said to be factually impossible when a person tries to commit it in such a way that makes it impossible to achieve.

> **EXAMPLE:** Lorena and her husband John are in bed. John's eyes are closed. Lorena goes to the closet and retrieves a hidden gun. Thinking that John is asleep, she points the gun at him and shoots him twice in the chest. What Lorena didn't know was that John died in his sleep an hour earlier. It was legally impossible for Lorena to kill John because he was already dead before she tried.

> **EXAMPLE:** Lorena and John are in bed. John's eyes are closed, but this time he's really just sleeping. Lorena goes and gets her gun. She points it at his chest and pulls the trigger. But Lorena didn't realize that she hadn't loaded the gun; it doesn't fire. In this case it was factually impossible for Lorena to kill John—you can't shoot someone to death with an unloaded gun.

Trying Counts. In almost all jurisdictions, neither factual nor legal impossibility is a defense. Despite the fact that it was impossible for Lorena to kill John, in each of the above examples she is guilty of attempted murder because she tried. Though the distinction between legal and factual impossibility has little practical meaning today, centuries of debate over the topic among judges and legal scholars spilled much ink and killed many trees.

 Legal Authority Examples

New York: It is no defense to a prosecution for attempting to commit a crime that the crime itself was impossible of commission, if the crime could have been committed had the circumstances been as a defendant believed them to be.

Minnesota: An act may be an attempt even if commission of the crime was not possible, unless the impossibility would have been clearly evident to a person of normal understanding.

Related terms: attempts; child pornography; *mens rea*; first degree murder (Murder One); statutory rape.

incest

Incest is a felony that occurs when sexual intercourse takes place between statutorily described family members. Incest laws prohibit voluntary sexual activity between consenting adults; courts have rejected the argument that incest laws violate the right to liberty protected by the Fourteenth Amendment of the U.S. Constitution. For legislators and judges, incestuous relationships are not truly consensual; they reflect unequal power relationships that undermine the family and invest sexual activity with an element of force or coercion.

While virtually every state forbids incest, states differ when it comes to the relationships that they consider incestuous. Sexual relations between parents and adult children and between siblings are incestuous in nearly every state. By contrast, sexual intercourse between first cousins and between step-parents and adult step-children is legal in some states, but not others. States also differ in their application of incest rules to adopted children.

 Legal Authority Examples

California: Persons being within the degrees of consanguinity within which marriages are declared by law to be incestuous and void, who intermarry with each other, or who being 14 years of age or older, commit fornication or adultery with each other, are punishable by imprisonment in the state prison.

Ohio: A person commits incest by engaging in sexual activity with a child (natural or adopted) or a step-child, or if the victim is the person's "guardian, custodian, or person in loco parentis of the other person." (A person in loco parentis of another has assumed parental status with regard to that person.)

incompetence to stand trial

See competence to stand trial.

indeterminate sentence

See sentencing (punishment options).

indigent (indigency)

See right to counsel.

informants

Persons who provide confidential information to the authorities about criminal activity are known as informants (or less politely, as "snitches" or "stoolies," depending on whom you ask). Commonly, informants have rap sheets of their own, and decide to inform on others' criminal activity in exchange for a benefit such as a lesser sentence on a pending charge. Typically, informants provide information leading to searches and seizures. The sections below focus on the role of informants in the Fourth Amendment context.

Probable Cause Determinations. Police officers may have first-hand knowledge of criminal activities that constitutes probable cause for an arrest or a search. Frequently, however, police officers obtain search warrants or conduct warrantless searches based in part on information provided to them by confidential informants. While judges recognize that informants may have axes of their own to grind and therefore may be of dubious credibility, they often consider information supplied by an informant when deciding whether to issue a search warrant or uphold a warrantless search.

> EXAMPLE: Officer McCloud receives a tip that three youths standing at a particular corner are in possession of illegal drugs. McCloud drives to the location, sees the three kids, and searches them for drugs. The search is illegal and any drugs that McCloud finds are not admissible in evidence. The tipster's

hearsay statement does not itself constitute probable cause to search. And other than verifying the obvious fact that the youths were at the corner, McCloud had no first-hand information suggesting that the youths possessed illegal drugs. However, McCloud would have had probable cause if he received the tip, drove to the location, and observed the three youngsters engage in brief transactions with drivers who pulled over at the corner. These actions are consistent with those of other drug dealers that McCloud has observed. After observing a number of transactions, McCloud accosts the youths and searches them for drugs. The search is legal because the tip as substantiated by McCloud's observations and experience establishes probable cause to believe that the youths possess illegal drugs.

Reliability of Informants. When evaluating how much weight to accord information provided by informants, judges typically consider whether an informant has on previous occasions provided information that turned out to be accurate. When police officers who rely on information from informants submit affidavits in support of applications for search warrants, they include information concerning an informant's past reliability whenever possible.

EXAMPLE: An informant who in the past has provided police officers with accurate information tells Officer McCloud that Williams, who is seated in a nearby car, has illegal drugs and a weapon on his person. Based on the tip, McCloud asks Williams to get out of the car, and frisks Williams for weapons. When the frisk reveals that Williams has an illegal weapon in his waistband, McCloud arrests Williams. Even though McCloud did nothing to verify the informant's information before frisking Williams, the frisk and arrest are valid. The informant's previous reliability does not provide probable cause for an arrest. But it is enough for McCloud to suspect reasonably that Williams is engaged in criminal activity, and therefore is sufficient to allow McCloud to stop and frisk Williams.

Related terms: search and seizure; warrantless searches; search warrants.

infraction

See hierarchy of criminal offenses.

inquest

This is a hearing conducted by a coroner seeking to collect information about the circumstances surrounding a victim's death. The advantage of an inquest over a police investigation is that a coroner can compel attendance through the issuance of subpoenas, and that witnesses have to answer questions under oath.

insanity

When defendants plead not guilty by reason of insanity, they are asserting an affirmative defense—that is, they admit that they committed a criminal act, but seek to excuse their behavior by reason of mental illness that satisfies the definition of legal insanity. People who are adjudged to have been insane at the time they committed a crime are neither legally nor morally guilty.

Historical Antecedents. The insanity defense has been around for centuries. A 1313 English court referred to insane people as "the witless, who do not have reason whereby they can choose the good from the evil." More colorfully, an 1812 English court decided that a man who had shot a Lord was insane because he was "a madman who … doth not know what he is doing, no more than a brute or a wild beast." Despite this lengthy pedigree, consensus on the proper definition of legal insanity still does not exist either among psychiatrists or among legal scholars, and the two professions don't have a lot of confidence in each other.

Definitions of Legal Insanity. Many criminal acts seemingly result from distorted mental processes. The criminal justice system continues to struggle for a method to distinguish offenders whose mental illness is so severe that society should not deem them morally responsible for their behavior from offenders whose actions, while perhaps objectively irrational, nevertheless merit punishment. The plethora of approaches makes the criminal justice system seem a bit, well, schizophrenic.

The *M'Naghten* Test. Many states define legal insanity according to the *M'Naghten* Test, developed in an 1843 English case. An offender is insane under this test if mental illness prevents the offender from knowing the difference between right and wrong. Other states have replaced the *M'Naghten* Test with a modified version known as the *Brawner* Test. Under this test, defendants are insane if, because of mental disease or defect, they lack the substantial capacity to appreciate the criminality of their actions or to conform their behavior to legal requirements. Some states supplement one of these tests with the "irresistible impulse" rule, under which offenders are insane if a mental disorder prevents them from resisting commission of an illegal act that they know is wrong.

> **EXAMPLE:** Manion, an army officer, returns home just as Quill races out the back door. Manion hurries inside and finds his wife Laura lying on the floor, raped and beaten by Quill. Manion picks up a gun, walks to Quill's place of employment, shoots and kills him, then calls the police. A defense psychiatrist testifies that Laura's injuries caused Manion to suffer a sudden psychic shock called dissociative reaction, and that dissociative reaction creates an unbearable tension that people may try to alleviate by taking immediate and often violent action. The psychiatrist's testimony supports a conclusion that Manion was legally insane under the irresistible impulse test. (This example is loosely based on the classic 1959 film, *Anatomy of a Murder*.)

Trial Procedures. Defendants have to advise prosecutors prior to trial if they plan to rely on an insanity defense. Typically, defense lawyers and prosecutors each obtain their own psychiatrists to examine a defendant and testify at trial. Judges appoint government-paid psychiatrists for indigent defendants. Defendants have the burden of convincing judges or juries by either a preponderance of the evidence or by the tougher standard of clear and convincing evidence that they were insane at the time they committed a criminal act. Evidence rules forbid defense psychiatrists from testifying to an opinion that a defendant was legally insane at the time a crime was committed. They can only provide a medical diagnosis concerning a defendant's mental illness.

No "Get Out of Jail Free" Card. Defendants found not guilty of severe crimes by reason of insanity are rarely set free. Instead they are almost always confined in mental health institutions. They may remain confined for a longer period of time than had they been found guilty and sentenced to a term in prison. States may compel defendants adjudged insane to remain in a mental health institution until they convince a judge that they are no longer legally insane.

A Hybrid Approach. Guilty, but mentally ill (GBMI) is a hybrid verdict that some states have adopted response to the widespread (and largely inaccurate) popular belief that the insanity tests let too many guilty people escape punishment. The general purpose of GBMI laws is to imprison offenders rather than place them in hospitals, and to afford them appropriate mental health services while they are incarcerated.

Myths and Truths. Research has dispelled many popular myths suggesting that the insanity defense is a boondoggle that lets criminals "get away with it" and get back on the streets immediately. Research consistently produces the following conclusions:

- Defendants offer an insanity defense in less than 1% of all felony cases, and are successful only about one-quarter of the time.
- Defendants found not guilty by reason of insanity are often confined in mental institutions for many years, and in some cases for a longer time than they would have been incarcerated had they been found guilty.
- Few offenders "fake" insanity; most defendants who plead insanity have a long history of mental illness and prior hospitalizations.

• In the large majority of cases, prosecution and defense expert psychiatrists agree on whether defendants are legally insane.

 Real-Life Illustration

Clad in body armor, wearing a gas mask, and carrying numerous guns, James Holmes entered a movie theater during a midnight screening of *Batman: The Dark Knight Rises* and fired his weapons randomly and indiscriminately. Holmes killed 12 patrons and wounded 58 others before police captured him without incident in the theater's parking lot. Holmes was charged with multiple counts of murder and attempted murder. Holmes's lawyers said that he would plead guilty to avoid the death penalty, but prosecutors rejected the offer. If the case goes to trial, Holmes's lawyers are likely to rely on a defense of insanity or diminished capacity. Shortly before the shootings, Holmes was able to legally buy two Glock .22 pistols, a Remington shotgun, a Smith & Wesson semiautomatic rifle, 3,000 rounds of ammunition for the pistols, 3,000 rounds for the semiautomatic rifle, and 350 shells for the shotgun.

 Legal Authority Examples

Texas: A person is legally insane if his criminal conduct was a result of severe mental disease or defect, so that the person did not know that his conduct was wrong. The term "mental disease or defect" does not include an abnormality manifested only by repeated criminal or otherwise antisocial conduct.

Pennsylvania: People are legally insane if at the time of the commission of an offense they are laboring under such a defect of reason, from disease of the mind, as not to know the nature and quality of the act they were doing or, if they did know the quality of the act, they did not know that what they were doing was wrong. Defendants relying on the insanity defense have the burden of proving by a preponderance of evidence that they were legally insane at the time of the commission of the offense.

Related terms: diminished capacity; sentencing (punishment options).

internal affairs

A unit within police departments that investigates claims of police officer misconduct.

interrogation tactics

Law enforcement officials, faced with the timeless task of acquiring information from suspected perpetrators, have developed a variety of interrogation tactics. If these tactics fail to meet the Fifth Amendment guarantee of due process then the interrogation is illegal and the results are usually inadmissible at trial. (One example of this principle in action is the *Miranda* decision, the U.S. Supreme Court case that gave rise to the "*Miranda* warnings" that police officers issue to suspects before interrogating them.)

The Fifth Amendment also bars police officers from using torture, violence, or threat of violence to coerce suspects into admitting guilt. Nor can police officers extract confessions by seriously misrepresenting the legal consequences of failing to confess.

> EXAMPLE: The film *In the Name of the Father* (1993) graphically depicts abusive police interrogation tactics that elicit a false confession that causes innocent suspects to spend years in prison. The film is based on the case of the "Guildford Four," who were wrongfully convicted of killing five people in a 1974 IRA pub bombing.

> EXAMPLE: Police officers arrest Rosa, a legal immigrant, for participating in an illegal immigration operation. After Rosa agrees to talk to the police officers, they tell her that if she doesn't confess, her entire family will be deported and the judge will double the length of her sentence. Such serious misrepresentations concerning legal principles are likely to

render any confession that Rosa may give involuntary and therefore inadmissible in evidence.

Voluntary Confessions Can Be the Result of Deception. Another ramification of the Fifth Amendment's due process clause is that confessions that suspects make to police officers are admissible in evidence at trial only if the suspects make them voluntary. Courts have decided that confessions can be voluntary even if they are a product of police officer deception. Some examples of the deceptions that are permitted include:

- **Leniency.** False statements about leniency are a common form of deception that judges generally allow.

  EXAMPLE: After booking Gully on a burglary charge and giving him his *Miranda* warnings, police officer Roos tells Gully, "If you agree to talk to me and confess to the burglary, I'll ask the prosecutor and the judge to give you leniency." Officer Roos has no intention of seeking leniency for Gully. Any confession that Gully makes as a result of Roos's misrepresentation is voluntary.

- **Detector Lies.** Misrepresenting the outcome of lie detector (polygraph) tests is another way police officers can coax confessions out of suspects without rendering them involuntary.

  EXAMPLE: After booking Gully on a burglary charge and giving him his *Miranda* warnings, police officer Roos offers Gully the chance to take a lie detector test. The polygraph operator tells Roos privately that Gully's test results are too equivocal for a conclusion as to whether Gully's claims of innocence are false or accurate. Nevertheless, Roos tells Gully, "The lie detector test shows that you committed the burglary. You might as well confess now and get it over with." Any confession that Gully makes is voluntary.

- **Singing Accomplices.** The arrest of two (or more) accomplices offers police officers the chance to use deceptive interrogation tactics to coax confessions out of them. (See *Frazier v. Cupp*, U.S. Sup. Ct. (1969).)

  EXAMPLE: Police officers arrest Corleone and Capone for conspiracy to smuggle illegal drugs into the country. The officers separate the suspects, neither of whom say a word to the officers. Nevertheless, the officers falsely tell each suspect, "Your friend is singing like a songbird. He's told us all about the smuggling ring. He says that you were running the show and that he played only a small role in the conspiracy. If you want to set the record straight and protect yourself, talk to us now and tell us what you know about the smuggling operation." If the deceptive tactics produce confessions, the statements are voluntary and admissible in evidence.

- **"We've Got the Goods."** A final common type of deception that courts generally allow involves police officers falsely telling suspects that the police have recovered crime-related evidence.

  EXAMPLE: Police officers arrest Dillinger for bank robbery. They tell him, "You really screwed up. A hidden camera shows you plain as day pointing a gun at the teller. We had a good laugh watching it. You might as well make life easier for us all by confessing." Even if no visual evidence exists, any confession that the misrepresentations produce is likely to be voluntary and admissible in evidence.

 Legal Authority Examples

Excerpt from the Fifth Amendment: "No person shall be … deprived of life, liberty or property without due process of law."

Dickerson v. United States (U.S. Sup. Ct. (2000)): Courts determine the voluntariness of a confession based on the "totality of the circumstances," including both the characteristics of an interrogated suspect and the details of the interrogation process.

Related terms: accomplices and accessories; polygraph machines (lie detectors); *Miranda* warning.

intoxication defense

Alcohol intoxication often features indirectly in the commission of many types of crimes. For example, wrongdoers may abuse alcohol and then engage in domestic violence or commit other assaults. Though collecting reliable data is difficult, estimates are that alcohol (and/or drug) abuse plays a significant role in the commission of at least a third of all serious crimes. Unless intoxication is involuntary, being drunk or drugged will rarely serve as a defense to the commission of a crime. However, in some states, intoxication may be a partial defense for crimes that require specific intent—for example, first degree murder.

Involuntary Intoxication. The criminal law punishes people whose actions are morally blameworthy. People who through no fault of their own become intoxicated to such an extent that they are not responsible for their behavior and commit a crime that they otherwise would not have committed are not morally blameworthy and therefore are not guilty. However, these scenarios are rare—for example, someone's cocktail is drugged.

Voluntary Intoxication. Suspects may try to claim, "I'm not guilty because the reason I committed the crime is that I had too much to drink (or took some drugs) and didn't know what I was doing." Suspects who commit crimes under the influence of alcohol or drugs that they have voluntarily ingested are generally as guilty as suspects who commit crimes when they are stone-cold sober. This makes sense because if it were otherwise, criminal law rules would motivate many people to abuse alcohol or drugs so that they could commit crimes with impunity. Also, voluntary intoxication is reckless behavior. If the intoxication leads to commission of a crime, moral blameworthiness exists. In other words, inebriation is no defense.

Voluntary Intoxication and Specific Intent Crimes. Courts have long wrestled with the impact of voluntary intoxication in the context of specific intent crimes. Specific intent crimes specify the purpose with which a wrongdoer must act in order to be guilty. For example, "assault with intent to kill" has traditionally been regarded as a specific intent crime because wrongdoers are guilty only if they carry out an attack with the purpose of killing their victims. At present, some states consider voluntary intoxication to be a partial defense to specific intent crimes. In other words, voluntary intoxication can negate the specific intent element of a crime. However, many states make no exception for specific intent crimes on the theory that people who ingest alcohol or drugs should be held fully responsible for the harms they cause.

> **EXAMPLE:** Soon after learning that he has been made redundant and thus is out of a job, Joe goes home and gets his handgun. Joe then goes to a tavern and gets drunk, breaks into his former workplace and shoots his former boss three times. His boss survives, and Joe is charged with assault with intent to kill. In some states, Joe would be guilty only of assault (with a firearm), and not the crime of assault with intent to kill, if the judge or jury concludes that he was intoxicated to such an extent that he didn't intend to kill his boss. In many states, Joe's intoxication would not constitute a defense to the specific intent portion of the crime and he could be convicted of assault with intent to kill. On the other hand, if Joe kills his former boss and is charged with first degree, premeditated murder, he may be guilty of second degree rather than first degree murder— provided that he was intoxicated to the extent that he was incapable of formulating a plan to kill his ex-boss.

Legal Authority Examples

New York: Intoxication is not a defense to a criminal charge, but intoxication of a defendant is admissible whenever it is relevant to negate an element of the crime charged.

Wisconsin: Involuntary intoxication is a defense to a criminal charge if the intoxication rendered the defendant incapable of distinguishing right from wrong. Voluntary intoxication is a defense to a criminal charge to the extent that it renders the defendant incapable of forming the specific intent to commit the crime.

Related terms: *mens rea*; first degree murder (Murder One); second degree murder (Murder Two).

invasion of privacy

Invasion of privacy laws seek to protect individuals' normal and reasonable expectations of privacy by punishing those who intentionally intrude into private spaces personally or electronically. These laws are based on the principle that the pursuit of "life, liberty, and happiness" includes the privacy of one's body and intimate personal activities. Nowadays, invasion of privacy increasingly involves the use of electronic devices such as webcams and mobile phones that reproduce and disseminate images, conversations, or other materials that are intended to be private or confidential. Invasion of privacy typically constitutes a felony.

 Real-Life Illustration

Anticipating that Tyler Clementi, his Rutgers University dormitory mate, would shortly engage in homosexual sex, Dharun Ravi opened the camera on his personal computer so that Ravi and others who logged onto his social media website could observe as the sexual activity took place. Clementi committed suicide in September 2010 after finding out what Ravi had done. Ravi was convicted of invasion of privacy (and other criminal charges) in 2012.

Privacy Expectations. Invasion of privacy statutes only protect those who have a reasonable expectation that they're free from being observed or disturbed by others—that is, they're involved in private activities. People that are publicly viewable with the human eye—for example, a couple in a public park—usually have no protectable expectation of privacy. Similarly, if a neighbor's sexual activity can be viewed through a high-rise window without the aid of binoculars, invasion of privacy does not occur because the neighbor has not taken reasonable steps to protect privacy.

Recording Private Conversations. In some states, such as California, parties to private conversations—whether in person or on the phone—cannot record what is said without the permission of all participants. In other states, parties can record conversations without permission so long as they are themselves participants in the conversation. One common exception to this rule is that some conversations can be recorded without consent if the recording is done pursuant to a search warrant.

> **EXAMPLE:** Following his arrest for conspiracy to distribute marijuana, Smokey decides to reduce his punishment by going undercover and helping the police gather evidence on other conspirators. The police attach a wire to Smokey that enables them to listen in and record everything that is said during a conspirators' meeting that Smokey attends. The tactic is valid only if the police have obtained a search warrant from a judge.

A Note About Peeping Toms. The quaint term "Peeping Tom" originates with the famous 11th century ride of Lady Godiva through the streets of Coventry, which the townsfolk were ordered not to watch. However, Tom peeped through his shutters and, according to legend, went blind. Nowadays, the term refers to the typically male offenders who invade privacy by surreptitiously observing women in private spaces.

Legal Authority Examples

Washington DC: It is a crime to record a phone call or conversation unless one party to the conversation consents.

Arizona: Knowingly photographing, videotaping, filming, digitally recording, or otherwise secretly viewing another person without that person's consent in a private location such as a bathroom, locker room, or bedroom while the person is dressing, undressing, nude, or involved in sexual intercourse or sexual contact is a felony.

Related terms: search and seizure.

J

jail

A jail refers to a locked facility. Jail populations comprise two principal communities. One community consists of convicted defendants serving sentences of up to a year. The second community consists of defendants charged with crimes who are unable or unwilling to post bail while they await resolution of their cases.

See booking procedures.

jurisdiction

Jurisdiction refers to a court's power to preside over a case. Courts generally have the power to preside over prosecutions involving crimes committed within the boundaries of the states in which they are located. Within states, county courts have jurisdiction over offenders who commit crimes within their counties. The federal government sometimes has exclusive jurisdiction over crimes committed on federal property and under certain statutes—for example, the federal government has exclusive jurisdiction over assaults on airline security agents at airport check-in gates.

Concurrent Jurisdiction. It is possible for a crime to be committed in two states—for example, a man in New York sends his ex-wife poisoned candy and she eats it in Connecticut. It is also possible for the same criminal act to violate state laws and federal laws. "Concurrent jurisdiction" exists when more than one state or both a state and a federal court have power over the same case. When concurrent jurisdiction exists, usually the first court to take control of a case retains exclusive jurisdiction until its proceedings conclude. Federal and state authorities can voluntarily relinquish jurisdiction to each other.

EXAMPLE: Rob is arrested by the FBI for robbery of a federally insured bank in Iowa. Rob is likely to be prosecuted in federal court. An Iowa state court also has jurisdiction to prosecute Rob for the same bank robbery. If Iowa intends to prosecute Rob for other robberies that violate state but not federal law, the feds might turn Rob over to Iowa so that one jurisdiction coordinates all the prosecutions.

Dual Sovereignty and Double Jeopardy. The constitutional prohibition against double jeopardy prevents the state or federal government from prosecuting the same person for the same crime more than once. But, the double jeopardy rule applies only to prosecutions by the same government, often described as the same "sovereign." (A government is sovereign if it draws its power from a source that is distinct from another entity. States draw their power from their constitutions and laws; the federal government draws upon the federal constitution and laws of Congress.) This means that both a state and the federal government can prosecute someone for the same criminal conduct (assuming that each has jurisdiction over the offense). However, such duplicate prosecutions are rare.

 Real-Life Illustration

In one of the first prosecutions in which a visual recording of an alleged crime scene played a prominent role, four Los Angeles police officers were charged in state court in 1992 with using excessive force to arrest Rodney King. A jury acquitted three of the officers and failed to reach a verdict on the fourth. Following widespread rioting primarily in the black community of Los Angeles, the federal government prosecuted the four police officers for violating King's civil rights. The charges were sufficiently distinct from the assault charges that the second trial did not violate double jeopardy. The federal trial resulted in conviction of two of the officers and acquittal of the other two.

Dragged Kicking and Screaming. Once defendants are in a court that has jurisdiction, judges usually don't question how they got there. Even the illegality of a defendant's apprehension may not detract from this issue. For example, a bounty hunter might violate laws in order to return a defendant to a specific state, but despite the illegality of the apprehension, the court will still have jurisdiction to prosecute the defendant.

 Legal Authority Examples

Iowa: The state has power to prosecute individuals for offenses that are committed either wholly or partly within Iowa; or if an individual's conduct outside Iowa constitutes an attempt to commit an offense within Iowa; or if an individual's conduct outside Iowa constitutes a conspiracy to commit an offense within Iowa; or if an individual's conduct within Iowa constitutes an attempt, solicitation, or conspiracy to commit an offense in another jurisdiction that is also illegal in Iowa. An offense may be committed partly within Iowa if conduct that is an element of the offense occurs within Iowa. If the body of a murder victim is found in Iowa, the death is presumed to have occurred within Iowa. If a kidnapping victim, or the body of a kidnapping victim, is found within Iowa, the confinement or removal of the victim from one place to another is presumed to have occurred within Iowa.

Related terms: double jeopardy; elements of a crime.

juror misconduct (pre and post verdict inquiry)

See trial by jury (jury trial); jury instructions.

jury instructions

Jury instructions are the vehicle through which judges advise jurors of legal rules and procedures, including the jury deliberation process. In a sense, jury instructions serve as a collection of principles that the jury should apply during their deliberations. Traditionally,

J

judges read instructions to jurors at the close of evidence and arguments. Because the effect of reciting these at length can be sleep-inducing, judges may read some instructions to jurors at the outset of a trial and others at its conclusion. Judges may also give jurors a complete copy of the instructions, in the form of either a written packet or an electronic file.

Pattern Jury Instructions. Most jurisdictions have compiled the principles constituting common crimes, defenses, evidentiary principles, and jury deliberation processes into books of standard and approved jury instructions, often called pattern jury instructions. Trial judges know that using approved jury instructions is a good way to prevent appellate court judges from reversing jury verdicts on the ground that a judge failed to properly instruct the jury. For example, if a judge deviated substantially from standard instructions on reasonable doubt, an appellate court would in all likelihood reverse a guilty verdict based on the erroneous instruction.

However, when defendants are charged with unusual crimes for which standard jury instructions do not exist, judges and lawyers have to craft case-specific instructions. For example, consider a defendant who is charged with violating a new law, for which a pattern jury instruction does not yet exist. The trial judge will probably ask both the prosecutor and the defense attorney to submit a proposed instruction, and will ultimately decide on the instruction's wording.

Elements of Crimes and Defenses. The most crucial function of jury instructions is to inform jurors of the legal rules they are to apply to evidence in order to arrive at a verdict. Instructions cover the elements of the crimes with which defendants are charged and of lesser-included offenses—crimes that involve the same activity as the principally charged crime. Instructions also explain the elements of any affirmative defenses that defendants have raised. However, judges have some discretion. For example, if a defendant's lawyer seeks a jury instruction on self-defense, but has not adequately raised that issue during trial, a judge can properly refuse to provide the instruction.

Evidentiary Principles. The criminal justice system has developed an array of principles that guide judges' and jurors' evaluation of evidence. In jury trials, judges issue instructions that advise jurors of relevant evidentiary principles—for example, a judge will instruct that a defendant is presumed innocent and that a charge against the defendant itself does not constitute evidence of guilt. Or, in the typical case involving both direct and circumstantial evidence, one of the judge's instructions would explain the difference between the two forms of evidence, and advise the jury that both are valid forms of proof that are entitled to whatever weight the jurors choose to give them.

> **EXAMPLE:** Teresa Mutter is charged with selling illegal drugs to an undercover police officer. Mutter testified in support of her defense that the police officer entrapped her. When the prosecutor cross-examined her, Mutter admitted to a previous conviction of perjury. The judge instructs the jurors that they cannot use the perjury conviction as evidence that Mutter sold drugs illegally, but can consider the conviction only for the limited purpose of evaluating Mutter's credibility as a witness.

Deliberation Processes. Judges seem to fear that in the absence of guidance, jurors will deliberate aimlessly and deceitfully rather than fairly and efficiently. Thus, jury instructions provide jurors with a general guide to the deliberation process. Certain "routine instructions" typically advise jurors to:

- choose a foreperson
- listen to each other's views
- keep an open mind
- not visit the scene where relevant events took place
- promptly report any improper behavior by a juror or an outsider to the judge
- not discuss the case with anyone other than during jury deliberations, and
- not give up an honest belief simply to get the case over with.

Listening Ears. Juror deliberations are private. Jurors do not have to explain the bases of their verdicts. As a result, judges may issue instructions by the carload but usually have no way to know whether jurors actually follow them. For example, a verdict will be final even if a jury acquits a defendant after misinterpreting a judge's instruction on reasonable doubt. (If, on the other hand, the defendant can establish that a conviction was the result of juror misconduct, an appellate court will reverse it.)

 Legal Authority Examples

California: Standard criminal jury instructions are compiled in book called CALCRIM (Judicial Council of California Criminal Jury Instructions.)

Federal Court, 11th Circuit: The pattern instruction on reasonable doubt instructs the jurors that "the Government's burden of proof is heavy, but it doesn't have to prove a Defendant's guilt beyond all possible doubt. The Government's proof only has to exclude any reasonable doubt concerning the Defendant's guilt. A reasonable doubt is a real doubt, based on your reason and common sense after you've carefully and impartially considered all the evidence in the case. Proof beyond a reasonable doubt is proof so convincing that you would be willing to rely and act on it without hesitation in the most important of your own affairs. If you are convinced that the Defendant has been proved guilty beyond a reasonable doubt, say so. If you are not convinced, say so."

Related terms: assault with a deadly weapon; burdens of proof; convictions, consequences of; affirmative defenses; self-defense; evidence; trial by jury (jury trial); lesser included offenses.

jury nullification

See trial by jury (jury trial).

jury selection

See trial by jury (jury trial).

juvenile court

This is a specialized court that hears cases involving crimes committed by minors (usually children less than 18 years old) as well as dependency cases (in which a county seeks to remove a child permanently or temporarily from the child's parents). If a minor is charged with committing an especially serious crime or if a minor has a lengthy juvenile court criminal record, a juvenile court judge may be able to transfer the case to a general criminal court, which has the power to try the minor as an adult.

K

kidnapping

Kidnapping consists of seizing and transporting a victim by force and against the victim's will. Though a kidnapper may demand payment (a ransom) in exchange for releasing a victim, such a demand is not an element of the crime. Kidnapping is a felony, one that in the past was punishable by death in some states. Statutes may establish degrees of kidnapping, with first degree or aggravated kidnapping punished more severely because it involves harm to a victim or use of a weapon.

> **EXAMPLE:** Abbie has been unable to obtain legal custody of her seven-year-old daughter, Connie, from her ex-husband. Abbie picks up Connie after school and takes her to a distant location, creates new identities for herself and Connie, and conceals their whereabouts from her ex-husband. Abbie's actions constitute kidnapping. Even though she is Connie's mother, Abbie had no right to take exclusive custody of Connie, and as a minor, Connie is too young to consent to Abbie's abduction.

Historical Antecedents. Laws against kidnapping go back at least to the book of Exodus, which deemed it to be a capital offense (Exod. 21:16.) In 1600s England, kidnapping frequently entailed abducting victims in order to sell them as slaves in the North American colonies. In the U.S., Bruno Hauptmann's 1932 apparent kidnapping and slaying of the one-year-old son of famed aviator Charles Lindbergh created national hysteria and resulted in Congress enacting the Lindbergh Law (18 U.S.C. § 1201–1202), which makes kidnapping a federal crime if a kidnap victim is transported across state lines.

Incidental Movement. Crimes often involve movement by victims. For example, assume that a robber accosts a victim in front of the victim's house. In order to carry out the robbery without being seen, the culprit forces the victim at gunpoint to go back into the house. If a judge strictly applied the language of the typical kidnapping statute to the robber's actions, the robber could be convicted not only of robbery but also of kidnapping. However, the general rule is that forcing a victim to move in the course of committing a crime does not constitute kidnapping if the movement is incidental to the commission of the crime. Thus in the robbery scenario, a judge may deem the victim's movement incidental to the commission of the robbery and disallow a kidnapping charge. However, if a victim has to move so substantially that the movement creates an increased risk of harm—for example a bank robbery hostage is driven to an isolated cabin in the woods and left there—a kidnapping likely occurred.

Don't Move. Typically, kidnapping involves substantial movement of a victim. However, under modern statutes a kidnapping may also take place if a perpetrator forcefully prevents a victim from leaving a location. For example, if one coconspirator holds an industrial night watchman in the watchman's office at gunpoint all night while confederates steal and carry off equipment, under some states all of the conspirators could be convicted of kidnapping in addition to other crimes.

See false imprisonment.

Kidnapping in Popular Culture. While kidnapping is a very serious and frightening offense, it has also been the subject of study and observation by psychologists, writers, and filmmakers. Because kidnapping involves emotional and physical duress, victims sometimes begin to identify with their captors, resulting in a psychological condition known as Stockholm syndrome, in which victims identify more with their captors than with their rescuers. This condition is commonly associated with the kidnapping of the heiress, Patty Hearst. A common theme in books and movies is that of kidnappers who got more than they bargained for—as in the O. Henry story, "The Ransom of Red Chief," where the kidnappers have to pay to return their unruly hostage; and in the film comedy *Ruthless People*, in which a naïve young couple learn that their hostage's vile husband is happy that his wife is gone.

 Real-Life Illustration

Ariel Castro kidnapped Amanda Berry, Gina de Jesus, and Michelle Knight between 2002 and 2004 and held them captive in the basement of his Cleveland, Ohio home for about a decade. Castro's neighbor, Charles Ramsey, heard Berry screaming from behind a locked door and helped Berry, her six-year-old daughter fathered by Castro, and the other two women escape. Prosecutors charged Castro with multiple counts of kidnapping and rape. They also charged him with a capital crime—meaning he would be eligible for the death penalty—because he physically abused his victims by assaulting them and induced miscarriages by kicking them in the stomach. But, with the agreement of prosecutors, Castro plead guilty in exchange for a sentence of life plus 1,000 years in prison, meaning that he would avoid the death penalty.

 Legal Authority Examples

Illinois: Kidnapping includes both forcing a victim to go from one place to another and confining a victim to a location against the victim's will. Confining a child 12 years old or younger without the consent of the child's parent also constitutes kidnapping. Aggravated kidnapping includes kidnapping for ransom and use of a weapon, and subjects a perpetrator to additional punishment. All forms of kidnapping are felonies.

knock and announce rule (knock and notice)

See arrests.

larceny

Larceny occurs when a thief takes another's personal property without permission and with the intent of depriving its owner or possessor of possession permanently. Larceny can be either a misdemeanor (sometimes referred to as "petty larceny") or a felony (referred to as "grand larceny") depending on the dollar value of the stolen property.

Historical Antecedents. Centuries ago in England, larceny was a felony if the value of stolen property exceeded 12 pence, which was then the going price for a whole sheep. By that standard, today theft of anything more valuable than a mini lamb chop would be a felony!

Possession Is Nine-Tenths of the Law. *Not!* For purposes of the law of larceny, a possessor of property may be an owner or simply a temporary possessor. So long as an owner or possessor has not abandoned property, an offender who takes it commits larceny.

> EXAMPLE: Walt tells a jewelry store clerk that he wants to examine a ring. When the clerk hands the ring to Walt, Walt dashes out of the store with it. Walt is guilty of larceny. The clerk did not give him possession of the ring, but only temporary custody for the purposes of examination.

Permanent Deprivation. Larceny law does not distinguish in regards to what a thief does with purloined property. So long as a thief intends for the owner or possessor not to get property back, larceny takes place. For example, an angry ex-girlfriend commits larceny when she removes her boyfriend's bicycle from his house and throws it over a cliff. Even though she did not keep the bicycle, she permanently deprived its owner of it. However, if a person does not intend to permanently deprive the owner of property, no larceny has occurred.

> EXAMPLE: Mavis contacts a rental car company on the day she is supposed to return the car. Mavis asks the company for permission to keep the car for two additional days before returning it, but the company refuses to give its permission. Mavis keeps the car for two additional days anyway and then returns it. Mavis is not guilty of larceny because she did not intend to deprive the rental car company of the car permanently. Nevertheless, Mavis is probably guilty of the less serious crime of joyriding. Also, at the behest of rental car companies, some states have enacted statutes that define failure to return a rental car on time as theft.

By the way, larceny also occurs if a thief steals property from a thief. (So much for honor among thieves.)

 Legal Authority Examples

Colorado: Theft is knowingly obtaining or exercising control over an owner's or possessor's property without authorization so as to deprive the other person permanently of the property's use or benefit. Theft is a Class 2 misdemeanor if the value of stolen property is less than $500, a Class 1 misdemeanor if its value is more than $500 but less than $1,000, a Class 4 felony if its value is more than $1,000 but less than $20,000 and a Class 3 felony if its value exceeds $20,000.

Connecticut: First degree larceny is a felony punishable by a term of imprisonment of not less than one nor more than 20 years.

Related terms: robbery; shoplifting.

lesser included offenses

Many criminal offenses have less harsh counterparts called "lesser included offenses." These are criminal charges that incorporate many of the same elements as the more serious crime but have a less severe penalty. For example, joyriding (taking a car without permission) is a lesser included offense of auto theft (taking a car without permission with intent to steal it). Similarly, the crime of driving under the influence of alcohol often includes the lesser offense of reckless driving. As part of plea bargaining negotiations, defendants often seek to plead guilty to lesser included offenses, thereby reducing the severity of the punishment. Judges generally accept guilty plea bargain agreements for lesser included offenses.

Trial Verdicts. Judges and jurors have the power to convict defendants of a lesser included offense rather than a charged offense. Judges rather than lawyers decide whether the evidence warrants instructing jurors about lesser included offenses, and in this way, judges can limit attorneys' opportunities to play strategic games at trial.

 Real-Life Illustration

In the controversial and internationally televised "Nanny Trial" of 1997, a 19-year-old British *au pair* babysitter was charged in Massachusetts with second degree murder. The murder charge was based on the government's contention that the babysitter shook a baby with such reckless violence that the baby died. The babysitter denied using violence. Consistent with Massachusetts law at the time of the trial, at defense counsel's request the judge did not instruct the jurors that they might convict the babysitter of involuntary manslaughter, a lesser included offense. The defense gambled on an "all or nothing" verdict, reasoning that if the jurors had no middle ground and had to choose between murder and acquittal, they would choose acquittal. The defense lost the immediate battle: the jury returned a verdict of second degree murder. Ultimately, the judge reduced the conviction to involuntary manslaughter anyway.

Double Jeopardy. Double jeopardy protections attach both to charged offenses and to lesser included offenses. This principle is sometimes called the "merger doctrine" because lesser and greater offenses merge into each other. This makes sense, because otherwise the government could prosecute a defendant multiple times for essentially the same conduct. If a jury acquits a defendant of a more serious offense but cannot agree about the defendant's guilt of a lesser included offense, the government cannot retry the defendant for the more serious offense. For example, a person charged and acquitted of second degree murder cannot later be charged with the lesser included offenses of voluntary and involuntary manslaughter, because the person would be placed in jeopardy twice for the same conduct. However, if a jury acquits a defendant of a more serious offense, for example, armed robbery, but is split in favor of convicting the defendant of the lesser included offense (robbery), the government can retry the defendant again for robbery, but not armed robbery.

 Legal Authority Examples

New York: In addition to instructing juries about the greatest offenses of which a defendant may be convicted, judges have discretion to instruct them about any lesser included offense that the evidence reasonably supports. A judge may not instruct about a lesser included offense when there is no reasonable view of the evidence that would support conviction of the lesser offense.

Texas: The crime of passing a bad check is not a lesser included offense of a crime of theft.

Related Terms: burglary; double jeopardy; intoxication defense; plea bargaining; manslaughter; second degree murder (Murder Two).

life without parole (LWOP)

See sentencing (punishment options).

loitering

See disorderly conduct.

L

M

magistrate

A magistrate is a public official with limited power (or "jurisdiction") to decide civil and criminal matters. Generally, a magistrate's power in criminal matters is limited to pretrial hearings (e.g., arraignment and bail) and trials for lesser crimes. Full-time magistrates in the federal court system are appointed for eight-year terms by district court judges. In state courts, a judicial officer who may be called a justice of the peace or a commissioner often carries out duties similar to those performed by a federal court magistrate.

Related term: commissioners.

malice

See mental states in criminal law.

malice aforethought

See first degree murder (Murder One).

manslaughter

Manslaughter consists of killings that are unlawful but occur under circumstances that reduce a killer's moral culpability for a victim's death. Most jurisdictions distinguish between voluntary and involuntary manslaughter, and as the names imply, voluntary manslaughter is the more serious of the two. All forms of manslaughter are felonies, and are generally punishable by a term of years according to the severity of the circumstances.

Manslaughter in the Spectrum of Killing Crimes. In the hierarchy of "killing crimes," manslaughter ranks behind first and second degree murder. This spectrum offers jurors and judges various choices when it comes to the difficult task of blame-assessment and punishment. A person whose conduct led to a victim's death may be charged with first-degree murder. It's then up to a jury to consider the evidence and evaluate the killer's behavior based on all of the circumstances. The jury may decide that even if the killing was unlawful, the circumstances do not justify a conviction for first degree or second degree murder, and may return a verdict of second degree murder or voluntary or even involuntary manslaughter. Jurors also have the right and the power to decide that a killing was not criminal and return a verdict of not guilty.

The point is that legal elements by which killing is judged, such as "malice aforethought," "extreme recklessness," "heat of passion," and "criminal negligence" are abstractions and are largely meaningless apart from their application to concrete scenarios. As the "conscience of the community," jurors have the often-difficult task of assessing a killer's blameworthiness and choosing which legal label best fits the circumstances of a particular killing. In this manner, manslaughter provides a reasonable alternative for a juror convinced that an unlawful killing has occurred but is not so clear as to the degree of blame.

Voluntary Manslaughter. Voluntary manslaughter is an intentional killing that would constitute murder but for the presence of mitigating circumstances that reduce a killer's moral culpability. In many situations, provocation by the victim is the factor that reduces a criminal homicide from murder to manslaughter. If a killer responds in what lawyers and judges often refer to as the "heat of passion" to a victim's provocative behavior, the killing is likely to constitute voluntary manslaughter rather than murder.

Consider three scenarios loosely based around the plot of the classic courtroom film, *Anatomy of a Murder*:

- **Scenario 1: Heat of Passion = Voluntary Manslaughter.** A man returns home from a meeting of his National Guard unit.

As he opens the front door, he hears his wife screaming "Get off me, get off me!" He rushes into the bedroom and sees a stranger sexually assaulting his wife. When the stranger spots the husband he jumps up and rushes out of the bedroom. The husband yells to stop, but when the stranger continues to run away the husband in a panic grabs his military revolver from a drawer and shoots and kills the stranger. The killing was unlawful because the stranger was running away and therefore no longer a threat. However, the sexual assault provoked the husband into shooting at him. The husband is guilty of voluntary manslaughter.

- **Scenario 2: Cooling-Off Period = Murder.** If the husband had not shot the stranger in the immediate aftermath and after witnessing the attack, but instead later learned the stranger's identity and went to his home and killed him, the husband would no longer have a legitimate "heat of passion" defense. The husband is expected to behave reasonably, and a reasonable person would have had time to cool down and call the police rather than personally seek justice. The husband is probably guilty of murder rather than voluntary manslaughter.

- **Scenario 3: Heat of Passion, Wrong Victim = Murder.** Assume again that the husband witnesses the attack, but the stranger escapes before the husband can stop him. However, the husband remains in such a rage that he stands outside his front door after the attack, firing his gun wildly in all directions. Unfortunately, one of the bullets strikes and kills a neighbor who was walking her dog. The husband is guilty of murder rather than voluntary manslaughter. He may have fired his gun at a time when he was in the "heat of passion," but the victim was not the person who provoked him.

Mistaken Self-Defense. Killers who kill in the reasonable but erroneous belief that deadly force is necessary to save their own lives also are typically guilty of voluntary manslaughter rather than murder. For example, an inebriated man would be liable for voluntary manslaughter if he mistakes another man's identical apartment for his own and enters, gets into a dispute with the real owner and accidentally kills the owner believing he is defending himself and his home.

Involuntary Manslaughter. Involuntary manslaughter arises when a killer's negligence rather than an intentional act results in a victim's death. To justify elevating an act of negligence that results in death from a civil tort to the crime of involuntary manslaughter, criminal statutes often require proof of "criminal," "gross," or "culpable" negligence. These are vague terms, but the idea is that a killer's conduct falls somewhere between the "extreme recklessness" that can produce murder charges and the "simple negligence" that is not criminal and instead often results in civil "wrongful death" lawsuits for damages.

> **EXAMPLE:** Sela is sending a text message on her mobile phone while driving, despite a state law making it illegal to do so. Sela makes a right turn without noticing the pedestrian who has just entered the crosswalk. Her car strikes and kills the pedestrian. Sela is probably guilty of involuntary manslaughter. Sela struck the pedestrian because she ignored the well-known risks of driving while texting. A jury may reasonably conclude that Sela was guilty of "gross negligence" that constitutes involuntary manslaughter. (Another term for this in some states would be "vehicular homicide.")

 Real-Life Illustration

A jury convicted Dr. Conrad Murray of involuntary manslaughter for providing reckless medical care that led to the death of famous pop singer Michael Jackson. Murray was paid a hefty monthly fee to provide virtually round-the-clock care to Jackson in his L.A. home as he prepared for an upcoming concert tour. On the day Jackson died, Murray injected him with a powerful sedative called propofol, which is typically administered only during hospital surgical procedures, with trained medical personnel on hand to deal with complications. Murray was sentenced to four years in prison and lost his license to practice medicine.

Legal Authority Examples

Pennsylvania: A person who kills an individual without lawful justification commits voluntary manslaughter if at the time of the killing he is acting under a sudden and intense passion resulting from serious provocation or if at the time of the killing he unreasonably believes the circumstances to be such that, if they existed, would justify the use of deadly force for self-defense. A person is guilty of involuntary manslaughter when as a direct result of the doing of an unlawful act in a reckless or grossly negligent manner, or the doing of a lawful act in a reckless or grossly negligent manner, he causes the death of another person.

California: Manslaughter is an unlawful killing of another person without malice. Involuntary Manslaughter is a killing that occurs during the commission of a misdemeanor or as the result of a lawful though dangerous act, that is done in an unlawful manner or without due caution or circumspection.

Related terms: first degree murder (Murder One); second degree murder (Murder Two).

marijuana offenses

Laws in all jurisdictions criminalize the cultivation, possession, and sale of marijuana (cannabis). Possession of a small amount of marijuana is punishable as either an infraction or a misdemeanor, while selling marijuana and possessing it for sale are generally felonies. Medical marijuana laws in a number of states authorize the sale of marijuana by licensed dispensaries with a doctor's prescription.

Legalization? Perhaps coincidentally, the end of Prohibition in 1933 was shortly followed by the criminalization of marijuana. Ever since, supporters of cannabis's legalization have argued that "weed" is no more addictive or harmful than alcohol or nicotine and should be legalized on the same basis. Their arguments have been aided by a growing sense that legalizing marijuana and taxing its growers and consumers can be a dandy way of providing governments with much-needed revenue streams.

Decriminalization. Laws decriminalizing marijuana are common but they are not the equivalent of legalization. Decriminalization means that possession of a small quantity of marijuana for personal use is a minor violation akin to a traffic ticket. Violators are subject only to a small fine. In states that have decriminalized marijuana, offenders receive citations and are not arrested unless they possess large amounts, posses it for sale, or are repeat offenders.

Size Matters. Punishment for marijuana possession typically varies according to the quantity of marijuana that a person possesses. Possession of marijuana almost always constitutes a felony rather than a misdemeanor when the quantity is large enough to indicate that it is held for sale rather than for personal use. Even if a defendant isn't caught with a substantial quantity of cannabis, simultaneous possession of materials such as packaging bags, scales, or ledgers (tracking who has paid and who hasn't) will likely trigger a felony prosecution for possession with intent to sell.

Minor Crimes. Selling or giving marijuana to minors typically results in enhanced punishment. So, for example, an "enlightened" dad who furnishes marijuana cigarettes to his teenage children and their friends may be charged with a felony even though he is doing so in his home and attempting to demonstrate the negative aspects of drugs.

Federalism. Federal laws also criminalize the cultivation, possession, and sale of marijuana. The federal government typically leaves enforcement of marijuana laws up to the states. However federal agents may act when large criminal enterprises are engaged in the marijuana trade. Federal prosecutors may also prosecute marijuana crimes that are legal under a state's law, though they rarely do so.

EXAMPLE: Pursuant to a medical marijuana law, a dispensary called The Joint is licensed by a state to sell marijuana to patients who have doctors' prescriptions. Nevertheless, federal agents can obtain a warrant to seize The Joint's supply of marijuana and The Joint's owners can be prosecuted in federal court for selling marijuana.

 Legal Authority Examples

Texas: Possession of two to four ounces of marijuana is a misdemeanor punishable by up to a year in jail and a fine of $4,000. Sale of any amount of marijuana to a minor is a felony punishable by imprisonment of two to 20 years and a fine of up to $10,000.

Montana: Possession of up to 60 grams of marijuana is a misdemeanor punishable by up to six months in jail and a fine of no more than $500. Cultivation of up to one pound of marijuana is a felony punishable by one year to life in prison and a fine of up to $50,000.

Michigan: Use of marijuana despite a cease-and-desist order is a misdemeanor punishable by up to 90 days in jail and a fine of up to $100. Free distribution of marijuana is a misdemeanor punishable by up to a year in jail and a fine of up to $1,000. Cultivation of up to 20 plants is a felony punishable by imprisonment for up to four years and a fine of up to $20,000. Cultivation of 20–200 plants is a felony punishable by imprisonment for up to seven years and a fine of up to $500,000.

Federal: Possession of any amount of marijuana is a misdemeanor that is punishable by up to a year in prison and a fine of up to $1,000 for a first offense; repeat offenders face harsher penalties. Sale or cultivation of 1,000 kilograms or more of marijuana is a felony punishable by imprisonment of ten years to life and a fine of up to $4,000,000.

 RESOURCE
For information on how each state defines and punishes marijuana offenses, go to www.nolo.com/marijuanacrimes.

Related terms: hierarchy of criminal offenses.

mayhem

Mayhem is an assault that results in the permanent disfigurement or impairment of a victim's body part. Many states do not include mayhem as a separate crime, instead punishing the infliction of injuries that constitute mayhem as aggravated assault. Whether defined as mayhem or aggravated assault, the crime is a felony.

Historical Antecedents. Mayhem's roots reach back at least as far as the Middle Ages, when kings punished mayhem to protect their interests in raising an army of able-bodied soldiers. (Apparently, one-armed archers didn't strike a lot of fear in enemy hearts.)

Eggshell Victims. To constitute mayhem, some states require a prosecutor to prove that an attacker intended to cause the injuries that resulted in a victim's permanent disfigurement or impairment. In these states, if a vulnerable assault victim suffers disfigurement or impairment that an attacker could not reasonably have anticipated, the crime is not punishable as mayhem. However, in other states attackers can be guilty of mayhem if an unlawful use of force results in unanticipated permanent injuries. For example, an employee elbows his boss hoping to cause momentary pain. The employee is unaware that his boss was born without three ribs on his right side. As a result, the employee's action damages the boss's right kidney so severely that it can no longer function. The employee would not be guilty of mayhem in states that require prosecutors to prove intent to cause permanent injuries. The employee would technically be guilty of mayhem in other states because his intentional attack of his boss resulted in injuries that constitute mayhem.

Permanency of Injuries. Mayhem can also result if injuries are severe enough to impact a victim's physical health for a substantial period of time that is less than "forever."

 Real-Life Illustration

In 1997, former boxing champion Mike Tyson bit off part of Evander Holyfield's ear during a boxing match. Tyson was not prosecuted for mayhem, but Holyfield's injury would have been permanent for purpose of a mayhem law even though doctors could later reattach the bitten-off part of his ear.

> **EXAMPLE:** Members of a college fraternity secretly lace a new recruit's drink with sleeping tablets. While the recruit is asleep, they tattoo "Mother's Little Helper" on his left forearm. The fraternity members are guilty of mayhem because the tattoo is sufficiently durable and difficult to remove that it is permanent for purposes of a mayhem statute.

 Legal Authority Examples

Washington, DC: An attacker who intentionally, knowingly, or recklessly causes significant bodily injury shall be fined not more than $3,000 or be imprisoned not more than three years, or both. For the purposes of the law, "significant bodily injury" means an injury that requires hospitalization or immediate medical attention.

California: Anyone who unlawfully and maliciously deprives a person of a body part, or disables, disfigures, or renders it useless, or cuts or disables the tongue, or puts out an eye, or slits the nose, ear, or lip, is guilty of mayhem. Mayhem is punishable by a prison term of two, four, or eight years and a fine of up to $10,000. Punishment is more severe if the victim is under age 14 or over age 65, or blind, deaf, or developmentally disabled.

Related terms: assault and battery.

mens rea

Mens rea, a Latin phrase that means "guilty mind," is the factor that identifies behavior as morally blameworthy and distinguishes criminal acts from other forms of noncriminal harmful behavior. (Despite the Latin derivation, the terminology is obviously intended for both genders.) In most states, children less than seven years old are legally incapable of having *mens rea* and therefore cannot be guilty of crimes.

For legal purposes, harmful behavior generally falls into one of three categories:

- **No Liability.** The behavior may be such that there is no legal liability whatsoever—for example, a taxi driver crashes into a storefront after swerving to avoid a woman who has fallen in the road.
- **Civil Liability.** The behavior may be tortious, and if so, actors are civilly liable and must compensate those they have harmed, usually by paying damages—for example, a taxi driver crashes into a storefront after taking unnecessary risks to deliver a pregnant passenger to a hospital.
- **Criminal Guilt.** The behavior may be criminal, and if so actors are guilty of crimes and subject to punishment—for example, a taxi driver intentionally crashes into a storefront after the store owner has insulted him with an ethnic slur. (Note: Some behavior may give rise to both civil liability and criminal guilt.)

General Intent and Its Equivalents. For most crimes, *mens rea* exists if an offender intentionally commits an act that a law makes illegal. These are known as "general intent" crimes because they don't require specific intent to cause a particular result—merely performing the criminal act is sufficient. *Mens rea* can also exist if a person acts recklessly or is grossly negligent. So, for example, a homeowner may not intend to cause ill health to her neighbors by wildly spraying a banned herbicide, but her recklessness likely constitutes a crime.

Ooops—My Bad. People who make innocent and reasonable factual mistakes (also referred to as "mistakes of fact") are not morally blameworthy and therefore lack *mens rea*. People who make mistakes about legal requirements, by contrast, do have *mens rea*.

- **Factual Mistake; No *Mens Rea*:** Merrie visits her son's elementary school, unaware that her ex-husband had returned to her house the previous night and hidden a small packet of marijuana in her jacket pocket. Merrie would not be guilty of possessing an illegal drug because she did not know and reasonably could not have known that the marijuana was in her jacket.

- **Legal Mistake; *Mens Rea*:** Merrie is guilty of illegal possession of marijuana if she knows that a small packet of marijuana is in her jacket pocket, but wears the jacket to school anyway because she mistakenly believes that possession of a small quantity of marijuana on school grounds is legal.

Inferring *Mens Rea* From Conduct. Despite the centrality of *mens rea* to criminal law, peoples' beliefs and intentions are not objectively observable. For example, no witness can testify, "I saw the shooter's mind and it sure looked guilty to me." As a result, judges and jurors must infer people's beliefs, intentions, purposes, and other mental states by evaluating their behavior in light of the circumstances. This is why evidence that bears on people's mental states carries the label "circumstantial evidence." Despite the plethora of TV and movie lawyers who denounce adversaries' claims as "based on nothing more than a bunch of circumstantial evidence," in actual courtrooms circumstantial evidence is perfectly legitimate and in fact is the most common form of evidence.

> EXAMPLE: Knowing that his friend Moe needs cash quickly to pay off a gambling debt, Shemp drives Moe in his pickup truck to a dark warehouse district. There, Shemp watches as Moe arranges for large cartons to be loaded into the truck's bed. As they drive off, Shemp tells Moe, "I don't want to know what's back there." A police officer pulls Shemp over for speeding, inspects the cartons and realizes that they contain stolen TV sets. A jury could convict Shemp of knowingly possessing stolen property because the circumstances permit an inference that Shemp knew that Moe picked up stolen goods. At best, Shemp was "willfully ignorant": He suspected but didn't want to know he was participating in a crime. Willful ignorance satisfies the *mens rea* requirement.

Specific Intent Crimes. A heightened *mens rea* requirement applies to what are called specific intent crimes. Specific intent crimes require prosecutors to prove that a defendant committed an illegal act for an explicitly forbidden purpose. Judges and juries rely on circumstantial evidence to determine a wrongdoer's purpose. So, for example, when a prosecutor seeks to prove that the purpose behind an assault was to kill the victim (a specific intent crime) the circumstantial evidence that the prosecutor presents to the jury might include the relationship between the perpetrator and the victim, their past dealings, and the severity of the attack.

Strict Liability Crimes. A few offenses dispense with the *mens rea* requirement altogether. Such offenses typically are called violations or infractions rather than crimes, and punishments are minimal. Strict liability crimes generally identify situations in which the desire to prevent undesirable consequences outweighs the reluctance to punish people who lack *mens rea*. An example in California is misbranding cattle—the crime doesn't require proof of intent to brand someone else's cattle or even knowledge that cattle being branded belong to another.

 Legal Authority Examples

Texas: Reckless driving consists of operating a vehicle with willful or wanton disregard for the safety of persons or property. Reckless driving is a misdemeanor punishable by up to 30 days in jail and/or a fine of up to $200.

New York (general intent crime): Robbery consists of the use of force to illegally obtain someone else's property.

California (specific intent crime): Possession of a controlled dangerous drug for purpose of sale is a felony punishable by imprisonment for two, three, or four years.

Related terms: strict liability crimes; *mens rea*.

mental state

Criminal law statutes frequently incorporate legal elements identifying a state of mind—for example, knowingly, willfully, intentionally, purposefully, and with malice aforethought—with which a defendant must have acted in order to be proved guilty of a crime. As lawyers have a penchant for exorbitant, unnecessary, excessive, pompous, and redundant verbosity (of which this introductory phrase is an example), a statute may incorporate at least two of these elements even though they have a virtually identical meaning.

Inferential Reasoning. Mental states such as intent and willfulness are not directly observable legal elements. Typically, judges and jurors have to infer defendants' mental states from their words and actions. For example, it is inferred that a perpetrator who picks a lock to enter a home and then runs away carrying a laptop computer entered the house with the intent to steal and therefore is guilty of both burglary and larceny.

Mental State Elements. The language defining mental states is typically built upon the following key terms: intent, knowing, willful, purposely, malice, and reckless.

- **Intent.** Characterizing mental state elements almost always begins with "intent." The reason is that *mens rea*, the mental state that so often justifies criminal punishment, typically consists of intent or its moral equivalents. Defendants act intentionally when they mean to commit an act.

    EXAMPLE: Arsenio is charged with arson and insurance fraud. To prove that Arsenio torched his barn intentionally in order to collect the proceeds of a fire insurance policy, the prosecutor offers evidence that Arsenio brought hay into the barn. Moments after Arsenio walked into the barn with a lighted torch, he ran out of the burning barn. The evidence leads to an inference that Arsenio intentionally set the barn on fire.

- **Knowing.** Defendants act "knowingly" or "with knowledge" when they engage in actions with the knowledge that activity is illegal or that an illegal consequence is virtually certain to occur.

  EXAMPLE: Fence is charged with receiving stolen goods. One of the crime's required elements is that Fence knew that the boxes of computers that were delivered to his warehouse were stolen. Evidence that the mailing label on each package identified the name and address of a national retailer would suggest that Fence knew that the packages had been stolen.

- **Willful.** "Willful" is usually just a synonym for "intentional." Prosecutors generally satisfy the element of willfulness by proving that a defendant acted intentionally.

  EXAMPLE: As Lucy walks through a cosmetics store, she surreptitiously removes small items from counters and shelves and drops them into an oversized purse. Under a law providing that willfully concealing unpurchased store merchandise constitutes evidence that the concealer intended to steal the merchandise, a judge or jury can infer from Lucy's actions that she intended to steal the items.

- **Purposely.** Defendants act purposely when they consciously intend to cause a forbidden consequence. Purposefulness is sometimes referred to as "specific intent," because statutes incorporating the element of purpose typically identify the specific intent that the statute criminalizes.

  EXAMPLE: Rayne uncovers the sheets in his hospital bed and exposes himself to a group of female interns. Under an indecent exposure statute that identifies a specific illegal purpose, Rayne may be guilty of a crime only if he exposed himself for the purpose of gaining sexual satisfaction. If Rayne exposed himself as part of an anatomy lesson, even though his act was intentional he would not be guilty because he did not expose himself with the specific purpose the statute requires.

- **Malice.** The legal element of "malice" does not require that defendants act out of dislike for a victim. Rather, as with willfulness, malice is usually simply a synonym for intent. Prosecutors generally satisfy the element of malice by proving that a defendant acted intentionally.

    EXAMPLE: Statutes typically define murder as an unlawful killing of a human being with malice aforethought. Prosecutor Smith satisfies the element of malice aforethought by proving that Sam, the defendant, intentionally killed a victim.

- **Reckless.** Defendants act recklessly when they bring about illegal consequences by disregarding a substantial and unjustifiable risk that they are or should be aware of. Statutes often provide for lesser punishment of defendants who act recklessly than of those who commit intentional crimes.

    EXAMPLE: Ray sprays graffiti on the side of an old building. The building ignites and burns to the ground when the paint on the building interacts with chemicals in the spray. Assuming Ray had no way of knowing about the risk of fire, Ray is guilty of vandalism (or "malicious mischief"), but not of the more serious crime of arson.

 Legal Authority Examples

Colorado: A person who knowingly sets fire to another's building commits first degree arson, a class 3 felony.

Idaho: The word "knowingly" requires only knowledge of the facts that make an act or omission illegal. It does not require knowledge that an act or omission is unlawful.

Pennsylvania: Indecent exposure consists of exposing one's genitals in any public place or in any place where other persons are present under circumstances in which the exposer knows or should know that this conduct is likely to be offensive or alarming.

Related terms: arson; elements of a crime; manslaughter; *mens rea*; first degree murder (Murder One); Second degree murder (Murder Two).

Miranda warning

In the 1963 case of *Miranda v. Arizona*, the U.S. Supreme Court decided that incriminating statements resulting from police officer questioning ("custodial interrogation") are inadmissible in evidence at trial unless the police first advise suspects of their constitutional rights (now referred to as "*Miranda* rights") and the suspects agree to talk. Referred to as the *Miranda* warning, or "Mirandizing a suspect," these rights are familiar because they are often depicted in movies and TV shows as follows:

"You have the right to remain silent. You have the right to have an attorney present when we question you, and if you cannot afford an attorney one will be appointed for you. If you waive these rights and talk to us, anything you say may be used against you in court. Do you understand these rights?"

The Supreme Court decided that advising suspects of these rights was a procedural safeguard that protects the Fifth Amendment constitutional privilege against self-incrimination.

A suspect's *Miranda* rights are triggered only by custodial interrogation. Whether a suspect is "in custody" for purposes of *Miranda* depends on whether that person reasonably feels free to terminate a conversation with a police officer and walk away. A judge may have to consider a variety of factors when deciding whether a suspect was "in custody," not simply the physical space in which questioning takes place. Even if police officers question a prisoner in a prison conference room, the prisoner is not "in custody" if the officers advise him that he is free to stop the questioning and return to his prison cell. (*Howes v. Fields*, U.S. Sup. Ct. (2012).) Similarly, if after being stopped by a police officer for speeding a driver blurts out, "Okay, I stole the car, you got me," the confession is admissible in evidence because no interrogation took place. On the other hand, a confession made after arrest and in response to police officer questioning that is not preceded by a *Miranda* warning and a suspect's waiver of rights is generally not admissible in evidence.

> EXAMPLE: Responding to a "stolen car" call, Officer Jones pulls Binder over and makes an arrest. While transporting the handcuffed Binder to the police station, Jones tells Binder, "Look, I'll recommend leniency if you tell me that you did it." If Binder confesses, the confession would not be admissible at trial. Binder was in custody, the confession was made in response to the officer's question, and the officer failed to advise Binder of the *Miranda* rights.

Nothing to Fear but Fear Itself? No sooner did the Supreme Court issue its *Miranda* decision than opponents denounced it as an example of activist judges weakening public safety. They argued that suspects would clam up once the police advised them of their *Miranda* rights, and that in the absence of confessions convictions would become much more difficult for prosecutors to obtain. However, many studies suggest that suspects commonly waive their rights to silence and the presence of counsel and talk to police officers. A variety of psychological factors may explain why most suspects wind up implicating themselves in criminal activity. Some suspects may believe erroneously that they can talk their way out of trouble. Other suspects may, like most of us, simply be conditioned to cooperate with interrogators who seek information from us. And police officers themselves are often quite capable of managing custodial circumstances so as to increase the likelihood that suspects will waive their *Miranda* rights. For example, a police officer may delay interrogating a suspect long enough for the suspect to become so anxious that the suspect wants to talk. Whatever the reasons for suspects so frequently waiving their rights and agreeing to answer police officers' questions, the reality is that *Miranda* has had nothing like the negative impact on law enforcement that its early opponents predicted.

Impeachment. Even when suspects' incriminating statements are initially inadmissible in evidence because of a *Miranda* violation, a prosecutor might be able to offer them into evidence later in the trial for "impeachment" purposes. This situation arises when a suspect testifies at trial and contradicts the story previously given to the police. Then the prosecutor can offer the suspect's incriminating statements into evidence as an attack on credibility. In this way, a *Miranda* violation does not necessarily mean that a prosecutor will be unable to offer a confession into evidence at trial.

> **EXAMPLE:** A suspect confesses to armed robbery, but the trial judge decides that the prosecutor cannot offer the confession into evidence because the police officer elicited it after ignoring the suspect's request to have an attorney present during questioning. Following this ruling, the suspect testifies to an alibi. Now the prosecutor can call the police officer as a witness and ask the officer to testify to the confession so as to attack the believability of the suspect's alibi defense.

Fruit That's Safe for Prosecutors to Eat. A U.S. Supreme Court-developed rule known as the "fruit of the poisonous tree" doctrine means that any evidence that police officers find as the result of an illegal search is not admissible at trial. If the Supreme Court applied the "fruit of the poisonous tree" doctrine to confessions, evidence that police officers uncover as the result of confessions that violate *Miranda* should likewise be inadmissible at trial. However, the Supreme Court has generally not applied the fruit-of-the-poisonous-tree doctrine to confessions taken in violation of *Miranda*. For example, a confession would not be admissible if a police officer elicited it by ignoring the suspect's request to have an attorney present. However, if as part of the confession, the suspect revealed the location of the gun used during the robbery, the subsequently found gun would be admissible in evidence.

If at First You Don't Succeed ... A suspect's refusal to respond to police officers' questions about a particular crime has a "shelf life" of two weeks. After that, the police officers can give the suspect a new set of *Miranda* warnings and interrogate a second time. If the suspect then makes incriminating statements, the statements are admissible in evidence.

 Real-Life Illustration

Michael Shatzer was in jail, serving a sentence for a theft conviction. After issuing *Miranda* warnings to Shatzer, a police officer questioned him about allegations that Shatzer sexually abused his stepson. Shatzer refused to answer the officer's questions. A few weeks later, another officer questioned Shatzer about the same sexual abuse allegations after again advising Shatzer of his *Miranda* rights. This time Shatzer agreed to talk and confessed to sexually abusing his stepson. Shatzer's confession was admissible in evidence. (*Maryland v. Schatzer*, U.S. Sup. Ct. (2010).)

Related terms: interrogation tactics.

miscegenation laws

Miscegenation laws (more accurately, "antimiscegenation laws") prohibited interracial marriage and even interracial sexual intercourse, at least when one participant was Caucasian and the other was African-American. The U.S. Supreme Court invalidated antimiscegenation laws in *Loving v. Virginia* (1967), ruling that they deprived individuals of their right to liberty.

misdemeanor

See hierarchy of criminal offenses.

misdemeanor manslaughter

Misdemeanor manslaughter is a doctrine followed in some states that provides that a death that occurs in the course of a misdemeanor violation constitutes manslaughter even if it would not otherwise do so. For example, assume that a store clerk is so shocked by witnessing a petty theft that she suffers a heart attack and dies. Under this doctrine, the petty thief might be convicted of manslaughter even though he could not reasonably have foreseen that the crime would lead to death.

Related terms: homicide; manslaughter.

mistake of fact

See mens rea.

motion

A motion is a request for a legal ruling that a lawyer (or *pro se* defendant) submits to a judge. While both prosecutors and defense lawyers may be the "moving party," defense lawyers often submit motions in support of defendants' constitutional and statutory rights. Motions vary from simple one-sentence oral requests to long written prayers accompanied by extensive discussions of legal authorities. Depending on the type of ruling sought, a lawyer may submit a motion before, during, or after a trial.

Naming Motions. Many motions are specialized in that they seek to accomplish a narrow purpose; lawyers and judges often use a common shorthand practice of referring to motions by the name of the generally known appellate court opinions that authorize the rulings.

> **EXAMPLE:** In the case of *Pitchess v. Superior Court* (1974), the California Supreme Court developed a policy regarding defendants' gaining access to police officer personnel files prior to trial. As a result, California defense attorneys may discuss with clients the making of a *Pitchess* motion.

Legal Authority Examples

Colorado: Applications to a court for an order shall be by motion. Motions made before or after a trial must be in writing unless a judge allows an oral motion. Written motions must state the grounds on which they are made and must set forth the ruling that they want a judge to make.

Related terms: motion *in limine*; motion concerning bail; motion for change of venue; motion to suppress evidence; motion for judgment of acquittal; motion for new trial; writ of *habeas corpus*.

motion concerning bail

Judges (or magistrates) ordinarily set bail at a defendant's initial court appearance, which may be a bail hearing or an arraignment. In response to changed circumstances, prosecutors or defense attorneys may submit a motion seeking upward or downward adjustments to bail amounts or conditions.

> **EXAMPLE:** Lou is charged with attempted robbery. A week after he posts bail, the prosecutor learns that Lou tried to buy a one-way plane ticket to a distant country. The prosecutor submits a motion asking the judge to revoke bail or to order Lou to forfeit his passport and to wear an electronic bracelet that allows the police to trace his whereabouts.

motion for change of venue

The term *venue* refers to a trial's location. Defendants may submit a motion for a change of venue when they believe that pretrial publicity has so poisoned a community's attitudes that a fair trial is impossible.

See jurisdiction.

motion for judgment of acquittal

When prosecutors "rest" (finish presenting evidence), defense attorneys may move for a judgment of acquittal. This motion asks a judge to rule that prosecution evidence is insufficient to constitute proof of guilt beyond a reasonable doubt. Jurors are not present when such a motion is made and argued, since they would almost certainly regard a judge's refusal to grant the defense motion as additional proof of a defendant's guilt.

> EXAMPLE: In a kidnapping case, the only dispute concerns whether Tracy, the alleged victim, voluntarily accepted a ride home from work with Dick, the defendant. Tracy testified that Dick forcibly shoved her into his car, but her testimony was evasive and vague. Moreover, during cross examination by Dick's lawyer, Tracy admitted that she had given the police conflicting accounts of the kidnapping. Dick's attorney moves for a judgment of acquittal, arguing that the evidence does not constitute proof beyond a reasonable doubt. The judge may take the case from the jury and grant the motion.

 Legal Authority Examples

Federal Rules of Criminal Procedure: After the government closes its evidence or after the close of all the evidence, the court on the defendant's motion must enter a judgment of acquittal of any offense for which the evidence is insufficient to sustain a conviction.

motion for new trial

Defendants can ask judges to set aside a guilty verdict and order a new trial. Common bases for new trial motions include newly discovered evidence, juror misconduct, and legal errors in evidence rulings and jury instructions.

EXAMPLE: A jury convicts Dick of kidnapping. A month later, Dick's attorney moves for a new trial based on a video showing the alleged victim leaving work and voluntarily entering Dick's car on the day of the alleged kidnapping. The motion includes an affidavit from Dick's attorney explaining why the attorney had no reasonable way to find out about the video's existence until after the trial was over. The judge has power to set aside the guilty verdict and order a new trial.

motion *in limine*

A motion *in limine* is a pretrial motion. A defense lawyer may submit an *in limine* motion in the hope of short-circuiting a criminal case entirely. More often, defense lawyers submit *in limine* motions in the hope that a judge will rule that specific prosecution evidence is inadmissible. Rulings on motions *in limine* often influence lawyers' trial strategies and their willingness to plea bargain. For example, a lawyer may submit a written motion *in limine* requesting a ruling that if the defendant testifies as a witness, the prosecutor will not be allowed to impeach the defendant's credibility with a seven-year-old felony conviction. The judge may defer ruling on the motion until the defendant testifies. But if the judge does rule on the motion before trial, whether or not the defendant testifies may depend on whether the judge grants or denies it.

motion to suppress evidence

Defense lawyers frequently submit motions to suppress to seek a ruling that evidence that prosecutors intend to offer into evidence at trial was obtained by police officers in violation of the Fourth Amendment or other constitutional rights and is therefore inadmissible.

EXAMPLE: Menos is charged with murder. Menos's attorney Dee argues that the police illegally seized a gun from Menos's house, and that the illegally seized gun induced Menos to confess to the police that the gun belonged to him. Dee also argues that a prosecution eyewitness's lineup identification of Menos as the killer is not admissible at trial because the police officers did not follow correct lineup procedures. Dee may submit a motion to suppress to ask the judge to exclude the gun, the confession, and the lineup identification from the evidence at trial.

Related terms: *Miranda* warning; plea bargaining; search and seizure.

motive (motive evidence)

In criminal cases, a motive is an explanation for why a defendant committed a crime. Motive is not generally a legal element of a crime. However, the criminal justice system expects judges and jurors to think rationally, and rational thought normally includes belief in cause-and-effect. Thus, prosecutors typically offer motive evidence to strengthen claims that a defendant committed a crime, and defendants point to lack of evidence of motive to argue that they are not guilty. For example, a prosecutor does not need to prove a defendant's motive to convict the defendant of murder, but a defense lawyer will seize on this "failure" when arguing that the prosecution did not prove guilt beyond a reasonable doubt.

Beneficent Motives. People sometimes act out of the best of altruistic motives. But if their conduct is illegal they may nevertheless be convicted of a crime. For example, Dr. Jack Kevorkian was a physician and right-to-die activist who furnished drugs to terminally ill patients who wanted to commit suicide. Dr. Kevorkian was convicted of second degree murder in 1999 and paroled in 2007.

Need for Money. Wrongdoers often commit crimes in order to acquire money or property. Thus, prosecutors might strengthen cases by offering evidence of defendants' need for money. Yet, the probative value of such evidence can be slight, because virtually everyone will admit to a need for more money. Such evidence can also be unfairly prejudicial if it leads a jury to convict a defendant based on the reason that the defendant needs money. As a result of balancing the probative value of "need-for-money" evidence against the risk of unfair prejudice to a defendant, judges often rule that such evidence is inadmissible.

> **EXAMPLE:** Robbins is charged with committing a robbery by demanding money from a drive-thru cashier at gunpoint. The prosecution claims that Robbins's motive was that he uses illegal drugs and needed money to purchase more drugs. The judge may exclude the evidence of Robbins's motive. The risk is substantial that the jury will be more inclined to convict Robbins because he uses illegal drugs. On the other hand, in the absence of evidence concerning the extent of Robbins's drug habit, his need for money may not be any greater than that of someone who needs a new car or to pay the rent. The result might be different if the prosecutor claims that Robbins's motive was that he owed his drug dealer $10,000, and that on the morning of the robbery the dealer had told Robbins that he would be beaten severely if he did not come up with at least half of what he owed by nightfall. In that case, the judge is likely to admit this motive evidence because its probative value is high and outweighs the risk of unfair prejudice.

Hate Crimes. Hate crime statutes provide for enhanced punishment for offenders who commit crimes out of an animus against protected social groups such as members of racial and sexual minorities. Thus, hate crime laws constitute an exception to the general rule that motive is not a legal element. For example, if a prosecutor has evidence that an arsonist's motive for targeting his victims was their status as immigrants, the prosecutor can charge the arsonist with a hate crime.

Legal Authority Examples

Federal Rule of Evidence 403: The judge may exclude relevant evidence if its probative value is substantially outweighed by the danger of unfair prejudice.

Related terms: elements of a crime; hate crimes; mental state; *mens rea*.

mug shot

A mug shot is a photo taken of an arrested suspect as part of the booking process. A mug shot documents an arrestee's physical condition and can be shown to witnesses for identification purposes.

mugging

This is the informal name for an assault, a purse-snatching, a robbery, or another crime of physical aggression that doesn't cause major physical injuries.

murder

See first degree murder; second degree murder.

N

necessity

The necessity defense arises when a person commits a relatively minor offense in order to avoid a greater and imminent peril—for example, a woman whose license has been suspended drives to a hospital emergency room to seek medical treatment for her gravely ill son. Some legal commentators refer to necessity as the "lesser of two evils" defense.

Necessity vs. Duress. The necessity and duress defenses are kissing cousins. Both defenses allow offenders to avoid punishment by blaming illegal conduct on an external threat. A duress defense arises when a threat emanates from a person. By contrast, necessity arises when a condition or natural force is the source of a threat. So, for example, a man forced to break into a building by a gun-wielding assailant is under duress; but a young girl wearing red shoes and holding a dog who breaks into a building to avoid being caught in a fast-approaching tornado acts out of necessity.

Cleanliness First. A necessity defense is not available to offenders with "unclean hands." That is, offenders whose wrongdoing or even sloth creates the mess that leads them to break the law can't avoid punishment by claiming necessity.

> **EXAMPLE:** Harry seeks refuge from a hurricane by breaking into a locked warehouse. Harry previously ignored official orders to evacuate the area in which the hurricane struck. As Harry was placed in peril because of his own misconduct, he cannot rely on the necessity defense.

Balancing the Harms. The necessity defense recognizes that breaking the law can sometimes be a morally responsible choice. But morality and the defense vanish if a wrongdoer commits a serious crime in order to avoid a relatively minor injury. For example, necessity would not be available as a defense if a man derails a train in order to prevent a rare gem from being crushed on the tracks.

 Real-Life Illustration

Orthodox wisdom is that necessity should not constitute a defense to murder. Fortunately, the issue has arisen almost always in the writings and musings of law professors, who excel at turning human tragedy into classroom and law review hypotheticals. Supporting the orthodox rule is a case known to generations of law students as "The Case of the Shipwrecked Sailors," which may strike you as the title of a Sherlock Holmes story. However, the notorious English case does have an official name, *Regina v. Dudley and Stephens* (1884).

After their ship sank, four surviving sailors were stranded at sea in a small open boat. At sea for about three weeks and without food and water for a week, they were near death. Two of the sailors killed a third, who was chosen not by lot but because he was the youngest and also was weak from drinking seawater. The three remaining sailors ate his flesh, and survived until they were rescued four days later. Charged with murder, the two killers relied on a defense of necessity. The jury rejected the defense and convicted them of murder. The judge sentenced the killers to death, but the government commuted the sentence to six months in prison.

 Legal Authority Examples

New York: The defense of necessity arises when a defendant commits a crime in an emergency in order to avoid an imminent public or private injury that came about through no fault of the defendant. Judged by ordinary standards of intelligence and morality, the desirability and urgency of avoiding the injury must clearly outweigh the desirability of avoiding the harm sought to be prevented by the statute defining the charged crime.

Related terms: duress; affirmative defense.

no contest (*nolo contendere*) plea

This is a plea in court signifying that the defendant will not contest the charge of a particular crime; it is also called "*nolo contendere*." Although it is not an official admission of guilt for the commission of a crime, a plea of "no contest" is typically treated as a guilty plea for sentencing purposes and the defendant's record. A no contest plea is often made in cases in which there is also a possible lawsuit for damages by a person injured by the criminal conduct (such as reckless driving, assault with a deadly weapon, aggravated assault). That's because it cannot be used in the civil lawsuit as an admission of fault.

nullification, jury

See trial by jury (jury trial).

N

opening statement

See trial phases.

opposing party statement (party admission)

See hearsay.

O.R. (own recognizance)

See bail.

panel attorneys

See defense counsel (defense attorney).

pardons

A pardon (also known as "executive clemency") occurs when the president or a governor forgives a party convicted of a crime and terminates the punishment associated with the conviction. The pardon power is one of the few absolutes in the criminal justice system. Judges have no power to review or override grants of executive clemency. In the U.S. only the country's presidents and state governors have the power to pardon wrongdoers. The pardon power allows chief executives to trump decisions made by the judicial branch of government and thus is inherently controversial in a system of government based on separation of powers.

Historical Antecedents. Thousands of years ago, Babylonian kings typically issued general discharges from criminal penalties when they acceded to the throne. In the U.S., George Washington granted the first pardons to the leaders of the Whiskey Rebellion. President Andrew Johnson's general pardon of Southern loyalists after the Civil War led to the first controversy over the extent of the presidential power of pardon.

Commuting Sentences. A limited form of pardon arises when sovereigns use the power of executive clemency to reduce wrong-doers' sentences. This is referred to as "commuting" a sentence. In these situations, convictions and attendant collateral consequences remain on the wrongdoer's record. In some cases, a sentence may be commuted to equal the time already served by the defendant, resulting in an immediate release from prison. In other cases, a sentence may be commuted to a less severe punishment—for example a death penalty changed to life in prison.

 Real-Life Illustration

On his last day as California's governor in 2011, Arnold Schwarzenegger aroused a storm of protest by commuting the 16-year sentence of Esteban Nuñez to a seven year term. Nuñez had pleaded guilty to participating in the murder of a college student. Nuñez's father was the former speaker of the California Assembly, and was Schwarzenegger's good friend and political ally. Though Schwarzenegger ignored a requirement that he consult the victim's family before issuing the commutation, his decision was final and nonreviewable by the courts.

Free and Clear. Full pardons result in the complete extinction of convictions and their collateral consequences. Chief executives can grant full pardons long after convicted people have finished serving their sentences although they typically grant them while the party is still incarcerated.

 Real-Life Illustration

Charles "Lucky" Luciano was a powerful Mafia kingpin. In 1936, New York City District Attorney Thomas E. Dewey successfully prosecuted Luciano for operating illegal brothels. Luciano was sentenced to a term of 50 years' imprisonment. During World War 2, while in prison, Luciano helped the United States military develop its plans for invading Italy. After the war, the governor of New York rewarded Luciano for his service by pardoning him on the condition that he leave the country and never return. The governor who pardoned Luciano was Thomas E. Dewey, Luciano's former prosecutor.

No Time Like the Present. Pardons can precede convictions. Pardoned individuals cannot be prosecuted for any activity encompassed by the pardon.

Real-Life Illustration

After the 1974 impeachment of President Richard Nixon for official misconduct in connection with the Watergate scandal, Vice President Gerald Ford succeeded Nixon as president. One of Ford's first official actions was to pardon Nixon for any crimes that he may have committed in connection with Watergate. At the time of the pardon, Nixon had not been charged with a crime.

Pardon Processes. Chief executives are typically anxious to avoid charges that they have exercised executive clemency unfairly in order to benefit powerful friends. As a result, many jurisdictions have established commissions, committees, or boards of advisors whose functions are to entertain and investigate pardon requests. Chief executives can insulate themselves against charges of favoritism by citing a committee's recommendation as the basis of a pardon grant.

 Legal Authority Examples

U.S. Constitution, Article II, § 2: "The President ... shall have power to grant reprieves and pardons for offenses against the United States, except in cases of impeachment."

Michigan Constitution, Article V, § 14: "The governor shall have power to grant reprieves, commutations and pardons after convictions for all offenses, except cases of impeachment, upon such conditions and limitations as he may direct, subject to procedures and regulations prescribed by law. He shall inform the legislature annually of each reprieve, commutation and pardon granted, stating reasons therefor."

Related terms: death penalty; three strikes laws; sentencing (punishment options).

parole

Parole consists of the early release of prisoners whom parole board members determine no longer pose a threat to society. Grants of parole are almost always accompanied by conditions that if violated can result in a parolee's return to prison. For example, a person convicted of aggravated assault involving a gun may as a condition of his eventual parole be required to meet regularly with a parole officer, to complete an anger-management program, to neither carry nor own a firearm, and to consent to random warrantless searches by police and parole officers.

At the same time, some sentences prohibit parole. For example, a sentence of life in prison without possibility of parole (LWOP) renders the convicted person forever ineligible.

Parole Procedures. Parole boards, whose members are typically appointed by states' governors, normally supervise the entire parole process. Boards conduct hearings and decide whether and when to release prisoners and what conditions to impose on those granted parole. When parolees violate conditions of release, boards conduct hearings and decide whether to revoke parole. The actual supervision of parolees is normally carried out by parole officers, who are part of a state's correctional system.

> **EXAMPLE:** Bessie is serving a life sentence for killing an abusive ex-boyfriend. The parole board reviews Bessie's status every two years. After Bessie has served eight years, the board decides to parole her to a halfway house run by an abused women's organization. Bessie has to meet regularly with a parole officer who has the authority to allow Bessie to move out of the halfway house.

Revocation. Media reports and research findings suggest that parole is revoked for more than half of all parolees. Technical violations of conditions of release, such as failing to notify a parole officer of an address change, sometimes result in revocation. More often and more disturbingly, the cause of revocation is a parolee's commission of additional crimes. Parole officers have discretion to respond to violations short of seeking parole revocation. In order to revoke parole, a parole board must convene a hearing at which a parolee is normally represented by an attorney and has a chance to present exculpatory evidence. (*Morrissey v. Brener,* U.S. Sup. Ct. (1972).)

A Reduced Role for Parole. Parole was largely a product of indeterminate sentencing, in which judges set lower and upper limits on prison terms and left it to parole boards to decide whether to release prisoners before their sentences expired. Many states have moved to determinate sentencing for crimes that are punishable by less than life in prison. With determinate sentencing, judges set fixed terms of imprisonment according to statutory guidelines. Prisoners may still be released before serving their full terms. But early release depends on fulfillment of statutory conditions rather than parole board discretion.

> EXAMPLE: Josh was convicted of aggravated assault involving use of a gun. The state's sentencing guidelines call for a two- or four-year prison term for aggravated assault. The judge sentences Josh to the upper term of four years because he used a firearm. Sentencing guidelines may also allow Josh to reduce his sentence by one day for every two days of good behavior as a prisoner.

 Legal Authority Examples

California: The Board of Prison Terms conducts hearings for all prisoners serving life terms who are eligible for parole. The Board sets terms and conditions of parole and conducts parole revocation hearings.

Texas: The Board of Pardons and Paroles determines which prisoners to release on parole, what conditions to place on parolees, and whether to revoke parole. The Board also advises the governor on whether to grant petitions from prisoners seeking clemency.

Related terms: sentencing (punishment options); probation.

party admission (opposing party statement)

See hearsay.

peremptory challenge

See trial by jury (jury trial).

perjury

Perjury consists of three elements: (1) making an intentionally false statement (2) about a material matter (3) while under oath. To obtain convictions, prosecutors have to prove each of these three elements beyond a reasonable doubt. Because perjury is a direct affront to justice, it is typically punishable as a felony. Below, consider each of the elements:

- **Intentionally False.** Perjury convictions require proof that witnesses knew that statements were false at the time the statements were made. Perjury prosecutions are relatively few in number because proving that a declarant knew that a statement was false can be difficult.
- **Material Matters.** Testimony is generally material if it is likely to have an important bearing on the outcome of a trial or other hearing. The element of materiality provides a degree of assurance that witnesses are subject to perjury charges only for testimony about important matters that they should have thought about carefully. So, for example, if a defendant in a murder trial lies about the source of money he used to buy a car, the false testimony probably has no bearing on his guilt and would not serve as the basis of a perjury charge.
- **Under Oath.** When witnesses are "sworn in" before testifying, they are in effect warned that a false statement might give rise to a perjury charge. Many affidavits also include oaths, so that declarants who make false statements in writing may also be prosecuted for perjury. Baseball player Roger Clemens was charged with perjury after he swore that he never used steroids

to a Congressional committee investigating steroid use among professional athletes.

Make-Up Cases. Perjury prosecutions can serve as a refuge for prosecutors who can prove that witnesses lied about illegal conduct in circumstances when they cannot convict the witnesses of engaging in the illegal conduct.

 Real-Life Illustration

In 2004, media guru Martha Stewart was convicted of perjury for falsely telling a federal investigator that she had not been told that the shares of stock she owned in a company called ImClone were going to be virtually worthless the day after she sold them. Instead of charging Stewart with the more complex crime of insider trading, the government chose an easier path by charging her with lying about the information she had been given.

Related Offenses. Making false statements is a crime in a variety of circumstances that do not necessarily constitute perjury because they are not made in court and under oath. For example, laws in most states make it a crime to call in a false report of a fire to a fire department, or to falsely claim that a consumer product has been tampered with.

 Legal Authority Examples

Indiana: Knowingly making a false and material statement under oath is perjury. Perjury is a Class D felony.

Federal: Knowingly making a materially false statement concerning a matter relating to a matter within the jurisdiction of any branch of the U.S. government is crime punishable by up to five years' imprisonment.

Related terms: burdens of proof.

perpetrator

A perpetrator is the person who commits a crime. The term is often abbreviated to "perp" by police investigators in TV crime shows).

petty theft v. grand theft

See shoplifting.

phishing

See cyber-crime.

pimping and pandering

See prostitution.

plain view searches

See warrantless searches.

plea bargaining

Plea bargaining consists of negotiations between prosecutors and defense lawyers about how to resolve criminal charges. Judges are sometimes part of the negotiation process as well. In well over 90% of all U.S. criminal cases, plea bargaining results in defendants pleading guilty or *nolo contendere* (a plea in which the party does not contest the charges but which carries the same legal consequences as a guilty plea).

Negotiate First, Litigate Second. Like virtually all successful negotiations, plea bargaining thrives because both prosecutors and defendants realize benefits. Prosecutors reduce their case loads and exchange the certainty of a guilty plea for the risk that they will be unable to obtain a unanimous verdict. Defendants exchange their constitutional right to a jury trial for definitive outcomes that often consist of reductions in the seriousness of offenses and the severity of sentences. Some plea bargains result only in a prosecutor agreeing to recommend a certain sentence to a judge, with the recommendation not binding on the judge. While plea bargaining typically takes place prior to trial, it may take place at any stage of a case, even when the case has already gone to trial and is on appeal.

 Real-Life Illustration

Russell Henderson and Aaron McKinney were charged with killing Matthew Shepard in 1998 because he was gay. Henderson pleaded guilty to murder and agreed to testify against McKinney in exchange for receiving two consecutive life sentences rather than risk being sentenced to death. After the jury in McKinney's case had convicted him of murder and was deliberating as to whether to sentence him to death, the jury was dismissed when McKinney agreed to a sentence of life in prison without possibility of parole.

A Deal's a Deal. Once both parties agree to its terms and the defendant pleads guilty or no contest, a plea bargain is binding. Buyer's remorse is not a valid excuse for voiding a negotiated plea.

> **EXAMPLE:** Dee pleads guilty to tax fraud in exchange for a negotiated sentence of 18 months in prison. Before she begins serving her sentence, Dee's friends convince her that she would not have been convicted had she gone to trial. Dee can't set aside the deal and reopen the case; the plea agreement is binding.

Good Cause to Withdraw a Plea. In limited instances, defendants can withdraw guilty or no contest pleas. In California, for example, defendants who demonstrate "good cause" can withdraw their pleas before the court enters judgment or within six months of being sentenced to probation rather than imprisonment. It's generally easier for defendants to withdraw their pleas if they entered them without the benefit of a lawyer. An example of "good cause" is the discovery of new evidence supporting the defendant's innocence. Inaccurate information from the attorney representing the defendant that the defendant relied upon in entering the plea can also constitute grounds for withdrawal. Appellate court judges sometimes fudge the seemingly set-in-stone time limits for withdrawing guilty pleas if the circumstances appeal to the judges' sense of justice and fairness.

Good-Faith Guilty Pleas. Agreeing to plead guilty is only part of the process. Judges are responsible for ensuring that a factual basis for a guilty plea exists. In order to assure themselves that defendants plead guilty because they really did break the law, judges typically question them in open court about the unlawful conduct that resulted in the criminal charge. Consider, for example, a defendant under questioning who tells a judge, "Sure, I'll plead guilty. I need to put this behind me and get back to work. But I really don't think I did anything wrong. That guy started the whole thing, I was really only defending myself." The judge will probably reject the offer to plead guilty because the defendant has denied that he committed a crime. But if the prosecution agrees to it, a judge might accept an "*Alford* plea*," which is a guilty or no contest plea in which the defendant either claims innocence or refuses to admit having committed the crime. (*North Carolina v. Alford*, U.S. Sup. Ct. (1970).)

Conflicting Perspectives. Debates over the pervasiveness of plea bargaining continue. Cynics charge that plea bargaining turns justice into swap meets, where buyers and sellers haggle over prices. They also contend that a negative result of the process is that prosecutors "overcharge," coercing defendants into guilty pleas by confronting them with more serious criminal charges than circumstances warrant and then offering them what in the distorted context seems like a deal that's too good to refuse. A third common attack on plea bargaining is that it penalizes defendants who refuse to plead guilty and insist on their constitutional right to trial by jury. The argument is that if defendants who accept plea bargains receive less punishment than similarly situated defendants who go to trial and are convicted, then plea bargaining punishes people simply for exercising their constitutional rights.

Supporters of plea bargaining argue that it promotes individualized justice, allowing prosecutors and defense lawyers to look beyond the facts of a case to a broad range of factors to produce an outcome that is fair and just. They argue that plea bargaining offers a legitimate benefit to defendants who take responsibility for their illegal behavior by pleading guilty. Finally, supporters also point out that without plea bargaining removing cases from the criminal justice system, the system would collapse.

Charge Bargaining and Sentence Bargaining. Charge bargaining consists of negotiations concerning the severity or number of charges to which defendants plead guilty or no contest. Sentence bargaining occurs when plea bargains indicate the sentence that a defendant will receive after pleading guilty. As sentencing is a judicial function, a judge may not abide by a prosecutor's recommended sentence. To protect themselves against unwelcome surprises, defendants often insist that an agreement include an understanding that if a judge refuses to follow a prosecutor's recommended sentence, the defendant can withdraw from the agreement.

> **EXAMPLE:** MaryAnn is charged with three counts of residential burglary. After negotiations, she agrees to plead guilty to one count of burglary if the other two counts are dismissed. As for sentencing, the prosecutor makes no representations except: "I won't oppose the sentence that the judge decides on after considering the probation officer's report." MaryAnn cannot withdraw her guilty plea if the judge's sentence is harsher than she expected. The plea agreement was not subject to the judge handing down a particular sentence.

I'll Have the Usual. Defendants should never plead guilty "straight up" without first investigating a prosecutor's plea bargaining policy. For example, a prosecutor's office may follow a policy of not seeking jail time for a first conviction of petty theft. In courtrooms as in commerce, what seems to be a bargain may be nothing more than a standard deal. Being represented by and receiving the advice of an attorney are crucial.

Effective Assistance. Defendants have a Sixth Amendment right to effective assistance of counsel during plea bargaining. (*Missouri v. Frye* and *Lafler v. Cooper*, U.S. Sup. Ct. (2012).) For example, a defense lawyer who neglects to advise an alien defendant that deportation is a likely consequence of a guilty plea provides ineffective assistance of counsel. The defendant can probably have the guilty plea set aside and insist on a trial.

 Legal Authority Examples

Plea bargaining is based on custom and practice and does not rest on explicit statutory authorization. Statutes and case law create procedures for entering guilty pleas and the consequences of doing so, but the length and timing of plea bargain negotiations are left to the discretion of prosecutors and defense lawyers. However, statutes that set mandatory minimum terms place limits on the terms of plea bargains:

California: A conviction for a second drunk driving offense within a ten-year period requires that the offender be sentenced to at least 96 hours in jail.

Related terms: hierarchy of criminal offenses; interrogation tactics; sentencing (punishment options); no contest (*nolo contendere*) plea.

police officers

Police officers have primary responsibility for maintaining public order. Their visible, uniformed presence on the street or in police vehicles may deter criminal acts from taking place. When crime does occur, police officers carry out investigations and apprehend suspects.

Discretion. Police officers enforce the law by exercising judgment within parameters established by departmental policies. Police officers may ignore minor violations that don't pose a threat to public safety or may choose to issue a citation to low-level lawbreakers rather than arrest them.

EXAMPLE: Officer Pat Roll observes a parent violating state law by driving with a child in the car who isn't belted in a car safety seat. State law allows the officer to arrest the parent. When a check of police records indicates no previous violations, the officer decides to issue a citation to the driver after the driver buckles the child into the seat.

EXAMPLE: Officer Cobb investigates a shoving match between two spectators at a sporting event. After interviewing the participants and nearby fans, Cobb is uncertain as to which participant was the aggressor. Moreover, neither participant was badly injured and neither is eager to press charges against the other. Cobb issues a warning to the participants but neither cites nor arrests them.

EXAMPLE: Officer Cobb enters an apartment in response to a domestic violence call involving a married couple. By the time Cobb arrives the altercation has ended. However, the wife has visible injuries and tells Cobb that her husband struck her after coming home drunk. Departmental policies in many jurisdictions call for "zero tolerance" of domestic violence. As a result, Cobb arrests the husband even though the wife asks him not to.

Charge! While police officers make arrests, charging decisions are for prosecutors. Like police officers, prosecutors are also vested with discretion.

EXAMPLE: Officer Krupke takes custody of Red Handed after Red was detained by a MayCee's Department Store security officer who observed Red leave the store with a pocketful of stolen watches. Krupke arrests Red for burglary. Reviewing

Krupke's arrest report a day later, the prosecutor decides to charge Red with the less serious crime of shoplifting.

The Feds. Federal law enforcement officials are generally referred to as agents rather than police officers. While many federal departments and agencies employ agents, perhaps the most well known are those of the Federal Bureau of Investigation (FBI).

Qualified Immunity. The doctrine of qualified immunity protects police officers from civil liability when they make reasonable mistakes.

EXAMPLE: Officer Tracy arrests a suspect who closely matches the description of the culprit who robbed a nearby jewelry store a few minutes earlier. Further investigation reveals that the arrested suspect had nothing to do with the robbery. Officer Tracy is immune from a civil damages lawsuit. While Tracy was wrong, his decision to arrest the suspect was reasonable.

polygraph machines (lie detectors)

A polygraph machine measures and records suspects' physiological reactions as they answer an operator's questions. Typically, polygraph machines measure a suspect's blood pressure, pulse, breathing rate, and the moisture content of skin. The notion is that deceptive answers produce predictable changes in suspects' physiological responses. Courts and legislators have traditionally considered the results of polygraph testing not to be reliable enough for admission into evidence in criminal trials. However, statutes in some states provide that lie detector test results are admissible if prosecutors and defense attorneys agree to admissibility before testing takes place.

Historical Antecedents. The quest for a reliable litmus test of truth-telling has gone on for centuries. Chinese authorities once used rice to distinguish liars from truth-tellers. On the theory that saliva dries up when people lie, authorities filled suspects' mouths with dry rice and then questioned them. Suspects who were unable to spit the rice out of their mouths were deemed guilty; their lies had caused them to lose their saliva.

Authorities in India relied on donkeys rather than rice. Suspects were left alone with a donkey in a pitch-black cave. Suspects were told that if the donkey brayed, it was a sign of innocence. Unbeknownst to suspects, the authorities had sprinkled black coal dust onto the donkey's tail before putting it in the cave. Suspects who came out of the cave with coal dust on their hands were deemed guilty; dirty hands indicated that they had pulled the donkey's tail to make sure that it brayed. Mechanical lie detector devices date to the late 19th century.

Reliability. In 1923, polygraph test results were deemed too unreliable to be admitted into evidence in New York by the first court to rule on the issue, in *Frye v. United States*. Courts' continued reluctance to admit polygraph test results was bolstered by a 2003 report issued by the National Academy of Sciences. The report concluded that while polygraph testing produces a better-than-chance likelihood of detecting liars, testing results in a large number of both false positives (indicating that truth-tellers are liars) and false negatives (indicating that liars are truth-tellers).

 Real-Life Illustration 1

Suspected of being the "Green River Killer," Gary Ridgway took and passed a polygraph test in 1984. After being confronted with DNA evidence 20 years later, Ridgway confessed to the crimes.

 Real-Life Illustration 2

Bill Wegerle was suspected of murdering his wife Vicki, especially after he failed two separate polygraph tests. Two decades later DNA analysis revealed that the culprit was serial killer Dennis Rader, nicknamed the BTK Killer.

Admissibility in Evidence. The United States Supreme Court decisions in *Daubert v. Merrell Dow Pharmaceuticals, Inc.* (1993) and *Kumho Tire v. Carmichael* (2000) condition admissibility of all evidence based on specialized training and knowledge on a showing that the methodology that produces the relevant conclusions is reliable. Judges' concerns about the reliability of polygraph test results have led courts to reject evidence of polygraph test results whether offered by either prosecutors or defense lawyers. However, statutes in some states authorize admissibility pursuant to stipulations by both parties.

> EXAMPLE: Verdad, who denies that he had any involvement in a sexual assault, voluntarily submits to a lie detector test. The operator concludes that Verdad's denial is truthful. Nevertheless, Verdad is charged with committing the crime. Verdad cannot call the polygraph machine operator as a witness to testify that Verdad passed the test. However, if the prosecutor and defense lawyer sign a written agreement before Verdad takes the polygraph test stating that the results will be admissible in evidence, the legal effect is different. In some states, the agreement means that the judge will allow the polygraph machine operator to testify that Verdad passed the test.

Legal Authority Examples

California Evidence Code: Polygraph test results are not admissible in any criminal case unless the parties stipulate to their admissibility.

Texas: A crime victim cannot be forced to take a polygraph test, and a victim's refusal to take a polygraph test cannot serve as the basis for refusing to charge a suspect with a crime.

Related terms: forensic science.

possession of illegal drugs

See drug offenses.

preliminary hearings

Preliminary hearings are an alternative to grand jury proceedings. In a preliminary hearing (also called preliminary examination), prosecutors present evidence to a judge in an effort to prove that probable cause exists to bring the defendant to trial. Suspects and their lawyers have a right to be present at preliminary hearings and can cross-examine prosecution witnesses, and suspects can present evidence in an effort to persuade judges that probable cause does not exist. Preliminary hearings are generally open to the public.

Comparing Grand Jury Proceedings to Preliminary Hearings. Preliminary hearings allow prosecutors to offer evidence sufficient to establish that probable cause (or a "strong suspicion") exists that a suspect committed a crime. Preliminary hearings are an alternative to grand juries in many states. In theory, both proceedings protect suspects against having to defend themselves against flimsy charges. Preliminary hearings differ from grand jury proceedings in a few important ways:

- In preliminary hearings, prosecutors present evidence to a judge; in grand jury proceedings, prosecutors present evidence to a group of 16–23 grand jurors.
- In preliminary hearings, suspects and their lawyers have a right to appear, present evidence demonstrating there is no probable cause, and cross-examine prosecution witnesses; in grand jury proceedings, the suspect and lawyer have no right to be present, or to offer evidence or cross-examine witnesses.
- Preliminary hearings are generally open to the public, while grand jury proceedings are closed and conducted in private.
- Grand juries issue "indictments," whereas prosecutors file "informations" following preliminary hearings. The difference is semantic and of no substantive importance.

Although the preliminary hearing provides the defendant with many opportunities that are not available at a grand jury proceeding, it

may not always benefit the defendant—from a strategic perspective—
to take advantage of these rights at the time of the hearing.

> EXAMPLE: At a preliminary hearing, the prosecutor offers
> evidence that Flood assaulted Bunning with a bat. Flood has
> a witness, Duke, who is prepared to support Flood's claim
> that Bunning started the fight and that Flood acted in self-
> defense. Flood is, however, unlikely to call Duke as a witness
> at the preliminary hearing. Because the prosecutor only has
> to establish probable cause to believe that Flood assaulted
> Bunning, the judge will probably ignore Duke's testimony
> when evaluating the sufficiency of the prosecutor's evidence.
> All Flood would accomplish by calling Duke as a witness at the
> preliminary hearing would be to give the prosecutor a preview of
> what Duke would say at trial and a chance to prepare to attack
> that testimony.

Strategic Choices. In states that provide for both preliminary
hearings and grand juries, prosecutors can choose which procedure
to follow in individual cases. Prosecutors often opt for grand juries
when they want to present witnesses in secret over a period of time
in order to obtain simultaneous indictments against a group of
suspects who are unaware that criminal charges are in the offing.
The principal advantage to prosecutors of preliminary hearings
involves the use of testimony at trial. Rules of evidence, including
the hearsay rule and the Sixth Amendment's Confrontation Clause,
prevent prosecutors from offering grand jury testimony into evidence
at trial. Depending on the circumstances, however, they can offer
testimony given at a preliminary hearing into evidence at trial.

> EXAMPLE: During the grand jury proceedings leading to Flood's
> indictment for aggravated assault on Bunning, Sam testified
> that Flood hit Bunning from behind. By the time of Flood's
> trial, Sam has developed sudden onset dementia and is unable to
> testify. The prosecutor cannot offer Sam's grand jury testimony

into evidence at trial. Had Sam testified at a preliminary hearing, the prosecutor could have offered his testimony into evidence against Flood at trial.

Informality. Though they normally take place in courtrooms before judges, preliminary hearings are often more informal than grand jury proceedings and trials. Some states authorize police officers to conduct preliminary hearings on behalf of the state. Hearsay is often admissible at a preliminary hearing to show probable cause, even if it is not admissible at trial to prove guilt. As a result, prosecutors can often protect crime victims and witnesses from having to appear in court repeatedly by asking a police officer to testify to what a victim and witnesses told the officer about the crime.

Preliminary Hearings and Double Jeopardy. A preliminary hearing does not place a suspect "in jeopardy." If a judge determines that a prosecutor's evidence does not establish probable cause to believe that a suspect committed a crime and dismisses the case, the prosecutor can refile charges based on additional evidence.

 Legal Authority Examples

California: At a preliminary hearing, the prosecution must establish probable cause to show that a suspect committed a crime. A preliminary hearing must be held within ten court days of an arraignment if a suspect is in custody unless the defendant waives that right.

Missouri: Prosecutors cannot file an information charging a person with a felony until the person has been accorded the right of a preliminary examination before an associate circuit judge in the county where the offense is alleged to have been committed.

Related terms: grand juries; double jeopardy; confrontation of prosecution witnesses.

presentence report

This is a report that a probation officer must prepare under court order to help the judge decide on an appropriate sentence. Judges often order a presentence report following a defendant's conviction, but they may also do so as a part of plea bargaining negotiations. Based on the contents of a presentence report, a judge might advise a defendant and a prosecutor of the sentence that the judge will hand down if the defendant pleads guilty. The indicated sentence may in turn help the defendant decide whether to plead guilty or go to trial. Presentence reports commonly include information about the circumstances of a crime and its impact on the victims, a defendant's background and criminal history, and a probation officer's recommended sentence.

Related terms: sentencing (punishment options).

presumed innocent

Defendants charged with crimes are presumed innocent until proven guilty. The Constitution does not refer to the presumption of innocence explicitly. However, the presumption is implicit in the Fifth Amendment's guarantee of due process of law. (*In re Winship*, U.S. Sup. Ct. (1970).) The presumption of innocence is the source of the rule that prosecutors must prove guilt beyond a reasonable doubt.

To emphasize the presumption of innocence during *voir dire* questioning, a defense lawyer may ask a prospective witness, "If you had to decide this case right now, before you heard any evidence, what would your verdict be?" The juror typically responds, "I can't decide the case now, I have to hear the evidence." To emphasize the principle of presumed innocence, the attorney typically counters with something like, "I realize that. My point is that the law presumes that my client is innocent. Because he is presumed innocent, and no evidence of guilt has been offered, if at this stage you were called on to decide the case you would have to find my client not guilty. If you are selected for the jury, will you follow this legal principle?"

Historical Antecedents. In his famous four-volume *Commentaries on the Laws of England* (1765-1769), William Blackstone identified the philosophy behind the presumption of innocence. Blackstone wrote, "[T]he law holds that it is better that ten guilty persons escape, than that one innocent suffer."

Bail. The presumption of innocence seems inconsistent with the practice of detaining suspects in jail until trials take place unless they post bail. Nevertheless, judges can detain suspects in jail pending trial. Moreover, when deciding on the amount of bail, judges can consider a suspect's potential dangerousness and the strength of the evidence suggesting that a suspect is guilty. While the judge can consider the threat that a suspect potentially poses, the judge must set bail in an amount that reasonably accounts for the threat's severity. The presumption of innocence does enter into bail decisions in the form of a requirement that bail be set at a reasonable amount.

Jury Instruction. Criminal defense lawyers and even prosecutors commonly remind jurors that defendants are innocent until proven guilty. To stamp the presumption with greater legal authority, judges' instructions to jurors always remind jurors of this principle.

> **EXAMPLE:** Near the end of his closing argument to the jury, defense lawyer Sabich tells the jurors, "As Her Honor will shortly instruct you, my client has been presumed innocent throughout this entire trial and is presumed innocent at this very moment." Sabich hopes that associating his argument with the judge's instruction will add force to the closing argument.

A Unique Presumption. In the legal system, virtually all presumed facts grow out of evidence. For example, consider the common presumption that a letter that was properly addressed and mailed has been received. The presumed fact that a letter was received requires evidence that it was properly mailed and addressed. By contrast, the presumption of innocence requires no evidence; the presumption is inherent in a criminal defendant's status.

Legal Authority Examples

Fifth Amendment, U.S. Constitution: "No person shall be ... deprived of life, liberty or property without due process of law."

Pattern Jury Instruction, Federal District Court, 11th District: The defendant is presumed innocent until proven guilty. The indictment against the defendant brought by the government is only an accusation, nothing more. It is not proof of guilt or anything else. The defendant therefore starts out with a clean slate.

Related terms: bail; burdens of proof; jury instructions.

priors

Priors are past convictions that defendants charged with or convicted of a crime have suffered. Priors are often set forth in a document called a "rap sheet." The usual effect of priors is to increase the severity of punishment. For example, a second conviction of DUI (drunk driving) may carry a mandatory jail sentence. Even more seriously, priors may mean that a new conviction constitutes a third strike that results in mandatory imprisonment for years. Juvenile convictions and expunged convictions can constitute priors.

prisoners' rights

The general rule is that restrictions on prisoners' civil liberties are valid if they are reasonably related to a legitimate government interest. This relatively low threshold means that judges uphold restrictions that are rationally related to officials' need to manage prisons effectively and safely.

Judges are generally reluctant to interfere in prison management. They recognize that corrections officials are in a far better position than they to balance inmates' privileges against the need to protect prisoners and correctional employees from harm. At the same time, as the U.S. Supreme Court has said, "Prison walls do not form a barrier separating prison inmates from the protections of the Constitution." (*Turner v. Safley*, U.S. Sup. Ct. (1987).)

When examining prison regulations, judges must determine if the rules are rationally related to prison safety. For example, consider a Missouri prison regulation that allows inmates to correspond freely with close relatives who are incarcerated in other prisons and with other inmates concerning legal matters, but otherwise places restrictions on inmates' correspondence with other inmates. The rule is valid because the distinctions it draws are rationally connected to prisons' need to maintain security.

Historical Antecedents. Stone Age Man probably used some of the first tools to create areas of confinement. As Nathaniel Hawthorne wrote in *The Scarlet Letter* (1850), "The founders of a new colony … have invariably recognized it among their earliest practical necessities to allot a portion of the virgin soil as a cemetery, and another portion of the site as a prison." Below are some of the common issues that judges must consider when evaluating prisoners' rights.

- **Religious Liberty.** Inmates can practice their religions in prison. For example, inmates are entitled to meet with clergy and wear ritual clothing. Observant Jews and Muslims are entitled to kosher or halal meals. But, prison management concerns do justify rational restrictions on religious practices. For example, prison officials can deny an inmate's right to wear a sword even if it is a necessary element of the inmate's religious rituals.

- **Search and Seizure.** Inmates have no reasonable expectation of privacy in their cells. Prison officials can conduct warrantless searches of prisoners and cells so long as they have a reasonable basis to do so. For example, if correctional officers find illegal drugs in a few prison cells, prison officials can conduct a blanket search of all prisoners and cells. The search is a reasonable response to the need to prevent prisoner access to illegal drugs.

- **Voting.** Almost all states deny felons the right to vote while they are incarcerated. Some states also deny voting rights

P

to parolees. In some states, an ex-inmate's voting rights are automatically restored when the prisoner completes a sentence. In other states, the ex-inmate would have to petition for restoration of voting rights.

- **Parental Rights.** Incarcerated parents lose physical but not necessarily legal custody of their children. Inmates who make satisfactory arrangements for their children's care usually incur no disruption of legal custody. A state must afford an inmate a hearing before terminating parenting rights. States normally appoint lawyers for inmates in such situations, though they are not legally required to do so.

- **Prison Assignment.** Prison officials have wide discretion when assigning inmates to prisons and a judge is unlikely to intervene if, for example, a prisoner complains that a prison assignment makes visits with a family prohibitively inconvenient.

 Legal Authority Examples

Vermont and **Maine:** Inmates retain the right to vote by absentee ballot even while they are incarcerated.

Federal Prison Litigation Reform Act: Judges can order the release of prisoners from overcrowded prisons only if less restrictive remedies to relieve overcrowding have been tried and failed. Inmates cannot file petitions in federal court unless they have exhausted all state avenues of redress. Indigent inmates lose the right to file court petitions for free after they have had three previous petitions dismissed.

North Carolina: Inmates may be given an early medical release from prison if they are diagnosed as permanently and totally disabled, terminally ill, or geriatric, or if they are incapacitated so that they do not pose a public safety risk. Inmates convicted of capital and certain other serious felonies are ineligible for a medical release.

Related terms: *habeas corpus*; parole; search and seizure.

privilege against self-incrimination

The Fifth Amendment provides that witnesses in all proceedings, criminal and civil, have a right to refuse to testify to any information that the government might use against them in a current or future criminal proceeding.

The privilege extends only to matters that if disclosed might lead to conviction for a crime. So, for example, a witness could refuse to testify about meeting with fellow robbers who were planning a robbery, but could not refuse to testify about meeting with a girlfriend simply because it would put the witness and his girlfriend in hot water with acquaintances.

Historical Antecedents. The right to avoid self-incrimination extends back at least to the early 1600s, when English judges invoked it to prevent the Catholic Church's ecclesiastical courts from trying to force prisoners to confess to heresy.

Communicative Information. The Fifth Amendment's reference to "witnesses" means that the privilege extends largely to assertive communications that resemble witness testimony. The privilege does not generally encompass "real" evidence such as business records, people's physical conditions, and other noncommunicative evidence. Here are two examples:

- A police officer advises a suspect, "If you don't agree to take a blood alcohol test, your refusal can be used in evidence against you in a drunk driving trial." The officer's advice is correct. The driver has no right to refuse to take a blood alcohol test because the government seeks physical evidence, not communicative information.

- Police officers can compel a robbery suspect to appear in a lineup and repeat the culprit's words, "Your money or your life." The suspect has no right to refuse. Neither appearing in the lineup nor repeating the robber's words constitute testimonial communications.

Police Interrogations. The privilege against self-incrimination is the basis of the famous case of *Miranda v. Arizona* (U.S. Sup. Ct.

(1963)). In *Miranda*, the Court ruled that confessions resulting from police interrogations are not admissible in evidence at trial unless police officers advise arrested suspects of their "*Miranda* rights" and those suspects agree to talk. The *Miranda* rights consist of the right to remain silent and to have an attorney present during questioning. The police must also advise suspects that anything they say can be used against them in court.

Silence in Court! The privilege against self-incrimination is also the basis of the rule that defendants have a right not to testify at trial. Prosecutors cannot call defendants as witnesses, nor can prosecutors ask judges and jurors to infer guilt from a defendant's failure to testify. For example, a prosecutor cannot argue to jurors that "The defendant would have testified if he didn't have something to hide." The prosecutor's argument is an improper comment on the defendant's reliance on his privilege against self-incrimination, and is likely to result in a mistrial. Note, however, that the prosecution may be allowed to comment on a suspect's silence in response to police questioning. The U.S. Supreme Court has decided that a suspect who is not yet in custody (and therefore likely hasn't been read the *Miranda* rights) must affirmatively invoke the right to silence in response to police questioning. So too must a suspect who is in custody and has received the *Miranda* warning. If the suspect doesn't say something to the effect of, "I invoke my right to silence," the prosecution can later argue at trial that the failure to respond to an officer's questions suggests guilt. (*Salinas v. Texas*, U.S. Sup. Ct. (2013); *Berghuis v. Thompkins*, U.S. Sup. Ct. (2010).)

Immunity. Because the Fifth Amendment bars the use of compelled information at trial, the government can overcome a witness's refusal to testify by a grant of "use immunity." Use immunity means that the government cannot introduce immunized testimony into evidence to prove that the witness committed a crime. Grants of use immunity extend to the so-called "fruits" of compelled testimony. This means that the government cannot offer into evidence any information or objects that the government finds out about as the result of compelled testimony. A grant of "transactional immunity," sometimes bestowed by prosecutors though not constitutionally required, provides even greater protection to witnesses. Witnesses given transactional immunity cannot be prosecuted at all for crimes about which they are compelled to testify.

> **EXAMPLE:** Hoffa is subpoenaed to testify at a congressional committee investigating labor union racketeering. Following Hoffa's Fifth Amendment refusal to testify, the committee chair grants him use immunity; the government cannot offer Hoffa's testimony into evidence against him in a future criminal trial. The grant of immunity negates Hoffa's Fifth Amendment privilege. If Hoffa continues to refuse to testify, Hoffa can be jailed for contempt of Congress. If, however, Hoffa testifies pursuant to the immunity grant and describes the location of a gun that he used to intimidate officials, the government, if it retrieves the gun, cannot use it as evidence against him. It is the fruit of compelled testimony and not admissible. If Hoffa testifies in exchange for a grant of transactional immunity, he cannot be prosecuted for any crimes encompassed by his testimony, even if the evidence of his guilt is in no way a product of his testimony.

 Legal Authority Examples

Excerpt from the Fifth Amendment to the U.S. Constitution: "No person … shall be compelled in any criminal case to be a witness against himself."

Federal Law (18 U.S.C. § 6002): Neither compelled testimony nor information directly or indirectly derived from such testimony may be used against the witness who gave it in any criminal case except a prosecution for perjury.

New York (Article 50, Criminal Procedure Laws): Witnesses who are compelled to testify after a grant of immunity are entitled to transactional immunity.

Related terms: *Miranda* warning.

privileges

Privileges refer to evidence rules that prevent witnesses from testifying to confidential information. Not surprisingly, a relationship protected by a privilege is called a privileged relationship. Common privileged relationships include attorneys and clients, spouses, priests and penitents, and doctors and patients. Private conversations between the parties to a privileged relationship may not be testified to in court. The existence of a privilege means that the legal system deems a privileged relationship more important than disclosure of "the whole truth" at trial. Privileges are created by statutes; judges have no power to create privileges on their own.

Related terms: spousal privileges; defense counsel (defense attorney); prosecutors; attorney-client privilege.

pro per (pro se)

See defense counsel (defense attorney).

probable cause

Probable cause means that enough reliable information exists to support a reasonable belief that a person has committed a crime. Probable cause is the standard that police officers (and other government agents) must have in order to carry out searches, seizure of evidence, and arrests of individuals, and to obtain search and arrest warrants. The term is used within the Fourth Amendment, which protects individuals against unreasonable searches and seizures by government agents.

Divining the Meaning of Probable Cause. There are thousands of judicial opinions describing the abstract term "probable cause" and linking these words to allegedly improper arrests and seizures of evidence. Based on these decisions, probable cause is something more than a mere hunch or suspicion of guilt and something less than belief beyond a reasonable doubt. In other words, probable cause is a complex concept that takes on meaning only in the context of judges' decisions that it did or did not exist in the circumstances of a case. The meaning can change from one context to another. Here are a series of examples:

- **The Hunch; No Probable Cause:** Patrolling a shopping precinct on foot, a police officer stops and searches a shopper because "she just had the look of a shoplifter." The search is unconstitutional because the police officer lacked reliable information to support a reasonable belief that a search would turn up evidence of a crime.

- **The Hopeful Arrest; Probable Cause:** A police officer intervenes in a brief scuffle. Based on his own observations, the officer has probable cause to believe that Andrew was the aggressor and arrests him, then searches him incident to the arrest. The police officer readily admits that the scuffle was minor, and that he really arrested Andrew because he hoped that a search would turn up evidence of other more serious crimes. Nevertheless, the police officer's conduct is constitutional. He had probable cause to arrest Andrew, and then had the right to search Andrew incident to the arrest. The fact that the real motive for the arrest was the hope of finding evidence of unrelated crimes is irrelevant.

- **The Unknown Tipster; Probable Cause Is Unclear:** Police officers receive a tip from an unknown caller stating that "The Bickersons are married drug dealers. They'll be picking up drugs from a courier outside the Main Street train station sometime in the next week." A few days later, a police officer who knows of the tip sees the Bickersons driving away from the train station and pulls their car over, then searches it. The officer's observations partially validate the tip. But whether these circumstances establish probable cause for the search cannot be answered merely by the language of the Fourth Amendment. Judges have to consider the harms the amendment was intended to prevent, past judicial decisions, the limits of individual freedom, and other factors in order to interpret the meaning of probable cause in this specific context.

- **The Housing Inspection as Pretext; No Probable Cause:** Housing inspectors conduct a routine search of an apartment in order to make sure that it meets building code requirements. Probable cause in this context does not require that the inspectors have reason to believe that they will find evidence of a crime. The state's general need to protect the public against hidden building defects provides probable cause for routine inspections. (*Camara v. Municipal Court*, U.S. Sup. Ct. (1967).) At the same time, the building inspectors could not use the inspection as a pretext to open a shoebox to look for drugs or weapons, because the shoebox is not related to building safety issues.

- **The Unknown Informant; No Probable Cause:** Police Officer Mertz is on routine patrol when a pedestrian waves him over and tells him, "I just saw Williams, who walked into that shop and molested a child last week." Mertz lacks probable cause to search or arrest Williams. Mertz did not personally observe Williams commit a crime, and Mertz knows nothing about the informant's reliability.

- **The Reliable Informant; Probable Cause:** An informant tells Police Officer Mertz that illegal human traffickers are using a specified location as a "safe house." Mertz surveys the house and observes activity that is consistent with the informant's report. Moreover, the informant has on a number of past occasions provided Mertz and other officers with accurate information related to illegal human trafficking. Mertz's corroboration of the tip and the informant's past reliability are factors indicating that Mertz has probable cause to obtain a warrant to search the house and arrest the traffickers.

In Summary, when it comes to information supplied by informants, judges consider both police officers' first-hand observations and information provided to them by informants, including an informant's past record of reliability, when deciding whether probable cause for a search or arrest exists. When it comes to police officer observations standing alone, the question is whether a reasonable officer in the same situation would have believed there was probable cause to act.

 Legal Authority Examples

U.S. Constitution, Fourth Amendment: "The right of the people to be secure in their persons, houses, papers, and effects, against unreasonable searches and seizures, shall not be violated, and no Warrants shall issue, but upon probable cause, supported by Oath or affirmation, and particularly describing the place to be searched, and the persons or things to be seized."

Related terms: search and seizure; arrests.

probation

Probation is conditional freedom, meaning that probationers remain in their communities so long as they conform to the conditions of probation that judges impose on them. A period of probation may be in lieu of or in addition to incarceration in jail. For example, a driver convicted of a second DUI, may receive a mandatory ten-day jail term and be placed on probation for four years.

Two Types of Probation. Offenders granted "summary probation" do not have to contact a probation officer or a court official during the probationary period. Judges may require "supervisory probation" for offenders convicted of more serious crimes or who have less-than-stellar past records. Supervisory probation normally requires a probationer to meet periodically (perhaps monthly) with a probation officer. While summary probation is less onerous, supervisory probation may be more beneficial in the long term. Regular meetings with a probation officer may help offenders with few family or community resources stick to crime-free programs. Offenders who develop a positive relationship with a probation officer may also gain a champion if a problem arises.

The Invisible Leash. Probation is an invisible leash that ties offenders to courts. Offenders who violate a condition of probation—by, for example, failing a drug test—may be arrested and taken to court for a revocation hearing. If a judge revokes probation, an offender may be resentenced on the same conviction that led to the grant of probation. Probationers facing incarceration may have the right to be represented by counsel at revocation hearings. Offenders whose violation of probation consists of conviction of another crime may be punished separately for the new conviction and for the conviction underlying the grant of probation.

> EXAMPLE: Herman is convicted of assault and sentenced to pay a fine and remain on summary probation for two years. During the probationary period, Herman is convicted of stalking. The court revokes Herman's probation and sentences him to four months in jail on the earlier assault conviction. The court also orders Herman to pay a fine and to serve six months in jail on the stalking conviction. The judge orders the sentences to run consecutively, meaning that Herman has to finish serving the assault sentence before he begins to serve the stalking sentence. The judge also places Herman on four years of supervised probation, to begin after he finishes serving both of the sentences.

Conditions of Probation. Judges have wide discretion when specifying the conditions that probationers must live by on pain of having probation revoked. Of course, limits exist. A condition that a probationer "achieve world peace" or "remain celibate" or "write a script for a novel romantic comedy film" would be unenforceable. Standard conditions require offenders to obey all laws, pay a fine, make restitution to victims, remain in a locality unless given permission to leave, and consent to reasonable requests by police officers or probation officials to conduct warrantless searches. Other conditions are reasonably related to specific convictions. For example, a man convicted of sexually abusing a child, may be sentenced to incarceration followed by probation, and a condition of probation may be that he not come within 500 feet of an elementary school. A man convicted of growing marijuana illegally may have to complete a court-approved drug treatment program and agree to random drug testing. A woman convicted of vandalizing a number of automobiles may as a condition of probation have to pay back the victims. But, if the total damages are substantial and the woman has no means of making restitution, the condition is illegal.

 Legal Authority Examples

Florida: Standard probation conditions include the following: no leaving a county of residence without permission; make restitution; avoid associating with lawbreakers; possession of firearms is forbidden. Standard conditions of probation for community control include house arrest (leaving the house only to work or perform community service) and wearing an electronic monitoring device.

New York: Offenders are entitled to advance notice of a probation revocation hearing, and are entitled to be represented by counsel but not to a jury. If a judge is convinced by a preponderance of the evidence (*not* beyond a reasonable doubt) that a condition of probation was violated, the judge may revoke or continue probation, or modify the original sentence.

Related terms: sentencing (punishment options); restitution; search and seizure; warrantless searches; presentence report.

prosecution

The party that represents the government in criminal proceedings. Prosecutors and not police officers take charge of a case following a suspect's arrest. For example, prosecutors decide whether to file charges, what charges to file, and whether to accept a defendant's proposed guilty plea. Many private defense lawyers are former prosecutors.

Related terms: prosecutors.

prosecutors

Prosecutors are lawyers who represent the government in criminal courts. Prosecutors decide such matters as whether to charge suspects with crimes, what charges to pursue, whether to accept defendants' offers to plead guilty to reduced charges or in exchange for lesser punishments, and what trial strategies to employ.

One Job With Many Names. Prosecutors' titles vary by jurisdiction and by an office's place in a prosecutorial hierarchy. For example, in urban areas in some states, a City Attorney's office may prosecute misdemeanors while a District Attorney's office prosecutes felonies. A state's Attorney General's office may take over the handling of cases when defendants appeal convictions. State prosecutors are commonly elected officials. The lawyers who work for them (who carry titles such as Assistant City Attorney and Deputy District Attorney) are hired as part of civil service systems.

In the federal system, the president of the United States appoints the Attorney General, a cabinet officer who heads the U.S. Department of Justice. The president also appoints United States Attorneys for each federal district; they in turn hire Assistants. United States Attorneys prosecute federal crimes.

Politics and Prosecution. When a state and the federal government both have jurisdiction over a case, state and federal prosecutors typically meet to decide which office will prosecute. Sometimes, the choice of whom to prosecute, or whether to prosecute at all, is a political decision that comes from above.

 Real-Life Illustration

During the George Bush administration, the Department of Justice controversially dismissed seven United States Attorneys for political reasons in 2006. Attorney General and fall guy Alberto Gonzales resigned because of the debacle. A Department of Justice report issued in 2008 concluded that the dismissal process was flawed and that it "raised doubts about the integrity of Department prosecution decisions."

Work Assignments. Prosecutors, especially in larger offices, tend to have discrete assignments that involve greater responsibility as they acquire experience and success. For example, charging prosecutors may make filing decisions after reviewing police reports and talking to police officers, victims, and others. In states that authorize the death penalty, a special group of charging prosecutors, including the head of an office, often decides whether to seek the death penalty. Newer prosecutors may be assigned to pretrial hearing and appearing before grand juries and at preliminary hearings. Prosecutors who try cases typically cut their teeth on ones that involve less serious charges and move up from there. Trial prosecutors usually conduct plea negotiations pertaining to their assigned cases, though they may have to obtain approval of plea arrangements from more experienced colleagues.

Prosecutorial Discretion. Prosecutors at all levels have virtually unlimited discretion over all aspects of the prosecution of criminal cases. Prosecutors consider such factors as the seriousness of a crime, the expense of prosecutions, and the "criminal temperature" of a local community when deciding whether and how to prosecute. Decisions about whom and how to prosecute may differ from county to county. For example, one county's district attorney may choose to use every felony as the basis of a three strike charge, while the district attorney of a neighboring county may charge a felony as a third strike only if it is serious or involved violence. As government representatives, prosecutors are immune from liability for their decisions.

> **EXAMPLE:** Seventeen years after a prosecutor convicts Jones of rape, DNA analysis reveals that Jones was innocent. Further investigation demonstrates that the prosecutor failed to reveal to Jones's lawyer that the principal prosecution eyewitness had at one point told the prosecutor that Jones was not the rapist. Prosecutorial immunity means that Jones cannot sue the prosecutor for damages.

Pursuing Justice. Prosecutors' ultimate responsibility is not to win cases, but rather to see that justice is done. Therefore, a prosecutor should not, for example, prosecute someone for a crime if the prosecutor is convinced that the evidence was seized illegally. No matter how unpopular a suspect, prosecutors should not charge crimes unless they are convinced that they can prove guilt beyond a reasonable doubt. Nor should prosecutors "overcharge," meaning that they should not coerce defendants into pleading guilty by filing charges that are more serious than the facts warrant.

 Legal Authority Examples

Kentucky: County and Commonwealth prosecutors may request assistance from the Attorney General in any criminal investigation or proceeding. The Attorney General may take such action as he deems appropriate and practicable under the circumstances.

Nevada: The district attorney shall attend the district courts held in his or her county, for the transaction of criminal business and conduct all prosecutions on behalf of the people for public offenses. A District Attorney must be an attorney who is licensed to practice in all Nevada courts. District attorneys are elected by the electors in their counties.

Related terms: grand juries; plea bargaining; preliminary hearings; three strikes laws.

prostitution

Prostitution is an illegal contract in which a party demands payment in exchange for sexual services. Some prostitution statutes also require acts in furtherance of sexual activity, even if sexual activity does not occur. Prostitution is typically punishable as a misdemeanor, but a person who engages in an act of prostitution with a minor can be prosecuted for a felony and if convicted may have to register as a sex offender.

EXAMPLE: An undercover police officer pulls over to a woman on a street corner and says, "How about going for a drive and having sex?" When the woman responds, "Fine, but it'll cost you $100," the officer arrests her for engaging in prostitution. The verbal agreement alone constitutes prostitution in some states, but not in others whose laws require concrete acts in furtherance of sexual activity in order for the crime to occur. However, if the woman responds to the solicitation by saying, "Fine, but it'll cost you $100," and then gets in the car and directs him to drive to a dark alley, the woman commits the crime of prostitution in states whose laws require concrete acts in furtherance of sexual activity. The man (a "john" in common lingo) is also guilty of prostitution.

Conflicting Attitudes. Whether or not prostitution is "the oldest profession," its longevity suggests that prostitution fills a market niche that criminalization does little to affect. Reformers argue against punishing a so-called victimless crime. Reformers also tend to support decriminalization and regulation of prostitutes as in The Netherlands and some counties in Nevada. They argue that health examinations and taxes on transactions would bring far greater benefits to communities as well as to prostitutes and their patrons. Feminist critics have long analogized prostitution to marriage. For example, two centuries ago Mary Wollstonecraft (the author of *Frankenstein*) described a wife's status as "legal prostitution." Defenders of criminalization argue that prostitution is far from a victimless crime, as prostitutes spread sexually transmitted diseases and undermine the social fabric of local communities. Many assert that prostitutes themselves are victims. Contributing to the debate are the diverse ways in which prostitutes earn their livings. Streetwalkers trying to support a drug habit and high-priced "call girls" paying for college by meeting clients by appointment in fancy hotels both practice prostitution, but they confront lawmakers with very different scenarios.

Pimping and Pandering. Pimping is a broad term that applies to a variety of crimes associated with the business of prostitution. These may include soliciting customers for a prostitute, arranging for a prostitute to meet with a john, or receiving payments from prostitutes for rendering services. Pandering typically refers to someone who solicits people to perform in the sex trade. Prostitutes often work under the direction of pimps and panderers, who take a portion of a prostitute's earnings in exchange for protection, customer lists, and the like. Pimping and pandering are typically punishable as felonies. Despite the illegal connotations of pimping and pandering, and the unsavory and cruel aspects of prostitution, pimps have been glorified in popular movies and music, and pimps who cater to the rich and famous are often considered celebrities.

 Real-Life Illustration

Sidney Biddle Barrows (the "Mayflower Madam") and Heidi Fleiss (the "Hollywood Madam") were convicted of prostitution-related offenses. They nevertheless became glamorous international celebrities for their economic success in furnishing wealthy and powerful clients with expensive and glamorous prostitutes.

 Legal Authority Examples

California: Pandering consists of procuring another person to engage in prostitution. Pandering is a felony punishable by a prison term of up to six years.

Illinois: Anyone who performs or agrees to perform any act of sexual penetration in exchange for anything of value commits an act of prostitution. Prosecution is a misdemeanor, but a second or subsequent violation of the law constitutes a felony.

Federal: The Mann Act prohibits transportation of people across state lines for purposes of prostitution. (Charlie Chaplin and boxing champion Jack Johnson were among the notable celebrities prosecuted under the Mann Act.)

RESOURCE

For information on how each state defines and punishes prostitution, pimping, and pandering crimes, go to www.nolo.com/prostitution.

public defenders (in some jurisdictions called legal aid lawyers)

See defense counsel (defense attorney).

public drunkenness

Public drunkenness laws allow police offers to arrest people in public spaces whose behavior interferes with others' use of those spaces. While drunk drivers pose a significant safety threat both to themselves and others on highways, public drunkenness laws protect primarily the safety of the drinker and more generally society's interest in unobstructed and safe use of sidewalks, parks, shopping malls, restaurants, and virtually any space that is open to the public.

> **EXAMPLE:** After attending a raucous bachelorette party in a club, Jenny walks outside and tries to hail a passing cab. Signs that Jenny had been drinking are obvious: She smells of alcohol, her eyes are bloodshot, and her speech is slurred and unusually loud. Yet she remains standing on the sidewalk while waiting for a cab and does not interfere with other passersby. Jenny is probably not guilty of being drunk in public.

Legal Authority Examples

Indiana: Public intoxication is a class B misdemeanor, punishable with up to 180 days in jail, and a $1,000 fine. Police offers can take a suspect to jail or transport a suspect to his or her home.

Kansas: People on a public thoroughfare whose blood alcohol content exceeds 0.08% are guilty of a misdemeanor.

 RESOURCE

For information on how each state defines and punishes public drunkenness, go to www.nolo.com/publicdrunk.

Related terms: drunk driving (DUI or DWI).

public intoxication

See public drunkenness.

public school searches

Recognizing that schools need to maintain discipline, enforce school rules, and protect students, and that children have fewer rights than adults, judges have granted public school officials greater freedom to investigate possible wrongdoing and search students than police officers have out on the streets.

Reasonable Suspicion. The Fourth Amendment protects students against random, suspicionless searches by school officials of their belongings and lockers. At the same time, school officials do not need "probable cause" to believe that a student has violated a criminal law or a school rule in order to justify an investigation and search. School officials who reasonably suspect that a student is engaged in wrongdoing can conduct a search of a student's belongings.

Real-Life Illustration

Arizona middle school officials received a tip from another student that 13-year-old student Savana Redding violated school rules by bringing a small amount of prescription pills to campus without permission from school authorities. School officials searched Redding's backpack and her outer clothing but found no evidence of pills. Officials then took Redding to a private office and demanded that she strip down to her bra and panties and shake them out. The tip that Redding brought prescriptions pills to school created a reasonable suspicion of wrongdoing that justified the search of Redding's backpack and outer garments. But the strip search violated Redding's rights under the Fourth Amendment. The excessively intrusive search was not justified by any need to protect student safety. (*Safford Unified School District v. Redding*, U.S. Sup. Ct. (2010).)

Suspicionless Searches. Public school officials can engage in wholesale drug testing of students who engage in competitive voluntary extracurricular activities even if they have no reason to suspect that any student uses drugs.

 Real-Life Illustration

The Delaware Valley School District adopted a policy that all middle school students who engage in any voluntary competitive extracurricular activity (including athletics, choir, band, and academic contests) had to submit to random drug testing. The U.S. Supreme Court upheld the policy on the ground that the interference with the students' privacy was minimal and that the policy was rationally connected to a legitimate goal of deterring drug use by children. (*Board of Education v. Earls*, U.S. Sup. Ct. (2002).)

Related terms: search and seizure; warrantless searches.

public trial (right to a public trial)

The Sixth Amendment guarantees defendants the right to a public trial in criminal cases. This right belongs to the defendant and cannot be asserted by others—for example, a television station that demands that a trial be publicly broadcast. The concept of a public trial is intended as a safeguard against government abuse, as history has shown that public officials are more likely to obey rules and do justice when outsiders can observe what they are up to.

Historical Antecedents. The founders' faith in public trials stems from their awareness of England's infamous Star Chamber, which was abolished by act of parliament in 1640. The court took its name from the gold stars that decorated the ceiling of the room in which it sat. English kings, most notoriously Henry VIII, hauled the rich and powerful into the Star Chamber. There, judges met privately and ordered the taking of their lands and often their heads. The Star Chamber was demolished in 1806, but portions of it were moved to and are still visible in Leasowe Castle in northwest England.

Please Be Seated. To be "public," a court must permit the public to attend and observe the proceedings. Typically, spectators and journalists ("the public") sit behind a bar in the courtroom and are thus separated from court officials, parties, and lawyers. (The courtroom divider explains why attorneys are "members of the bar.") Spectators may include friends and family members of defendants and crime victims. Even people who just want to come in out of the rain or cold have a right to observe trials. Judges have the power to limit attendance and make other orders to ensure that the public's right to attend doesn't interfere with the parties' right to a fair trial. For example, the judge may order spectators not to wear or carry messages, or may segregate seating to prevent family members of various parties from fighting in the courtroom. In other cases, for example cases involving sexual crimes, the judge may take certain precautions during the trial to preserve privacy, such as having certain parties testify via closed-circuit cameras.

In Media Res. The right to a public trial combined with the first amendment freedom of speech means that the media has a broad right to attend and report on trial proceedings. (*Richmond Newspapers v. Virginia*, U.S. Sup. Ct. (1982).) But the media does not have the right to televise trials or photograph trial participants. Since the 1995 double murder trial of O.J. Simpson, few judges allow the televising of criminal trials. Many believe that the trial unnecessarily continued for approximately nine months because everyone in the courtroom was playing to an international viewing audience.

 Real-Life Illustration

The right to a public trial may have affected the outcome of celebrity O.J. Simpson's trial for the murder of his ex-wife Nicole Brown Simpson and her companion Ron Goldman in Los Angeles in 1995. The trial was shown live internationally. To accommodate TV crews, journalists, and other spectators, the trial had to be moved from Santa Monica to a downtown courtroom. As a result, jurors were drawn from the racially diverse central district of Los Angeles rather than the more homogeneous and Caucasian beach communities. Nine of the 12 Simpson jurors were black, as was Simpson. Many experts ascribed Simpson's acquittal to the composition of the jury.

Who Can Be Denied Access? The judge has the power to bar certain parties from a public trial, and in other cases may sequester witnesses—that is, order them to remain outside the courtroom until after they have testified. Unlike witnesses, defendants ordinarily have a right to be present in court throughout all proceedings. Prosecutors are normally entitled to designate a police officer who can remain at the prosecution counsel table throughout a trial.

 Real-Life Illustration

Brian David Mitchell was convicted in 2010 of kidnapping teenager Elizabeth Smart and forcing her into a polygamous marriage. In the courtroom,

Mitchell constantly interrupted court proceedings with religious chants and loud talking. The judge routinely excluded Mitchell from the courtroom and had him placed in a separate room where he could watch the trial on closed-circuit television.

 Legal Authority Examples

Sixth Amendment: "In all criminal prosecutions, the accused shall enjoy the right to a speedy and public trial."

In re Oliver **(U.S. Sup. Ct. (1948)):** The Sixth Amendment right to a public trial is binding on all states.

Related terms: child sexual abuse.

P

R

racial profiling

See stop and frisk.

rap sheet

See priors.

rape

Rape is traditionally defined as the "carnal knowledge of a woman" forcibly and against her will. Many states have replaced this traditional definition with gender-neutral language that substitutes the phrase "sexual assault" for "rape" and defines the crime as sexual penetration of a person without consent. While lack of consent remains an element of rape, the revised laws recognize that victims do not have to demonstrate their unwillingness to engage in sexual activity by trying to physically fight off an attacker.

Thus, perpetrators of "date rape"—when the victim knows or has dated the victim—or perpetrators who have drugged or threatened their victims cannot avoid conviction simply because the victim did not resist or remained silent. Such responses do not constitute consent.

On the other hand, deceptively inducing a person into sexual activity—for example, by promising to marry or reward someone for sex, and then reneging—does not constitute rape.

Punishment. Many states provide for degrees of sexual assault and punish it according to the severity of the circumstances. For example, statutes may define first degree rape as a sexual assault accompanied by infliction of serious physical injuries, use of a weapon, or kidnapping. First degree rape is a felony that may be punishable by imprisonment for life and registration as a sex offender. The U.S. Supreme Court decided in *Coker v. Georgia* (1977) that rapists cannot be constitutionally subjected to the death penalty.

Force and Consent. In many states, a rape conviction requires proof both of an attacker's use of force (or threat to use force) and a victim's lack of consent. Though these are separate elements of the crime of rape, they are related in that evidence of force can provide reassurance that sexual activity was truly nonconsensual. In states that have eliminated the force requirement, rape can be proved if one party does not consent to sexual activity.

> **EXAMPLE:** Bob and Sheila go out for a dinner date. When Bob invites Sheila to go to his place after dinner, Sheila responds that she is tired and needs to be at work early the next day. Nevertheless, she drives with Bob to his flat and goes inside. When Bob starts to kiss her, Sheila says things like "we hardly know each other" and "this may not be a good idea," but embraces Bob. If kissing moves on to sexual intercourse, Bob is not guilty of rape in states that require that an attacker use force. Nor do Sheila's actions demonstrate lack of consent in most states, because her words were ambiguous and she continued to participate in sexual activity.

Date Rape. Date rape signifies sexual assault claims that arise when the parties to sexual activity know each other and perhaps have had a prior dating or even sexual relationship. Lawyers often refer to date rape cases as "he says, she says" types of cases, because invariably the only witnesses are the parties themselves and forensic evidence cannot prove or disprove the claim of rape. Determining whether sexual activity was consensual in these circumstances can be difficult because parties may interpret each other's behavior differently. Popular slogans such as "no means no" and "what part of no don't you understand?" often do little to help judges and juries resolve conflicting versions of social interactions that result in sexual activity. Date rape cases can be difficult for prosecutors to win.

EXAMPLE: Dick and Jane meet for dinner in order to discuss rekindling their romantic relationship. They have a few drinks and the evening culminates in sexual intercourse. Dick believed that his charm and genuine interest in renewing a relationship with Jane led to consensual sexual activity. Jane believed that Dick had plied her with alcohol and refused to give sufficient credence to her position that they should not rush back into a sexual relationship. Jane goes to the police and reports that Dick raped her. A medical examination confirms that sexual intercourse took place, but fails to uncover physical signs of injury. The prosecutor is likely to have a difficult time convincing a jury that Dick is guilty of rape.

Spousal Rape. Historically, rape law was intended to preserve a husband's right to exclusive sexual access to his wife. This perspective gave rise to what was known as the "marital exemption," a rule that a man was legally incapable of raping his wife. Virtually all states have abolished the marital exemption, and a husband who sexually assaults his wife can be convicted of rape.

 RESOURCE
For information on how each state defines and punishes spousal rape (also known as marital rape), go to www.nolo.com/ maritalrape.

Related Crimes. States have enacted an array of statutes to punish different forms of illegal sexual activity. Related crimes include sodomy, oral copulation, sexual battery, sexual molestation, child molestation, assault with intent to commit rape, and statutory rape.

R

Real-Life Illustration

Former Penn State assistant football coach Jerry Sandusky was convicted of 45 counts of molesting ten boys over a 15-year period. Sandusky met the molestation victims through a nonprofit organization that he had helped establish, "The Second Mile." An investigation by former FBI director Louis Freeh concluded that Penn State officials, including beloved head football coach Joe Paterno, were aware of Sandusky's molestations but remained silent in order to protect the university's football program.

 RESOURCE
For information on how each state defines and punishes sex crimes that aren't covered by rape statutes, go to www.nolo.com/ sexualbattery.

 **Legal Authority Examples**

Indiana: Rape is a Class B felony that consists of sexual intercourse when the other person is compelled to engage in intercourse by force or imminent threat of force, or when the other person is unaware that the sexual intercourse is occurring, or when the other person is too mentally disabled or deficient to consent to sexual intercourse. Rape is a Class A felony if the attacker uses or threatens to use deadly force, or is armed with a deadly weapon, or causes serious bodily injury, or drugs the victim.

New York: First degree rape consists of sexual intercourse accomplished by means of forcible compulsion, or sexual intercourse with a person who is incapable of consenting, or sexual intercourse with a person who is less than 11 years old. First degree rape is a Class B felony, and is punishable by imprisonment for not less than five nor more than 25 years.

Related terms: statutory rape.

rape shield laws

Rape shield laws prevent defendants charged with rape from attacking a rape complainant's sexual character. All states and the federal government have enacted rape shield statutes as part of their rules of evidence. Such laws would prevent the defendant in a rape case, for example, from offering evidence that a rape complainant often dressed or acted provocatively, or frequently had consensual sex with strangers, or worked as an exotic dancer.

The Historical Context. Prior to the enactment of rape shield laws, men charged with rape whose defense was that the complainant consented to sexual intercourse often cross-examined the complainant about her sexual history. For example, complainants would often be asked about when they started dating, how many lovers they'd had, and how often they'd engaged in sexual intercourse. The purported relevance of these questions was that evidence of a complainant's past willingness to engage in consensual sexual activity bolstered the defendant's claim that she consented to sex with him. In practice, the frequent effect of such questions was to make women fearful of being "raped a second time by the criminal justice system." Many women decided not to report a rape for fear of having to answer humiliating questions about their sexual character in open court. Thus, one motivation behind rape shield laws was to encourage women to report rapes to the police and cooperate in the prosecution of their attackers. A second motivation was to protect rape complainants from irrelevant questioning. Women's choices of sexual partners are personal and private, and a woman's consenting to sexual activity with one partner is irrelevant to her decision to have consensual sexual relations with a different partner.

Exception #1: Sexual Activity With an Accused Rapist. Rape shield laws do not prevent an accused rapist from offering evidence of his previous consensual sexual activity with the complainant. The exception is consistent with the policy behind rape shield laws, because the evidence does not constitute an attack on a rape

R

complainant's general sexual character. However, to claim this exception, a defendant must offer the defense of consent.

> **EXAMPLE:** Ramon is accused of raping Jill. Ramon's defense is consent; he claims they had consensual sex when they went out on a date to discuss rekindling their relationship, which had fallen apart a few months earlier. Ramon can offer evidence that during the period that they were romantically involved with each other, he and Jill regularly engaged in consensual sexual activity. However, if Ramon's defense is mistaken identification, he will not be able to claim the exception. For example, let's say that Ramon claims that he was out of town on the night that Jill was raped. Ramon cannot offer evidence that during the period that they were romantically involved with each other, he and Jill regularly engaged in consensual sexual activity. Since Ramon's defense consists of an alibi rather than a claim of consent, past sexual activity between Jill and him is irrelevant.

Exception #2: Sexual Behavior Explaining a Complainant's Physical Condition. Rape shield laws also do not prevent an accused rapist from offering evidence that a rape complainant's physical condition (such as physical injuries and the presence of semen) resulted from sexual activity with someone other than the rapist. This exception is consistent with the policy behind rape shield laws because the evidence relates specifically to the circumstances surrounding the alleged rape and thus does not constitute an attack on a rape complainant's general sexual character.

 Real-Life Illustration

In 2003, Katelyn Faber accused professional basketball great Kobe Bryant of rape. Bryant claimed that his sexual activity with Faber was consensual. Investigation by Bryant's defense team uncovered information that Faber had had sex with another man very close in time to the alleged rape. The rape shield law would not have prevented the defense from offering evidence of Faber's other sexual activity at trial, because it tended to explain the traces of vaginal blood that the police found on her underpants. However, the rape shield issue never arose because the prosecution dismissed the charges before the case came to trial.

Assessment. Despite the exceptions, rape shield statutes have in many rape cases prevented defense lawyers from hectoring rape complainants with irrelevant and degrading questions about their sexual history. Whether their enactment has made women more willing to report rapes is uncertain. Current estimates are that rape remains the most underreported of violent crimes.

 Legal Authority Examples

Federal Rule of Evidence 412: Evidence of an alleged sexual assault victim's sexual behavior or sexual predisposition is not admissible in cases involving sexual misconduct. However, evidence of specific instances of an alleged victim's sexual behavior is admissible to prove that a person other than the accused was the source of semen, injury, or other physical evidence. Also, evidence of specific instances of an alleged victim's sexual behavior with the person accused of the sexual misconduct is admissible to prove that the victim consented to sexual activity.

Related terms: rape; statutory rape.

R

reasonable doubt

See burdens of proof.

receiving stolen goods

Buying or keeping stolen property is referred to as receiving stolen goods. To convict a defendant of receiving stolen goods, the government has to prove that property in the defendant's possession was stolen, and that the defendant acquired the property knowing that it was stolen. As is typical when a statute requires proof of state of mind, the government usually has to rely on circumstantial evidence. Usually, the government's case relies on evidence that would have alerted any reasonable person that the items were stolen.

reciprocal discovery

See discovery.

reckless child endangerment

Reckless child endangerment occurs when someone carelessly but not intentionally places a child in a situation that potentially harms the child. For example, leaving dangerous drugs or a weapon in a location where a young child might access it are forms of reckless child endangerment. The crime is more serious if the potential harm occurs. For example, if a caretaker leaves a child alone in a car and the child dies, the caregiver might be charged with involuntary manslaughter or even second degree murder.

Related terms: child abuse and neglect; child sexual abuse.

reeve

In ancient Anglo-Saxon and later Norman England, shire reeves were peace keepers. The title lives on in its modern form, "sheriff."

See sheriff

restitution

Restitution is compensation that a judge orders an offender to pay to a victim. Restitution is in addition to any other punishment a court might order, such as imprisonment, a fine, community service requirements, and a period on probation. Restitution orders are worth little when, as is often true, wrongdoers have few assets and no regular source of income.

What's a Remedy Like You Doing in a Place Like This? Criminal courts function primarily to punish wrongdoers for the harms they inflict on society through such means as confinement in jails or prisons and by imposition of fines paid to the government. Civil courts function primarily to impose liability on wrongdoers for the harms they inflict on individuals, through such means as ordering them to pay damages to those they harm. Restitution involves a criminal court ordering a wrongdoer to compensate victims for their losses, and thus blends together the functions of civil and criminal courts.

 Real-Life Illustration

Once-respected financier Bernard Madoff pleaded guilty in 2009 to running the biggest Ponzi scheme in U.S. history. Madoff made off with investors' money, defrauding them out of billions of dollars. District Judge Chin deferred making a formal order of restitution because "the lack of proper record-keeping, and the scope, complexity and duration of the fraud make it impossible at this time to determine whether restitution is practicable." If the judge were unable to identify victims and their losses adequately for restitution purposes, the government would sell the assets it had seized from Madoff (such as his real property) and distribute the proceeds equitably among identified victims.

Restitution Compared to Civil Court Awards. Restitution orders and civil court judgments are similar insofar as victims can enforce both by garnishing a wrongdoer's wages, placing liens on real property that the wrongdoer owns, and using other legally permissible enforcement tools. However, restitution orders are not fully equivalent to civil court judgments. For example, restitution orders generally extend only to a victim's out-of-pocket losses. Judges cannot generally include noneconomic losses such as "pain and suffering" in restitution orders. Nor can restitution orders include the civil remedy of "specific performance" (forcing someone to carry

R

out a legally required act). Crime victims seeking remedies such as these have to obtain civil court judgments.

> **EXAMPLE:** Roger is convicted of a racially motivated assault on a college student. The student's financial losses include out-of-pocket medical expenses and lost wages from her job as a research assistant. As a result of the assault, the student suffers from recurrent nightmares, has difficulty focusing on her coursework, and is unable to maintain social relationships. A restitution order could compensate the student for medical expenses and lost wages, but not for the psychological damages.

No Debtors' Prisons. Judges cannot put offenders in jail for failing to comply with restitution orders if those offenders don't have the financial ability to comply. That would constitute imprisonment for debt, a Dickensian-era form of punishment that has long been illegal in the U.S. However, if an offender on probation refuses to comply with a restitution order even though the offender has the financial ability to do so, a probation officer can petition the court to revoke probation and imprison the offender.

Government-Sponsored Victim Compensation. Restitution, compensation that judges order offenders to pay personally to victims, differs from government-sponsored victim compensation. California adopted the first victim compensation scheme in the U.S. in 1965, in part because the likelihood of victims obtaining money through restitution orders is low. Most states have adopted victim compensation schemes. These schemes require victims to apply for assistance, including identifying their direct financial losses. These schemes have "caps" and tend to be severely underfunded; few victims recoup their actual financial losses from the government.

 Legal Authority Examples

Virginia: Judges must order offenders convicted of identity theft to make restitution as the court deems appropriate to any victim or the victim's estate. The restitution order may include actual expenses associated with correcting inaccuracies or errors in credit reports or other identifying information. Restitution is in addition to any other punishment.

California: The Victim Compensation Program provides for financial reimbursement for up to $70,000 per person for victims (or their family members) of specified crimes, including assault with a deadly weapon, sexual assault, domestic violence, drunk driving, robbery, and murder. Victims may also be eligible for reimbursement for the expenses of psychological counseling. Victims have to file an application for compensation within a year of the crime and must be California residents, the crime must have occurred in California, and the victim had to have cooperated with the police and court officials.

Related terms: civil compromise.

right to counsel

See defense counsel (defense attorney).

right to remain silent at trial

See privilege against self-incrimination; failure of proof.

robbery

Robbery consists of the taking or attempted taking of property by force or fear. Because the crime consists of an immediate and violent confrontation between a culprit and a victim, the risk that a victim will suffer bodily injury or even death is high. Thus, robbery is a felony that typically merits a harsh sentence.

A defendant is guilty of robbery even if the victim has no property to give. A gun-wielding assailant who demands money from a victim who has no money is guilty of the crime. Although some statutes define a crime as robbery only if the robber inflicts or threatens immediate harm to a victim, many states interpret robbery to occur under any circumstances that could reasonably lead the victim to feel threatened and to believe that a demand for money was made.

On the other hand, if the incident occurs so fleetingly that the victim is not fearful—for example, a street thief grabs a handbag and runs off—the crime of larceny has occurred, probably not robbery.

Mine Forever. Robbery is a crime of both violence and thievery. A common element of theft crimes is that a thief intends to deprive a victim of the stolen property forever. Some but not all robbery laws contain this element.

> EXAMPLE: Al wants to impress his old pals by wearing a great-looking jacket to his ten-year high school reunion. Hours before the reception is to begin, he sees a man his size approaching him; the man is dressed in a jacket that Al had recently seen on the cover of *GQ*. Al accosts the jacket's owner and forcibly takes the jacket, but tells the owner to "be at this exact spot in 48 hours." After the reception, Al has the jacket cleaned, then gives it to a friend and asks the friend to deliver the jacket to its owner at the address on the label sewn into the jacket. Al may be guilty of robbery in some states, but not in others because at the moment he stole it, he intended to return the jacket to its owner. Of course, even if Al could not be convicted of robbery or theft he could be convicted of assaulting the jacket's owner. If, on the other hand, Al intends to keep the jacket forever when he steals it, but changes his mind and gives it back, he would be guilty of robbery in all states because he intended to keep the jacket at the moment he stole it.

Aggravated Robbery. A variety of factors can elevate the crime of robbery to what is typically referred to as aggravated robbery or first degree robbery. These factors include use of a dangerous weapon such as a gun or knife and inflicting serious physical injuries on a victim. Convictions for aggravated robbery typically result in harsher sentences compared to those for ordinary or second degree robbery.

Bank Robbery. Robbery prosecutions typically take place in state courts. However, state and federal courts often have "concurrent jurisdiction" in bank robbery cases, which means that either the state or the federal government can prosecute a bank robber. The reason is that robbery of a banking institution that is a federal association or is federally insured is a federal crime. When the same criminal act violates both state and federal laws, federal and state prosecutors decide which office will take charge of a case. In rare cases, the federal government may retry a bank robber who is tried and acquitted in state court. Double jeopardy (discussed separately) would probably not prevent the federal court prosecution because the state is an independent governmental entity.

Carjacking. Carjacking is a form of robbery in which a robber steals a car from a driver or passenger. The inherent danger to victims of carjacking is one reason for the special statutes that many states have enacted. Another reason is that carjacking statutes define carjacking as robbery even if the carjacker intends only to keep a car temporarily.

 Legal Authority Examples

California: First degree robbery includes armed robbery; robbery of bus or taxicab drivers or of their passengers; robberies that take place inside people's homes; and robberies of customers using automatic teller machines. First degree robbery is punishable by imprisonment for three, six, or nine years. Second degree robbery includes all other forms of robbery and is punishable by imprisonment for two, three, or five years.

New York: First degree robbery includes using or displaying a weapon to commit a robbery, or robberies that result in serious physical injury to a victim in the course of committing a robbery. First degree robbery is punishable by imprisonment for a minimum of five years, with a maximum punishment of 25 years. Second degree robbery includes robberies carried out by two or more persons, carjacking, and robberies that result in physical injuries to a victim. Second degree robbery is punishable by imprisonment of up to 15 years. Third degree robberies are all robberies that are not robberies of the first or second degree, and are punishable by imprisonment of between two and seven years.

Related terms: shoplifting; burglary; receiving stolen goods.

R

S

sale of alcohol or cigarettes to minors

Virtually all states criminalize the sale of alcohol or cigarettes to minors, though the age of minority can vary from one state to another. Sale of prohibited items is often a strict liability crime, meaning that a seller who neglects to demand identification can be guilty even if unaware that a purchaser was a minor. The crime is normally punishable as an infraction or a low-level misdemeanor, though repeated violations can result in more serious penalties, including loss of a sales license.

sale of illegal drugs

See drug offenses.

Sarbanes-Oxley Act

See securities fraud.

search and seizure

Search and seizure law emanates from the Fourth Amendment and refers to the government's power to search individuals and their property, and to arrest people and confiscate their property. The Fourth Amendment provides that the government cannot unreasonably search or seize people or their property, and that it must establish probable cause in order to make arrests. Thus. the scope of the government's search and seizure power depends on judges' balancing the government's obligation to protect the social order against the individual's right to be free from unwarranted intrusion. By making a rule protecting essential freedoms dependent on the uncertain meaning of the abstract terms "unreasonably" and "probable cause," the Founding Fathers guaranteed at least two results:

- The rule is flexible enough to apply both to situations that existed when the rule was approved in 1791 (such as papers concealed under floorboards) and to those that exist presently (such as electronic data hidden in the digital universe).
- Judges and lawyers forever have to engage in arguments about the application of "unreasonably" and "probable cause" to concrete situations.

Below are some of the central themes that judges use to interpret the meaning of and enforce the Fourth Amendment.

Privacy. At its core, the Fourth Amendment protects privacy. Government agents need to convince judges that they have legitimate bases for snatching people off the streets or out of their homes, or for grabbing or even examining their papers and other property. Individuals' own actions and expectations help shape the concept of privacy. For example, if police install a visual recording device in a public restroom, ordinary expectations of privacy mean that the device's installation constitutes a search that is subject to the Fourth Amendment. However, if police officers look through trash bins in the alleyway behind a suspect's residence, the officers' actions do not constitute a search that is subject to the Fourth Amendment, because people cannot reasonably expect their trash to be private.

The Exclusionary Rule. Judges enforce the Fourth Amendment by forbidding the government to use improperly seized evidence at trial (known as the "exclusionary rule"). Judges regard the exclusionary rule as a method of deterring police officers from carrying out unreasonable searches and seizures. Influenced by critics' argument that "it makes no sense for a criminal to go free because a constable has erred," courts have reduced the exclusionary rule's scope. For example, if a police officer pulls over a suspect in good faith based on information that the officer believed was accurate—for example, police headquarters mistakenly informed the officer that there was an outstanding warrant on the suspect—the exclusionary rule does not apply.

What Do They Know and When Do They Know It? Searches cannot be justified by their results. That is, a police officer who has a hunch about a suspect's possession of drugs cannot avoid the exclusionary rule simply because the officer's hunch proved correct. A search's reasonableness depends on information that police officers have before they conduct a search.

Poisonous Fruit. To act as an added deterrent to violations of the Fourth Amendment, judges created the "fruit of the poisonous tree" rule. The rule provides that if improperly seized evidence leads the government to seize additional evidence, the additional evidence is also inadmissible.

> EXAMPLE: A police officer improperly breaks into Sharkey's home and finds a map showing where Sharkey buried a bag of stolen loot. Using the map, the officer digs up the loot. The officer's illegal search is the poisonous tree and the loot is its fruit. Neither the map nor the loot is admissible in evidence.

Inevitable Discovery. When the police find evidence through an illegal search that they would undoubtedly have found in the course of a lawful investigation, that evidence is admissible. The prosecution must prove by a preponderance of the evidence that police discovery of the evidence through lawful means was inevitable.

> EXAMPLE: While in her patrol car, Officer Jan notices that the registration tag on the car in front of her is poorly affixed to the license plate. Jan asks her dispatcher to determine whether the car is registered; the dispatcher tells her it's not. So, she pulls over the vehicle and requests the driver's registration and license. The driver fails to produce either, insists he has both, and instead produces a birth certificate in the name of "Dangerous Jones" as proof of his identity. Jan suddenly, and without permission, lunges for and grabs the driver's wallet out

S

of his front pocket. In it is a driver's license in the name of "Alex Jones." Jan asks her dispatcher to determine whether "Dangerous Jones" has a valid driver's license; the dispatcher tells her that there is no record of such a name. The dispatcher also tells her that "Alex Jones" is wanted for armed robbery. Jan then arrests Jones. The wallet, even though the product of an illegal search, is admissible in evidence. Jan would have learned that Jones had given her a false name when she asked her dispatcher to check whether "Dangerous Jones" had a valid driver license. The wallet would inevitably have been discovered in a search incident to arrest based on the giving of a false name.

Private Parties. The Fourth Amendment regulates only governmental activity. Private parties are outside its scope.

EXAMPLE: On a hunch that Bill, a computer programmer, is stealing company equipment, a Giggle Software supervisor acting without the police's knowledge searches Bill's car and finds boxes of stolen electronic equipment. If Bill is arrested and charged with theft, the equipment is admissible in evidence.

So Sue Me! Individuals victimized by an illegal search or seizure have the option of filing a civil suit for damages against the government official who broke the law. But civil lawsuits are infrequent and largely ineffective. Thus, the exclusionary rule remains the criminal justice system's most effective deterrent to violations of the Fourth Amendment.

Searches Without Reasonable Suspicion. Fourth Amendment doctrine requires police officers to have probable cause to believe that they will find evidence of criminal activity before they can make arrests, obtain search warrants, or conduct warrantless searches. But, pursuant to Fourth Amendment court rulings, police officers can temporarily detain and frisk individuals if they have a lower level of belief that they will find evidence of criminal activity that courts refer to as "reasonable suspicion." Below are common scenarios in which police officers do not even need reasonable suspicion to conduct searches. Judges often justify these scenarios by emphasizing that suspicionless searches are valid because officials' primary purpose is not to catch criminals, but rather to further society's interests in health and safety.

- **Sniffer Dogs.** You've no doubt seen police cars with "K-9" markings. The designated canines are often sniffer dogs that are trained to detect the presence of illegal substances. Police officers can use sniffer dogs' sense of smell to "search" cars, airport luggage, and other objects even if they have no reason to suspect the presence of illegal substances. (*Illinois v. Caballes*, U.S. Sup. Ct. (2005).) For example, a search is valid if, during a traffic violation, a sniffer dog barks at the suspect's car trunk and police officers open the trunk and find drugs. The officers needed no suspicion to use the dog, and the dog's reaction furnished probable cause for the search of the trunk. But, dog sniffs sometimes constitute Fourth Amendment searches that require probable cause (and perhaps a warrant)— for example, a dog sniffing the front door of a suspected marijuana grow house.

- **Sobriety Checkpoints.** Police officers may legitimately set up checkpoints through which all drivers on a road have to pass. Police officers have the right to stop drivers randomly at checkpoints, even in the absence of any information suggesting that a stopped driver is under the influence of alcohol or drugs. If an officer detects symptoms consistent with DUI, the officer can pull the driver off the road for further investigation.

EXAMPLE: A police officer stops Nitti's car at random at a sobriety checkpoint. The police officer observes that Nitti's eyes are red and watery and that her speech is slurred. The police officer motions Nitti's car off to the side. The officer searches the interior and trunk of Nitti's car on a hunch that Nitti might be transporting illegal weapons. The police officer had the right to make a suspicionless checkpoint stop of Nitti. Moreover, Nitti's symptoms furnished probable cause for the police

S

officer to investigate her for DUI. But the search for weapons was invalid because a DUI offense does not furnish probable cause to believe that Nitti's car contained illegal weapons. Any evidence the search turned up would not be admissible in evidence.

- **Border Searches.** Numerous checkpoints exist at or near the Mexican and Canadian borders. As with sobriety checkpoints, government border agents can detain vehicles at random and conduct cursory investigations. Judges explain that the government's interest in preventing illegal immigration and deterring crime outweighs the brief intrusion of a suspicion-less detention. Of course, if an investigation uncovers suspicious circumstances, agents can prolong the detention and carry out a more thorough search.
- **Administrative Searches.** In order to ensure compliance with health and safety regulations, government agents can carry out reasonable suspicionless inspections of restaurants and other buildings.

EXAMPLE: A county health officer conducts a routine inspection of a restaurant that specializes in raw fish dishes. The inspection gives the officer reason to suspect that the restaurant serves Sei whale meat in violation of a federal law that bans the use of an endangered species for food. Follow-up inspections by other officers confirm that the whale meat is illegal and the restaurant's owner is charged with violation of the law. The county health officer's initial suspicionless inspection is valid because its primary purpose was to enforce local health laws. The officer's findings constitute a reasonable basis for the follow-up investigation.

- **Searches of Probationers and Parolees.** A common condition of probation and parole is that a person agrees to submit to a government agent's warrantless and suspicionless search. Judges generally uphold such searches on the ground that punishment for crime results in a reduced amount of freedom as well as reduced expectations of privacy.

EXAMPLE: Investigating a robbery of the Last National Bank, a police officer pulls over a car driven by Bonnie. Bonnie had served time on a bank robbery conviction and was recently paroled. The police officer has no information connecting Bonnie to the Last National robbery. Nevertheless, pursuant to a condition of parole that Bonnie agree to a reasonable search by police officers, the police officer searches both Bonnie and her car for evidence that might connect her to the robbery. The search is valid because the police officer has a legitimate reason to search Bonnie. Any evidence that the police officer uncovers would be admissible in evidence against her.

 Legal Authority Examples

Fourth Amendment: "The right of the people to be secure in their persons, houses, papers, and effects, against unreasonable searches and seizures, shall not be violated, and no Warrants shall issue, but upon probable cause, supported by Oath or affirmation, and particularly describing the place to be searched, and the persons or things to be seized."

Related terms: automobile searches; public school searches; informants; stop and frisk; search warrants; electronic surveillance.

search incident to arrest

See warrantless searches.

search warrants

The Fourth Amendment requires that government officials establish probable cause for the issuance of search warrants and that searches be reasonable. But, the Fourth Amendment does not say that search warrants are required in order for searches to be reasonable. In the great majority of cases, judges rule that searches are valid under the Fourth Amendment because the police officers acted reasonably, even though they did not obtain a search warrant.

Identifying when the Fourth Amendment requires police officers to obtain a search warrant is a reductive process that requires carving out all the circumstances in which judges permit warrantless searches and looking at what remains. As a general rule, search warrants are primarily required for nonurgent searches of dwellings. So, for example, if a police officer receives a tip from a confidential informant that a suburban home is a "grow house" in which marijuana is grown and harvested, the officer needs to obtain a search warrant in order to enter the home without the occupant's permission.

Warrant Procedures. To obtain a warrant, police officers provide judges with written affidavits signed under oath that establish probable cause to believe that the search will turn up evidence of crime. Affiants may include police officers, informants, crime victims, and others who may have information pertaining to criminal activity. In some situations, a judge may ask a police officer to amplify orally on the information in the affidavits. Applications must identify the places to be searched and the items to be seized "with particularity," and search warrants limit officers to those places and items. But the four corners of a search warrant do not necessarily control the scope of a search. For example, police officers can seize evidence or contraband that is in plain view even if it is not listed in a warrant. Similarly, police officers can protect themselves by conducting limited searches of people who happen to be in the searched premises.

EXAMPLE: A police officer seeks the issuance of a warrant to search the premises at 8871 Westgate Avenue to look for items stolen during a jewelry store robbery. Affidavits provided by the officer and a sibling of one of the suspects establish probable cause that the officer will find stolen jewelry at that address. The warrant is valid if it identifies the location to be searched by its street address and the items to be seized as "men's and women's gold and silver rings, necklaces, diamond earrings, and other jewelry items." If numerous pieces were stolen, the warrant need not identify exactly how many pieces of jewelry the officer may look for and seize, nor provide exact descriptions such as the carat weights and fair market value of individual pieces. The authorization to search the premises includes the power to look into places where stolen jewelry might reasonably be concealed, such as inside dresser drawers. If the police officer happens to find a gun that might have been used in the robbery while searching a drawer, the officer can seize the gun as evidence even though it wasn't listed in the search warrant. And the police officer can detain and conduct at least a limited pat-down search of anyone who happens to be in the premises at the time the search takes place.

Knock Knock: Who's There? Before entering a location to execute a search warrant, police officers are required to announce their presence and their intention to conduct a search. Courts do not require this bit of quaint politeness if advance warning would risk harm to police officers or if the affidavits establish that advance notice is likely to result in occupants' disposing of evidence.

> EXAMPLE: A police officer obtains a warrant to search a residence suspected of being a drug dealer's base of operations. Based on activity detailed in the police officer's affidavit suggesting that advance notice will give the occupants time and opportunity to dispose of any illegal drugs, the search warrant may authorize the police officer to execute the warrant without giving advance notice to the occupants.

Legal Authority Examples

Fourth Amendment: "The right of the people to be secure in their persons, houses, papers, and effects, against unreasonable searches and seizures, shall not be violated, and no Warrants shall issue, but upon probable cause, supported by Oath or affirmation, and particularly describing the place to be searched, and the persons or things to be seized."

Related terms: warrantless searches.

second degree murder (Murder Two)

Second degree murder, (or "Murder Two"), is an unlawful intentional or extremely reckless killing that does not constitute first degree murder. Second degree murder is a felony that is typically punishable by up to life in prison.

First Degree Murder vs. Second Degree Murder. Most states provide for two degrees of murder because even in the universe of intentional killers, lawmakers believe that some deserve harsher punishment than others. First degree murder is reserved for society's most morally blameworthy killers.

> **EXAMPLE:** In the musical comedy *Chicago* (2002), Roxie Hart aspires to fame as an actress in 1930s Chicago. She carries on an affair with Fred Casely because he has promised to make her a star. When Casely tells Roxie that he wasn't serious and starts to walk out on her, Roxie impetuously grabs a gun and kills him. Although in the movie Roxie was acquitted, in real life she would be guilty of second degree murder. She killed Casely intentionally but without premeditation. If, however, Roxie found out from a friend that Casely was a liar, then purchased a gun, invited Casely to her apartment, and killed him, she would be guilty of first degree murder.

S

Heart Problems. Extreme disregard for human life often functions as the equivalent of intent to kill. In other words, killers whose actions reflect what statutes or judges refer to as an "abandoned and depraved heart" or a "malignant heart" are deemed by law to have demonstrated intent to kill. As a result, regardless of their actual intent, killers who exhibit extreme disregard for human life can be convicted of second degree murder, depending on states' criminal law rules. For example, a man who, during an argument with another man, draws out a handgun and accidentally discharges it, killing the other man, could be convicted of second degree murder. So too could a dog owner who allows her overpowering and dangerous pet to be out in public and near another person whom the animal kills.

Murder or Manslaughter? "Malignant heart" second degree murder and involuntary manslaughter both occur when a defendant unintentionally kills someone through a criminal act. Malignant heart murder is the more serious offense, as it requires that the defendant act with a conscious disregard for the lives of others. Involuntary manslaughter, on the other hand, involves gross negligence. In practical terms, differentiating between the two forms of homicide can be tough.

 Real-Life Illustration

In April of 2009, Andrew Gallo killed three people, including Major League Baseball pitcher Nick Adenhart, in a drunk driving collision. Gallo, with a previous DUI conviction, had a blood-alcohol level nearly three times the legal limit at the time of the crash. He spent hours drinking beers and shots at three bars before the accident. Friends, family, and court officials had repeatedly warned him of the hazards of drinking and driving. A California jury convicted Gallo of three counts of second-degree murder (among other crimes), rather than a version of involuntary manslaughter specifically tailored for drunk driving scenarios. The jury decided that his conduct was so outrageous that it merited the more serious convictions.

Great Bodily Injury. Second degree murder also occurs when an individual intends to greatly injure a victim but instead causes the victim's death. So, for example, if a drug dealer hires a goon to beat up a slow-paying customer and the customer dies from the beating, the dealer and the goon would be guilty of second degree murder.

Circumstantial Evidence. Defendants frequently defend themselves against murder charges by arguing that they did not intend to kill. Yet, direct evidence of a killer's actual intent is virtually impossible to obtain. Thus, judges and jurors typically look to circumstantial evidence when evaluating the mental state of a defendant charged with murder.

> **EXAMPLE:** In the "Nanny Murder" trial that took place in Massachusetts in 1997, a 19-year-old British *au pair* ("mother's helper") was charged with second degree murder for intentionally shaking the baby who was in her care so violently that the baby died. The *au pair* contended that the baby's death was a tragic accident that resulted from her shaking the baby normally. The jury inferred from the circumstantial evidence that the *au pair* used extreme violence and convicted her of second degree murder. After the jury was excused, the trial judge evaluated the evidence independently and concluded that the *au pair* had behaved carelessly but not with extreme recklessness. The judge reduced the conviction to involuntary manslaughter.

Felony Murder Rule. The felony murder rule provides that a death that occurs in the course of the commission of a dangerous felony is murder. A killing may be first degree murder or Murder Two under the felony murder rule, depending on the severity of the underlying felony.

 Legal Authority Examples

Colorado: Murder in the second degree consists of knowingly causing a person's death. Second degree murder is generally a class 2 felony.

Florida: The unlawful killing of a human being, when perpetrated by any act imminently dangerous to another and evincing a depraved mind regardless of human life, although without any premeditated design to effect the death of any particular individual, is murder in the second degree and constitutes a felony of the first degree, punishable by imprisonment for a term of years not exceeding life.

Related Terms: felony murder rule; manslaughter; *mens rea*; first degree murder (Murder One); drunk driving (DUI or DWI).

securities fraud

Securities fraud is an umbrella term for various white-collar crimes involving intentional or reckless misrepresentations about shares of stock and related investments. Some securities fraud schemes involve false representations intended to attract investments from individuals and entities. Other schemes involve manipulating the value of companies, stock holdings, or investments based on secret information that is unknown to the general public. Securities fraud schemes generally involve large amounts of money and are almost always punishable as felonies.

Follow the Money. Courts can levy fines on companies that violate securities laws, and sometimes can even shut them down. But if courts are to send wrongdoers to prison, prosecutors have to identify the corrupt individuals responsible for the violations. In huge multi-level corporations filled with insiders and independent advisors who have lots of fingers to point at each other, tying illegal practices to specific suspects can be extremely difficult.

 Real-Life Illustration

Jeffrey Skilling was the former CEO of Enron Corp. After Skilling and other Enron insiders became millionaires many times over, Enron went bankrupt in 2001 when the accounting scams it had used to make the company seem profitable unraveled. The government spent years sifting through complex financial documents and ultimately convicted Skilling, former Enron President Kenneth Lay, and former Enron CFO Andrew Fastow of securities fraud. (Lay's death from a heart attack before he had a chance to appeal wiped his conviction off the books.) In 2006, Skilling was convicted of insider trading, securities fraud, and other crimes. In 2010, the U.S. Supreme Court overturned Skilling's conviction for the crime of depriving Enron of the intangible right of honest services. In 2013, Skilling's original sentence of more than 24 years in prison was reduced to 14.

Cooked Books. Deceptive accounting practices that overstate a company's financial condition are a common form of securities fraud. Investors lose money when they pay inflated prices for securities that can ultimately be worthless. For example, in the case of Enron, the company and its accountants hid losses in the books of subordinate offshore entities. The scam made Enron seem highly profitable when actually it was incurring huge losses. In addition to losing their jobs, most Enron employees also lost their life savings because the company had invested nearly all of the employees' retirement funds in Enron stock that was ultimately worthless. Thousands of investors who knew nothing about the corrupt accounting practices and bought Enron stock also were victims of the sham accounting practices.

Insider Trading. The concept of a free market in publicly traded stocks includes all potential investors having equal access to information that might affect the value of companies' stock. Insider trading consists of corporate insiders buying or selling stock in their own companies based on private information that has not been publicly disseminated.

 Real-Life Illustration

Media mogul Martha Stewart owned stock in a company called ImClone Systems. In March 2004, on the day before the company announced publicly that its stock was worthless, Stewart sold all of her stock in the company based on a tip that she received from ImClone's president. The president, who had also sold his ImClone stock before it became worthless, pleaded guilty to insider trading and was sent to prison. A jury convicted Stewart of a lesser crime of lying to federal agents about receiving the tip. Stewart served a few months in prison.

Churning Things Around. Churning consists of stock brokers buying and selling stocks for clients primarily to earn commissions. Churning is illegal—regardless of whether it enhances the value of a client's accounts—because brokers take advantage of investors' relative ignorance and abuse their fiduciary duty to put clients' financial interests above their own.

Ponzi Schemes. Operators of Ponzi schemes lure investors to part with money by promising uncommonly large and regular profits. Because actual investments would not produce the promised benefits, operators pay off existing investors with money raised from later investors. Ponzi schemes inevitably unravel when the number of existing investors grows so large that the operators are no longer able to attract enough money from new investors to pay off the existing investors.

 Real-Life Illustration

Bernard Madoff, who once headed a national stock market, pleaded guilty in 2009 to operating the largest Ponzi scheme ever uncovered. Estimates are that investors lost about $65 billion.

 Legal Authority Examples

Rule 10b-5, promulgated pursuant to the Securities Exchange Act of 1934: In connection with the purchase or sale of any security, it is unlawful to use any instrumentality of interstate commerce to employ any scheme or device to defraud, or to make an untrue statement of a material fact or to omit to state a material fact, or to engage in any act that operates as a fraud or deceit upon any person.

Rule 10b5-1, promulgated pursuant to the Securities Exchange Act of 1934: It is unlawful knowingly to purchase or sell a security on the basis of material nonpublic information about the security in breach of a duty of trust or confidence that is owed to the issuer of the security or its shareholders, or to any other person who is the source of the material nonpublic information.

Securities Exchange Act of 1934: Individuals who willfully violate the securities laws or regulations are punishable by a fine of up to $5,000,000 and/or imprisonment of up to 20 years. Corporations that willfully violate the securities laws may be fined up to $25,000,000.

Sarbanes-Oxley Act: Among other provisions relating to publicly traded companies, the law provides for oversight of public accounting firms, limits conflicts of interest between accountants and the firms they audit, makes senior company executives personally responsible for the accuracy and completeness of financial reports, and requires disclosure of companies' financial transactions and processes. Knowing violations of the law can result in fines and imprisonment for up to 20 years.

Related terms: fraud.

self-defense

S

Self-defense recognizes a right to protection from imminent physical harm and is a complete defense to a criminal charge. This means that defendants who use a reasonable amount of force to protect themselves from an aggressor's attack are not guilty.

Reasonable Force. How much force is reasonable for self-defense depends on how much force an aggressor uses. And force that is initially a legitimate exercise of self-defense can turn into an unlawful assault if the use of force continues after an aggressor no longer poses a threat of physical harm. Here are two examples of how the principle is applied.

Invalid Self-Defense: No Threat and Unreasonable Force. While Rhoda is at a stoplight, a bicyclist rides next to Rhoda's convertible, lightly shoves her shoulder once with his hand, and tells her that she almost ran him into a parked car because she was on her mobile phone while she was driving. Rhoda screams, "Get away from me," repeatedly slams her car door into the bicyclist and knocks him to the ground, then pours hot coffee on him and speeds off. Rhoda is prosecuted for assault and claims to have acted in self-defense. Her defense is invalid for two reasons. One, she used an unreasonable amount of force in response to one light tap on her shoulder. Two, as the bicyclist did not pose a threat to Rhoda after he had been knocked to the ground, she did not act in self-defense when she poured coffee on him.

Valid Self-Defense; Reasonable Force. Jane's abusive ex-boyfriend breaks into her home and in a drunken rage begins to choke her. Jane clubs him with a vase and kills him. Jane's actions constitute reasonable self-defense. Her use of deadly force was reasonable because the attacker used deadly force.

Imminent Harm. You don't have to wait to be attacked in order to defend yourself. If circumstances would suggest to a reasonable person that an attack is imminent, you can use self-defense to protect yourself. So, for example, deadly force as a self-defense would be justified against someone brandishing a deadly weapon in a threatening manner. Self-defense may also be justified against someone who acts aggressively, makes verbal threats, and prevents the victim from leaving. If someone uses self-defense in response to a perceived threat, but one that isn't actual or imminent, based on a history of abuse, it is often referred to as "imperfect self-defense."

Imperfect Self-Defense. Defendants who actually, but unreasonably, believe that they need to defend themselves with force can claim imperfect self-defense. Imperfect self-defense also applies when defendants reasonably believe that force is necessary to defend themselves, but use far too much force than the circumstances merit.

The imperfect self-defense doctrine doesn't lead to an acquittal, but it does allow for conviction of a lesser crime.

> EXAMPLE: Chapman and Vause exchange harsh words. Vause clenches her fists and begins to walk menacingly toward Chapman. Chapman, terrified by the much smaller Vause, pulls out a gun and shoots Vause, killing her. Chapman's actual but unreasonable belief that she needed to shoot Vause negates the "malice aforethought" state of mind required for murder. But her use of force was excessive, so she can still be convicted of manslaughter.

 Real-Life Illustration

Brothers Erik and Lyle Menendez relied on a defense of "imperfect self-defense" in their notorious and nationally televised 1993 and 1995 trials for brutally murdering their parents Jose and Kitty Menendez. The brothers testified that their parents had abused them sexually for years, and that they shot Jose and Kitty in the belief that the parents were intending to kill them to cover up the abuse. Had the jurors accepted the imperfect self-defense claim, the Menendez brothers would have been guilty only of manslaughter, not murder. The 1993 trial ended with a hung jury. The brothers were tried on the same charges in 1995, convicted of murder, and sent to prison for life.

See abuse excuse.

S

Stand Your Ground. State rules vary when it comes to whether self-defense is an acceptable defense if a defendant had a reasonable opportunity to avoid harm by retreating. Florida and California are two of the many states that don't impose a "duty to retreat" on people threatened by immediate harm. Florida's "stand your ground" rule, for example, allows a person faced with serious and immediate physical harm to meet force with force. The threatened person need not retreat even if he or she can safely do so. How much force is reasonable depends on the level of the aggressor's force.

Real-Life Illustration

African American teenager Trayvon Martin was walking through a largely Caucasian residential neighborhood in Florida when George Zimmerman began to follow him. Zimmerman was a Neighborhood Watch volunteer. A short and violent altercation between the two ended with Zimmerman fatally shooting Martin. Zimmerman told the police that he was forced to protect himself by shooting the unarmed Martin, who attacked him. Florida's stand your ground law initially appeared to be at issue, but Zimmerman's defense team ultimately didn't rely on it. Rather, his lawyers argued that Zimmerman had no option to retreat and that he shot Martin while under attack—they relied on a classic self-defense theory. Jurors had the option of convicting Zimmerman of second degree murder or manslaughter, but acquitted him.

Defense of Others. The right of self-defense extends to the defense of other people who are under attack or threatened with an attack. So, for example, a man who witnesses another man being beaten, may use reasonable force to stop the attack.

Defense of Property. Reasonable force is also justified when necessary to prevent a theft or other crime against property.

> **EXAMPLE:** Tikva comes home to find a man about to run out the back door with a large plastic bag filled with her personal possessions. Tikva pushes the man to the floor and threatens to hit him with a frying pan to prevent him from escaping while she dials 911 and obtains help. Tikva's use of force constitutes legitimate self-defense.

Character Evidence. Trials involving self-defense claims often turn on judges' and juries' beliefs as to who "started it": the defendant or the purported victim. To support a defendant's claim that the supposed victim was actually the aggressor and that self-defense was necessary, evidence rules allow defendants to offer evidence that a victim has a past history of violence and aggression. The risk of this strategy for defendants is that once they attack a victim's character for violence, prosecutors can launch an attack on their character.

Trial Procedures. Defendants who plan to rely on a self-defense claim typically have to allow prosecutors to prepare for trial by advising them of their plans before trial starts. Defendants do not necessarily have the burden of proving that they acted in self-defense. The burden in some states remains on the prosecutor to prove beyond a reasonable doubt that a defendant committed a charged crime.

 Legal Authority Examples

New York: A person may use physical force upon another person in self-defense or defense of a third person, or in defense of premises, or in order to prevent larceny ... or in order to effect an arrest or prevent an escape from custody.

Illinois: The use of force against another is justified when reasonably necessary for self-defense or the defense of another person against the imminent use of unlawful force, or to prevent or terminate unlawful entry into a dwelling. Force that is likely to cause death or great bodily harm is justified only if reasonably necessary to prevent imminent death or great bodily harm, or the commission of a forcible felony.

Related terms: assault and battery; burdens of proof; character evidence; abuse excuse.

self-incrimination

See privilege against self-incrimination.

sentencing (punishment options)

After a defendant is convicted of a crime, the judge issues a sentence—a court order setting out the punishment. The most common punishments are incarceration in a jail or prison and fines. Other common components of sentences, which often are in addition to incarceration and fines, include probation, community service, and restitution (money that a defendant is ordered to pay to a victim).

Bounded Discretion. When judges issue sentences they usually operate with bounded discretion—sentences are limited by boundaries set by the Eighth Amendment, and by state and federal statutes. Bounded discretion is derived from two oft-conflicting approaches to punishment.

- **Let the Punishment Fit the Crime.** Under this approach, offenders who commit the same crime should receive the same punishment. For example, a state statute may provide that all those who are convicted of a second DUI/DWI will automatically have their driver's licenses revoked.

- **Let the Punishment Fit the Criminal.** Under this approach, a judge can consider factors like offenders' backgrounds, ages, and criminal records when deciding on appropriate punishment.

Judges typically balance these two standards when issuing sentences. For example, a statute may set forth a minimum and maximum period of incarceration and allow judges to consider the circumstances of individual cases to decide on an appropriate length of incarceration. In addition to statutory constraints, the Eighth Amendment's prohibition of cruel and unusual punishment sets an outer limit on judges' sentencing discretion.

However, punishment policies are fluid. Factors such as public attitudes toward crime, the costs of incarceration, and the widespread belief that prisons fail to rehabilitate inmates continue to alter punishment policies and options. For example, the Supreme Court has interpreted the Eighth Amendment prohibition of cruel

S

and unusual punishment to mean that offenders who are under age 18 at the time they committed a crime cannot be subjected to capital punishment. (*Roper v. Simmons,* U.S. Sup. Ct. (2005).) And individualized justice allows for dramatic variations in states' use of the death penalty. For example, in 2008, 37 Death Row prisoners were executed in the entire country. All but two of these executions took place in Southern states. Texas accounted for 18 of the 35 Southern state executions.

Fines. Fines are a common form of punishment; virtually every sentence is likely to include a fine. However, an indigent offender can't be put in jail simply because of inability to pay a fine. (*Tate v. Short*, U.S. Sup. Ct. (1971).) As Justice Black wrote in the case of *Griffin v. Illinois* (U.S. Sup. Ct. (1956)), "There can be no equal justice where the kind of trial a man gets depends on the amount of money he has."

Restitution. Restitution is compensation that a judge orders an offender to pay to a victim. Courts order convicted defendants to pay restitution to a wide variety of victims, including individuals, businesses, charities, and government agencies. Restitution is in addition to any other punishment a court might order, such as imprisonment or a fine. Restitution orders have little value when a defendant has no assets or income.

Imprisonment: Misdemeanors, Felonies, and Wobblers. Punishment for misdemeanors may include confinement in a county jail for up to a year. Punishment for felonies usually carries confinement for more than a year in state prison. Some crimes are "wobblers," meaning that they are punishable as either a misdemeanor or a felony. In these cases, the sentence determines the category of crime. For example, if a defendant is convicted for burglary in a state in which burglary is a wobbler, and the judge sentences the defendant to nine months in county jail (rather than state prison), the conviction is for a misdemeanor.

Probation. Offenders are often placed on probation for a period of years, either in lieu of or following a period of incarceration. Probation may be "summary," in which case a probationer doesn't have to check in with a probation officer during the term of probation, or "supervised." Grants of probation come with conditions. Some conditions, such as "obey all laws" and "engage in at least 100 hours of community service," are standard. Others are offense-specific. For example, a condition for an offender on probation for spousal abuse may be "do not contact the victim." An offender who violates probation may be resentenced on the original charge that led to the grant of probation.

> EXAMPLE: Adam climbs a fence to eat an apple and pleads guilty to trespass. His punishment consists of a $100 fine and a year of summary probation. Six months later, Adam commits the same crime. The judge can revoke probation and resentence Adam on the original charge. Adam may also be convicted and punished for the second trespass offense.

Suspended Sentences. Suspended sentences often accompany grants of probation and indicate the length of time an offender has to serve if the offender violates probation or other court order.

> EXAMPLE: Art is convicted of spraying graffiti on public buildings. The judge sentences Art to 30 days in jail suspended, and orders Art to complete 100 hours of community service in cleanup campaigns within a year. If Art fails to complete his community service obligation, the judge can order his arrest and put him in jail for 30 days.

Mandatory Minimum Sentences. Legislatures may limit judges' discretion by requiring minimum sentences for specified convictions. For example, a DUI (Driving Under the Influence) law may provide that a defendant convicted of a second DUI within five years after a first offense has to serve at least ten days in jail. A judge might sentence a repeat offender to more than ten days in jail under this law, but not less.

In 1984 Congress passed the Federal Sentencing Guidelines in an effort to promote uniform sentences and to force federal judges

S

to "get tough on criminals." In the case of *United States v. Booker* (2005), the U.S. Supreme Court curtailed the Guidelines' influence by ruling that they were advisory, not mandatory.

Three Strikes Laws. These laws mandate lengthy prison sentences for convicted felons who have previously committed two or more serious or violent felonies.

Life Without Possibility of Parole (LWOP) and the Death Penalty. An LWOP sentence guarantees that an offender is never released from prison (except for the occasional "compassionate release" when death is imminent). Before the development of LWOP sentences, juries sometimes handed down death penalty verdicts because they feared that a murderer sentenced to life in prison would someday be paroled. LWOP provides judges and jurors with an alternative to a death sentence that protects communities.

 Real-Life Illustration

Jodi Arias was convicted in Arizona of murdering her former boyfriend, Travis Alexander. The details were lurid: Arias allegedly shot him in the head, stabbed him at least 20 times, and sliced his neck from ear to ear. Arias first told the police that she knew nothing about how Alexander had died, then later told them that intruders had killed him and wounded her. At trial she testified to a third story: Alexander had abused her and she killed him in self-defense. The jury quickly convicted her. During the sentencing hearing, Arias initially said that she wanted to be executed, but later asked the jury to spare her so as not to cause additional anguish to her family members. The jurors heard testimony from Alexander's family members about the immensity of their loss. The jury will decide whether to recommend that Arias be sentenced to death or life in prison without the possibility of parole.

Determinate and Indeterminate Sentences. Determinate sentences are for a fixed term, such as "90 days in county jail" or "Eight years in state prison." Indeterminate sentences indicate a minimum and a maximum term of imprisonment, such as "not less than three nor more than 14 years in prison." Indeterminate sentences require a second agency, such as a board of parole, to decide when release is appropriate. Factors that typically affect the length of confinement include the severity of a crime and an offender's behavior while in prison.

Consecutive and Concurrent Sentences. Offenders convicted of multiple crimes may be punished for each. For example, a defendant who was tried for a string of burglaries may wind up with a string of convictions and be sentenced separately for each conviction. If a judge orders the sentences to run concurrently, a defendant serves all of the sentences at the same time. If a judge orders the sentences to run consecutively, an offender must finish serving one sentence before beginning to serve a second sentence, and so on. When a defendant suffers multiple convictions for a single course of conduct involving one objective—for example, convictions for both simple assault and assault with a deadly weapon for the act of pointing a gun at one person—the sentences must generally run concurrently.

Diversion. Diversion programs, typically offered to first-time drug offenders, seek to promote rehabilitation by substituting education for incarceration. Diversion programs commonly offer an important carrot: upon completion of a program and probation, charges are dismissed and the offender's criminal record is cleaned.

> EXAMPLE: Kevin pleads guilty to possession of methamphetamine and is sentenced to complete a diversion program. If Kevin completes the required educational program and has no further arrests during the probation period, the case is dismissed. If asked by educational institutions or prospective employers or landlords whether he has ever been convicted of a crime, Kevin can answer, "No."

Sentencing Procedures. Sentencing is largely the responsibility of judges. However, judges can impose harsher punishment for "aggravating factors" (such as an offender's use of a gun to commit a crime) only if the jury finds beyond a reasonable doubt that those factors exist. (*Cunningham v. California*, U.S. Sup. Ct. (2007).) Judges often order probation officers to prepare reports and recommend sentences. Judges may also conduct sentencing hearings in which both sides can call witnesses to support their argument for a desired sentence. Defendants are entitled to legal representation at sentencing hearings.

What Is the Justification for Sentencing? Why does the state punish wrongdoers? This may seem like an academic question, but it has practical implications because it is sometimes at the heart of a judge's sentencing decision.

The "morality" of punishment can be viewed from two perspectives: utilitarianism and retributivism.

- **Utilitarianism.** Utilitarians focus on laws' consequences. For utilitarians, punishment exacts pain, not only for offenders but also for society. Society's pains include the costs of police forces, courts, and prisons. For utilitarians, punishment is morally justifiable if its benefits outweigh such costs. In this manner, imprisoning violent criminals is justifiable to the extent that the fear of punishment deters future violent crimes, including those that a punished offender might commit. At the same time, the death penalty is not justifiable if its added deterrent effect over and above a sentence of life in prison without possibility of parole does not outweigh the ultimate pain that it inflicts on offenders and the additional heavy costs that it imposes on society. Finally, prosecuting and incarcerating offenders who commit minor crimes is not morally justifiable if society can inflict less pain while deriving greater benefits from counseling and educating such offenders.

- **Retributivism.** Retributivists generally focus on "just deserts." Wrongdoers deserve to be punished according to the moral gravity of their misdeeds regardless of whether punishment deters others from committing crimes or produces other social benefits. Under this approach, if a victim of spousal abuse reports an incident and then later wants to drop the charges, her wishes are irrelevant. Someone who has physically abused the victim deserves to be punished. At the same time, the death penalty is justifiable if killers' actions are morally repugnant enough. The death penalty's ostensible deterrent effect and its costs are largely irrelevant to retributivists.

Neither utilitarians nor retributivists have carried the day; the U.S. criminal justice system reflects both perspectives. If nothing else, the criminal justice system's compromises and inconsistencies honor the contributions of virtually every moral legal philosopher who ever lived and ensure a continuing target for future moral philosophers.

Consider the Federal Sentencing Guidelines, adopted in 1987. The Guidelines were retributive, because they required judges to issue sentences that conformed to prescribed factors that determined the seriousness of every offense. In *U.S. v. Booker* (2005), the U.S. Supreme Court ruled that the sentences specified in the guidelines were advisory only; judges have the power to depart from them. By giving judges the discretion to issue sentences that take into account such factors as an offender's likelihood of rehabilitation, the *Booker* decision added utilitarian perspectives to the retributivist guidelines.

 Legal Authority Examples

California: Burglary in the first degree is punishable by imprisonment in state prison for two, four, or six years. Burglary in the second degree is punishable by imprisonment in the county jail not exceeding one year or in the state prison.

Texas: Possession of less than one gram of MDMA (an illegal drug) is a felony with a mandatory minimum of 180 days in county jail up to two years and a fine of up to $10,000. Punishment increases for higher amounts; possession of 400 grams or more of MDMA results in a mandatory five-year minimum and possible life imprisonment.

Related terms: death penalty; probation; expungement of criminal records; three strikes laws; restitution.

sequestration

At attorneys' requests, judges typically issue "sequestration orders" that require witnesses to remain outside a courtroom until after they have finished giving testimony, and to avoid discussing their testimony with other potential witnesses. Sequestration orders reduce the likelihood that witnesses will change their testimony to fit the stories of other witnesses. "Sequestration" may also refer to the practice of keeping juries away from the public in order to shield them from outside influences such as the media. Jury sequestration orders are rare.

sex offender

See convictions, consequences of.

sexual assault

See rape.

sheriff

Sheriffs are typically elected county officials who have a variety of legal and peace-keeping responsibilities. These duties include operating county jails, maintaining order in courtrooms, and serving legal papers on litigants. Sheriffs also provide police services in unincorporated county areas, and smaller municipalities often contract out police duties to sheriffs. Sheriffs in political hot water may also throw out the ceremonial first pitch at a baseball game.

Related terms: police officers; reeve.

shoplifting

Shoplifting is the popular name for a form of petty theft involving merchandise of relatively low value. Commonly, the theft of merchandise is petty theft when its value is less than $500, but dollar amounts can vary from state to state. Shoplifting is a misdemeanor that is punishable by a fine, confinement in jail for no more than a year, or both.

Petty Theft vs. Grand Theft. The same act that constitutes petty theft may be the more serious crime of grand theft if stolen merchandise is worth more than a state's petty theft threshold. Lack of knowledge as to the item's value is not a basis for categorizing a theft as petty or grand theft. So, if a shoplifter steals a pair of jeans, unaware that they are made by famous designer Fabrizio Della Over Prezzio, and are worth far more than $1,000, the shoplifter would be guilty of grand theft. Also, statutes in some states include theft of particular types of property (such as cars) as grand theft no matter what their monetary value. These statutes echo the laws in the Old West that regarded horse thievery as a particularly vile form of theft that often merited the death penalty.

Shoplifting Can Be Not-So-Petty Theft. Burglary is entering a building for the purpose of committing a crime. Thus, a prosecutor has the discretion to elevate an ordinary shoplifting case into burglary, a felony, if the prosecutor can prove that a shoplifter came into a store with the intent to steal merchandise. Also, if a defendant charged with shoplifting has been previously convicted of shoplifting, prosecutors in many states have discretion to charge the defendant with a felony popularly called "petty with a prior." Fortunately for most defendants, prosecutors often forgo the chance to lodge felony charges against defendants who have allegedly stolen merchandise of limited value.

Ability to Pay Is No Defense. Many shoplifters can afford to pay for the merchandise that they steal. But the ability to pay, or the offer to pay, once caught, will not serve as a defense. For example, in 2001, the financially successful movie actress Winona Ryder was convicted of grand theft for taking more than $5,000-worth of merchandise from Saks Fifth Avenue in Beverly Hills. (Ryder's sentence was a substantial fine, three years' probation, and hundreds of hours of community service.)

S

Potential Insecurity for Security Guards. With shoplifting somewhat low on the police priority list, many businesses employ private security guards. However, most states accord security guards only the same rights as any other citizen when it comes to making arrests. Security guards ordinarily cannot arrest suspected shoplifters and take them to jail. Instead, guards can detain them long enough for a police officer to arrive and arrest a suspect based on information provided by the guard.

Laws in all states generally protect police officers from being sued for false arrest so long as they have valid reasons for arresting suspects who turn out to be innocent. But these laws do not protect private citizens, including security guards. If a security guard makes a mistake and detains an innocent suspect, the detained individual may sue both the guard and the shop that employed the guard for damages in civil court.

 Legal Authority Examples

Pennsylvania: Pennsylvania's term for shoplifting is retail theft. Punishment for retail theft varies according to the value of stolen merchandise and a person's rap sheet. A first offense of retail theft of merchandise worth less than $150 is a summary offense rather than a misdemeanor, and the maximum penalty (undoubtedly rarely imposed) is 90 days in jail. If stolen merchandise is valued between $150 and $2,000, retail theft is a first degree misdemeanor punishable by up to five years in prison. If retail theft involves property worth in excess of $2,000, or if the stolen property is a car or a gun, or if a conviction is a culprit's third retail theft conviction, the crime is a third degree felony punishable by up to seven years in prison.

 RESOURCE

For information on how each state defines and punishes shoplifting and petty theft, go to www.nolo.com/shoplifting and www. nolo.com/pettytheft.

sobriety checkpoints

See search and seizure.

sodomy

Sodomy in the early common law era was a felony consisting of a variety of sexual practices that church leaders considered unnatural. To protect delicate minds from the sordid details of the illegal practices, sodomy was often vaguely referred to as "the infamous crime against nature." Generally, sodomy encompassed sexual activities such as inserting a penis into another's anus, oral-genital contact, and bestiality (sexual contact between people and animals).

The Infamous Crime of Selective Prosecution. In the United States, prosecutors and courts rarely applied sodomy laws to consensual sexual activities involving heterosexual adults. But, in Southern states, homosexual males were often targets of sodomy prosecutions, even if they were consenting adults. The U.S. Supreme Court ended these selective prosecutions with its decision in *Lawrence v. Texas* (2003). The Court ruled that sodomy laws could no longer be applied to consensual adult behavior because to do so would violate the right to liberty protected by the Fourteenth Amendment to the U.S. Constitution. Nonconsensual sodomy and sodomy involving a child remain enforceable felonies.

solicitation

Solicitation occurs when an offender invites, asks, or even commands another person to commit a crime, fully intending the crime to actually take place. The crime is complete at the moment of solicitation, regardless of whether the solicited person commits the solicited crime. Solicitation can be a misdemeanor or a felony, depending on the gravity of the solicited crime.

Specific Intent. Solicitation is a specific intent crime. This means that a person is guilty only if the solicitor intends a person to commit a crime. So, for example, a frustrated driver who screams, "I wish someone would blow up that traffic light," did not specifically intend for anyone to commit a crime. He didn't direct his request to a particular person, and the circumstances are more redolent of frustration than of actual criminal intent. Even if someone hears the driver's request and acts on it, destroying the traffic light, the driver is still not guilty of solicitation.

Accomplices. When a solicited crime takes place, the solicitor and the solicited offender are accomplices. As accomplices, they are equally guilty of the solicited crime. The crime of solicitation merges with the crime that took place, meaning that the solicitor is off the hook for the solicitation. So if a man offers $500 to a woman to steal a car, and the theft occurs, both are guilty of car theft. The man is not separately guilty of solicitation.

Closing the Barn Door After the Horse Escapes. After soliciting a crime, offenders may change their mind. They can escape punishment for solicitation if they fully renounce their intent for a crime to occur and succeed in preventing the solicited crime from occurring. Alas, if renunciation occurs too late to prevent the solicited crime from taking place, the solicitor's guilt remains.

 Legal Authority Examples

Alabama: A person is guilty of criminal solicitation if, with the intent that another person engage in conduct constituting a crime, he solicits, requests, commands, or importunes such other person to engage in such conduct. A person is not liable if, under circumstances manifesting a voluntary and complete renunciation of his criminal intent, he (1) notified the person solicited of his renunciation and (2) gave timely and adequate warning to the law enforcement authorities or otherwise made a substantial effort to prevent the commission of the criminal conduct solicited. Criminal solicitation is a Class A felony if the offense solicited is murder; a Class B felony if the offense solicited is a Class A felony; a Class A misdemeanor if the offense solicited is a Class C felony; and a Class B misdemeanor if the offense solicited is a Class A misdemeanor.

Related terms: accomplices and accessories; conspiracy; *mens rea*; sentencing (punishment options).

specific intent crimes

See mens rea.

speedy trial, right to

All parties to a criminal proceeding, including prosecutors, defendants, crime victims, witnesses, and even society as a whole, have an interest in the expeditious resolution of criminal cases. In most jurisdictions, three different sets of rules govern the timeliness of criminal prosecutions. They include a constitutional right to a speedy trial, a statutory right to a speedy trial, and statutes of limitations.

The Sixth Amendment. The Sixth Amendment to the U.S. Constitution provides for speedy trials. This does not mean that judges and lawyers have to talk really fast (although they may do so anyway). Instead, the amendment promotes fair trials and society's interest in effective punishment by establishing a policy that trials should take place while evidence is fresh and witnesses are available. The amendment also protects people against the unfair anxiety and loss of reputation that can occur when they carry the label of "accused criminal" for prolonged periods of time. Violation of defendants' constitutional right to a speedy trial typically results in permanent dismissal of criminal charges.

> EXAMPLE: Mae is an investment advisor. A grand jury indicts her for securities fraud, but the government neglects to arrest her for the crime until over two years later. Mae doesn't engage in any allegedly illegal conduct after her indictment. During the prolonged period when she was accused but proceedings were at a standstill, her client base and income disappeared. The judge grants Mae's motion to dismiss the case on the ground that the long and unjustified delay violated her speedy trial rights.

Start the Clock Ticking. The Sixth Amendment's clock does not start to tick until an individual becomes an "accused." As a general rule, an arrest or an unsealed grand jury indictment is the triggering event that turns an individual into an "accused." So if a prosecutor does not unseal (make public) an indictment for six months, at which point the suspect is arrested, the suspect became an "accused" for speedy trial purposes on the date of the arrest, not on the date the indictment was created by the grand jury.

Balancing Act. The Sixth Amendment contains no concrete time limits. As a result, judges generally balance the length of a delay, the reason for a delay, and prejudice to an accused when deciding whether to dismiss a case for violation of the constitutional right to a speedy trial.

 Real-Life Illustration

Doggett was arrested eight years after a grand jury indicted him for violating drug laws. Doggett was out of the country for the first two years. But for the last six years of the gap between indictment and arrest, he lived in the U.S. under his own name, was unaware of the indictment, and had not committed further violations. The extensive delay was presumptively prejudicial to Doggett's ability to defend himself and thus violated his speedy trial rights, even though the cause of the delay was the government's carelessness rather than its bad faith. (*Doggett v. U.S.*, U.S. Sup. Ct. (1992).)

Statutory Speedy Trial Rights. Many jurisdictions supplement the constitutional right to a speedy trial with statutes that establish precise time limits for bringing cases to trial. Typically, the clock on statutory speedy trial rights begins to tick only after an individual is formally charged in court. However, defendants are not entitled to dismissal if their own misconduct causes the delay. Moreover, dismissals based on a violation of a statutory speedy trial right are typically not final. Prosecutors can refile charges and start the clock ticking all over again.

Dismissal Granted: Stephanie is charged with petty theft for stealing cosmetics and pleads not guilty. The case is set for trial within the statutory time limit of 60 days. On the day set for trial, the prosecutor calls in sick and the judge continues the trial to a date that is beyond the statutory time limit. The judge grants Stephanie's motion to dismiss the case. However, the prosecutor's office can refile the charge.

Dismissal Not Granted: Stephanie fails to appear in court on the date that the case is originally set for trial. The judge issues a warrant for Stephanie's arrest, and she is not arrested and brought to court until after the statutory 60-day time limit expires. Stephanie is not entitled to dismissal of the petty theft case because her own unexcused absence caused the delay.

Justice Delayed Is Justice. Far from insisting on a speedy trial, defendants often seek to delay trials for as long as possible. Typically, defendants offer to "waive time for trial" to a date beyond statutory time limits in the hope that the extra time will allow for better preparation of a defense or more successful plea negotiations, and that the prosecutor or prosecution witnesses will lose their zeal for the case. However, speedy trial rights run in favor of prosecutors as well as defendants. Judges may refuse defendant's attempt to prolong a case when delay is likely to prejudice the prosecution.

 Real-Life Illustration

In 1995's infamous double murder trial of celebrity O.J. Simpson, the defense team surprised the prosecutors by insisting on a speedy trial. The early trial date limited the prosecutors' time to prepare for trial and may have contributed to the inept and confused presentation of evidence that many legal experts cited as a primary reason for Simpson's acquittal.

Statutes of Limitation. Virtually all crimes (murder being an exception) are subject to statutes of limitation, which fix time limits for charging alleged wrongdoers with crimes. Statute of limitations clocks start to tick on the date that crimes are committed. The expiration of a statute of limitations cuts off any possible prosecution.

> **EXAMPLE:** Police officers arrest Moore for an attempted rape that took place five years earlier. The jurisdiction's statute of limitations for attempted rape is four years. Moore cannot be charged with attempted rape. Though Moore did not become an "accused" until the date of his arrest, and though his statutory speedy trial rights were not violated, the expiration of the statute of limitations prevents his prosecution.

 Legal Authority Examples

Sixth Amendment to the U.S. Constitution: "In all criminal prosecutions, the accused shall enjoy the right to a speedy and public trial …"

California: A defendant charged with a felony who is not brought to trial within 60 days of arraignment is entitled to have the charge dismissed, unless the prosecution establishes good cause for the delay. Defendants can waive the 60-day time limit.

Related terms: arraignment; grand juries; statutes of limitations.

spousal privileges

In most jurisdictions, spouses have a right not to testify against each other. The privilege exists so long as the spouses are legally married at the time of trial, even if they were not married at the time the relevant events occurred. In most jurisdictions, the choice of whether to testify lies entirely with the subpoenaed spouse. A few jurisdictions give one spouse an independent power to prevent the other spouse from testifying, even if the other spouse wants to do so.

The spousal privileges are an exception to the general duty of all people with information relevant to a criminal charge to come to court and testify in response to a subpoena. The privileges reflect a Norman Rockwell-like philosophy that such values as "family harmony" and "the sanctity of the home" should trump the criminal justice system's desire to provide judges and jurors with all available evidence.

Spousal Privilege: Bonnie sees her husband Ramon toss a handgun down a trash chute. At Ramon's trial for attempted murder, the prosecutor subpoenas Bonnie to testify to what she saw. Bonnie has a spousal privilege and can refuse to testify against Ramon.

Spousal Privilege: Bonnie and Ramon were not married at the time that Bonnie saw Ramon toss the handgun down the trash chute. However, they are legally married by the time of trial. If the prosecutor subpoenas Bonnie to testify to what she saw, Bonnie has a spousal privilege and can refuse to testify against Ramon.

No Spousal Privilege: Bonnie and Ramon were married at the time that Bonnie saw Ramon toss the handgun down the trash chute. However, at the time of trial they are legally separated. If the prosecutor subpoenas Bonnie to testify to what she saw, she does not have a spousal privilege. The judge can hold Bonnie in contempt of court if she refuses to testify.

Waiver of Spousal Privilege: Bonnie and Ramon were married at the time that Bonnie saw Ramon toss the handgun down the trash chute and they remain husband and wife at the time of trial. Nevertheless, Bonnie can choose to waive (give up) the privilege and testify to what she saw. In a few jurisdictions, Ramon would have an independent right to claim the privilege and could prevent Bonnie from testifying against him.

Confidential Marital Communications: A separate privilege protects confidential marital communications from disclosure at trial. Generally, communications between a husband and wife are confidential if they talk to each other in a private setting in a manner that signals their intent to keep information to themselves. The privilege exists so long as the spouses were legally married at the time of communication, even if they are no longer married at the time of trial. Each spouse can prevent the other spouse from testifying to a confidential marital communication.

Confidential Marital Communication: Standing at the window of their home, Ramon sees his wife Bonnie quickly pull into the driveway of their home and hose off the car's front bumper. When she comes inside, Bonnie tells Ramon that "I think the guy I hit will be okay, but I had to get out of there." Bonnie and Ramon remain married at the time of Bonnie's trial for hit-and-run driving. The prosecutor subpoenas Ramon to testify to what he saw and heard. In most jurisdictions, Ramon alone has the power to waive the privilege not to testify and can testify to seeing Bonnie pull into the driveway and hose off the car's front bumper. However, Bonnie's statement to Ramon constitutes a confidential marital communication. Bonnie can exercise her legal right to protect that statement from disclosure at trial and prevent Ramon from testifying to it.

Confidential Marital Communication: Bonnie and Ramon are divorced at the time of Bonnie's trial for hit-and-run driving. Nevertheless, Bonnie's statement to Ramon constitutes a confidential marital communication because they were legally married at the time she spoke to him privately. Bonnie can prevent Ramon from testifying to her statement to him.

No Confidential Marital Communication: Ramon's friend Buck is chatting with Ramon when Bonnie comes into the house and says, "Sorry to interrupt you, Buck. Ramon, I think the guy I hit will be okay, but I had to get out of there." Buck's presence means that Bonnie's statement was not a private conversation between spouses. The privilege for confidential marital communications does not exist in this situation. Ramon (and of course Buck) can testify to what Bonnie said.

Same-Sex Couples. Spousal privilege rules are nearly everywhere limited to husbands and wives. Even states that allow same-sex couples to register as domestic partners generally do not extend spousal privileges to domestic partners. Spousal privileges probably extend to married same-sex couples in states that legitimize gay marriage. Also, federal courts apply the privilege rules of the states in which they are located and are therefore likely to extend the spousal privileges to same-sex couples who are legally married under state law.

 Legal Authority Examples

Tennessee: In criminal proceedings, confidential marital communications are privileged if confidentiality is essential to the full and satisfactory maintenance of the relation between the spouses and if the injury to the marital relationship by disclosure of the communications outweighs the benefit of a correct outcome of a trial. A confidential marital communication is inadmissible in evidence at trial if either spouse objects. The privilege does not exist in proceedings concerning spousal or child abuse.

Vermont: The spousal privileges are available to same-sex couples in civil unions or marriages.

Related terms: attorney-client privilege; privileges.

stalking

Stalking consists of engaging in a course of conduct that typically includes intentionally and repeatedly following, watching, contacting, or threatening a victim in circumstances that reasonably lead the victim to experience fear or psychological distress. The federal Interstate Stalking Punishment and Prevention Act of 1996 punishes stalkers who cross state lines to commit their crimes. Stalking can be either a misdemeanor or a felony depending on the severity and extent of the incidents. Conviction of stalking typically entails an order to cease the behavior, which if violated is itself a crime.

 Real-Life Illustration

John Hinckley, Jr., who attempted to assassinate President Ronald Reagan in 1981, was a multiple stalker. In 1980 he enrolled in a Yale University writing course so that he could be close to famous actress Jodie Foster. Hinckley repeatedly sent letters and poems to Foster, describing his obsessive devotion to her. Hinckley then turned his attention to President Jimmy Carter, appearing at many of Carter's public appearances. Hinckley later began stalking President Reagan, finally shooting him and others nearby in Washington, DC, in March of 1981. Hinckley was charged with a variety of crimes, was found not guilty by reason of insanity (which led to a change in the federal insanity laws), and was committed to a mental institution.

Historical Antecedents. Unlike many traditional crimes that date back at least to Biblical days, stalking is a new legal concept. Most states did not criminalize stalking until after California enacted the first antistalking statute in 1990. By that time police and mental health professionals had recognized that stalking was destructive to victims and often the precursor to violent physical attacks.

Cyber-Stalking. Cyber-stalkers conduct their obsessive behavior electronically instead of (and sometimes in addition to) in person. Cyber-stalkers, who often are pedophiles, send repeated messages to victims. The messages tend to increase in intensity over time, and cyber-stalkers often eventually demand to meet personally with victims.

> EXAMPLE: Joe is angry at his colleague Maggie because their company promoted Maggie and not Joe to a supervisorial position. Joe sends a series of email messages to Maggie, accusing her and her friends of sabotaging his chances of promotion with lies, and making threats along the lines of "We'll see how long you last around here" and "I'd be careful getting into my car if I were you." Sometimes Joe forwards news articles to Maggie describing incidents of workplace violence. Joe's messages to Maggie often include a final note along the lines of "Only kidding, just keeping you on your toes." For her part, Maggie fears that Joe might be serious, and she sometimes responds to his messages by telling Joe not to contact her directly. Joe's behavior constitutes cyber-stalking. Joe knew that his messages scared Maggie but he nevertheless continued to send them.

Protective Orders. Before the filing of criminal charges, stalking victims often try to stop the stalking behavior by going to court and obtaining a civil protective order. Protective orders, however, are often ineffective and sometimes incite stalkers to ramp up their obsessive acts. A stalking victim need not obtain a protective order before initiating criminal charges by reporting a stalker's actions to the police.

 Legal Authority Examples

California: Stalking consists of intentionally and repeatedly following or harassing another person and making a credible threat with the intent to place that person in reasonable fear of their safety or the safety of their family, whether in person or electronically. Simple stalking can be charged as either a felony or misdemeanor and as a misdemeanor is punishable by up to a year in jail and fines of up to $1,000.

status offenses

See disorderly conduct.

statutes of limitations

Statutes of limitations establish time limits for charging defendants with crimes. The statutory time limits reflect several legal principles, including the Sixth Amendment guarantee of speedy trials for criminal defendants, as well as the desire to proceed with prosecutions while memories are fresh and evidence and witnesses are still available.

When attorneys think about clocks, often they conjure up visions of billable hours. But attorneys may also think about clocks in the context of statutes of limitations. An attorney's statement that "the clock is running" means that an act has occurred that has triggered an applicable statute of limitations. "The clock has been tolled" means that the calculation of the time period cannot begin or has been temporarily stopped due to some condition—for example, a crime perpetrator fleeing the jurisdiction.

 Real-Life Illustration

Sara Jane Olsen, formerly Kathleen Soliah, was wanted for attempting to murder Los Angeles police officers in 1976 by planting bombs under their police cars. Olsen fled California for Minnesota, began a new life, and evaded capture for 23 years. She was arrested in 1999 and charged with various felonies, including attempted murder. Olsen pleaded guilty to a reduced charge in 2001. The charges were not barred by the applicable California statute of limitations because the clock did not run (was "tolled") while Olsen was living in Minnesota.

Dismissal Following Expiration. When the police charge a defendant with a crime after the statute of limitations has expired, the defendant can have the charges dismissed.

Statute of Limitations Has Expired: Stan, a patron at a sporting event, reports an assault by Lee to the police before leaving the stadium. The police interview Lee, but Lee hears nothing further until more than two years go by. Lee then receives a citation indicating that he is charged with misdemeanor assault and ordering him to report to court for arraignment on or before the date set forth in the citation. If the state's statute of limitations for charging defendants with misdemeanors is two years, a judge must grant Lee's petition to dismiss the charges.

Statute of Limitations Has Expired: Stan, a patron at a sporting event, is assaulted by Lee before leaving the stadium. Stan does not immediately report the assault to the police. Instead, he tries to obtain an apology from Lee during a series of meetings. When more than two years have gone by and Lee has steadfastly refused to apologize, Stan reports the assault to the police. The prosecutor charges Lee with misdemeanor assault the very next day. Again, if the state's statute of limitations for charging defendants with misdemeanors is two years, a judge must grant Lee's motion to dismiss the charges. Even though the police and prosecutors knew nothing about the claimed assault, more than two years elapsed between the time the crime occurred and the time that Lee was charged with it.

Why Hurry? According to a popular phrase, "Justice delayed is justice denied." The phrase suggests that statutes of limitations protect both prosecutors and defendants by providing some assurance that witnesses and documents needed to prosecute or defend charges are available. Nevertheless, defense attorneys sometimes advise clients to "waive time" and agree to postponements of trials. The thinking is that more time means better preparation (including investigation) and better odds at a favorable plea bargain.

Counting the Days. The clock normally starts ticking on time limits set forth in statutes of limitations on the date that a crime takes place, and normally stops ticking on the date that the defendant is charged. However, when crimes unfold over periods of days, months, or even years, prosecutors and defense attorneys often put forth conflicting positions to judges about when clocks start and stop.

> **EXAMPLE:** Four members of a local gang are charged with conspiring to rob and robbing 15 banks over a period of the last 15 years. Relying on the jurisdiction's six-year statute of limitations for serious felony offenses, the defense attorneys petition for dismissal of charges for the nine oldest robberies. The prosecutor responds that the individual robberies were all part of a single conspiracy by gang members to support themselves by robbing banks, and that since the conspiracy continued until their arrest for robbery No. 15, the statute of limitations has not expired.

Murder. Murder is the only criminal charge that is nowhere subject to a statute of limitations. Statutory time limits for other crimes vary from one state to another. In general, the more serious a criminal charge, the longer a limitations period is likely to be.

Speak Now or Forever Lose Your Defense. A claim that the statute of limitations has expired is an affirmative defense. This means that judges do not take it upon themselves to review cases for possible limitations problems and dismiss charges when they detect violations. Instead, defendants have to protect themselves by petitioning for dismissal based on a violation of a statute of limitations.

 Legal Authority Examples

Excerpt, Sixth Amendment: "In all criminal prosecutions, the accused shall enjoy the right to a speedy and public trial."

Illinois: No statute of limitations exists for a variety of serious felonies, including first and second degree murder, reckless homicide, arson, forgery, or offenses involving sexual conduct, so long as the victim died or reported the crime to the police within two years of its occurrence. For other offenses, the statute of limitations is three years for felonies and 18 months for misdemeanors.

Florida: No statute of limitations exists for the crimes of murder, perjury in capital prosecutions, or any felony punishable by death or life imprisonment. For most felonies, the statute of limitations is three years. The statute of limitations for misdemeanors is two years for first degree misdemeanors and one year for second degree misdemeanors. For sexual offenses, a statute of limitations begins to run when a victim either reports a crime or becomes 16 years old, whichever is earlier.

Related terms: affirmative defenses; speedy trial, right to.

statutory rape

Statutory rape consists of sexual intercourse in which one of the parties is a minor under a state's age-of-consent law. A common age of consent is 18, but the definitions vary from state to state, with the definition and seriousness of the offense often dependent not only on the participants' ages but also on the age difference between the participants. Statutory rape is a nonviolent form of unlawful sexual intercourse in which an underage minor's outward consent to intercourse is irrelevant because underage minors cannot legally give consent. Other common labels for unlawful sexual contact with a minor include sexual assault of a minor, sexual abuse of a minor, and contributing to the delinquency of a minor. Statutory rape can be either a misdemeanor or a felony.

Strict Liability vs. *Mens Rea*. Some states regard statutory rape as a crime requiring *mens rea*, and criminalize consensual sexual intercourse with a minor only if the other participant knows or reasonably should have known that the minor was too young to give consent. Other states regard statutory rape as a strict liability crime, punishing sex with a minor no matter the wrongdoer's knowledge.

> EXAMPLE: Maria is a dancer in a strip club in which a sign advises patrons that "all performers are over the age of 18." Juan meets Maria for the first time after she finishes a performance, and after she assures him that she is over the age of 18, they engage in consensual sexual intercourse. Juan is not guilty of statutory rape in some states even if it turns out that Maria is under the age of 18 because he reasonably believed that she was old enough to give legal consent. In states in which sexual intercourse with a minor remains a strict liability offense, Juan would be guilty of statutory rape regardless of his reasonable belief that Maria was an adult.

Teenager Loves Teenager. Technically, two underage teenagers who engage in consensual sexual intercourse can both be guilty of statutory rape. Luckily for our already-overcrowded jails, such situations are far more likely to fall within the purview of angry or uncertain parents than letter-of-the-law prosecutors. Some states minimize the chance that teenage love will turn into a crime by providing that statutory rape is a crime only if the difference in age between the participants is at least two or three years.

The Male Perspective. For many years, statutory rape laws applied only to men. The laws reflected the common image of older male Lotharios who seduced underage and vulnerable females into sexual intercourse. Modern statutory rape laws are gender-neutral, making women the equal of men when it comes to the possibility of conviction of statutory rape.

 Real-Life Illustration

Washington State elementary school teacher Mary Kay Letourneau was the defendant in one of the country's most notorious older female/younger male statutory rape cases. LeTourneau pleaded guilty to raping her student

Vili Fualaau; the relationship began when Fualaau was 12 years old. When she pleaded guilty in 1997, Fualaau had fathered a child by LeTourneau and she was pregnant with his second child. After LeTourneau was released from prison, the couple married in 2004.

Registration as a Sex Offender. Whether an offender convicted of a statutory rape offense has to register with the police as a sex offender varies from one state to another and often according to the nature of the offense. For example, in California a conviction of sexual intercourse with a minor does not require the wrongdoer to register as a sex offender if the crime was punished as a misdemeanor, but does require registration if the crime was punished as a felony.

 Legal Authority Examples

California: Sexual intercourse between a person under age 18 and another person who is not more than three years younger or older is a misdemeanor punishable by confinement in jail for up to one year. If sexual intercourse occurs between a person under age 18 and a person more than three years older, the older person is guilty of either a misdemeanor or a felony.

Pennsylvania: Sexual intercourse with a person under the age of 13 is a felony punishable by imprisonment of up to 20 years.

New York: Sexual intercourse between anyone age 21 and older and someone younger than age 17 constitutes third degree rape that is punishable by imprisonment for up to four years.

 RESOURCE

For information on how each state defines and punishes statutory rape, including whether the state recognizes "reasonable mistake of age" as a defense, go to www.nolo.com/statutoryrape.

Related terms: rape; strict liability crimes; *mens rea*.

stop and frisk

Police officers who reasonably suspect that an individual may be guilty of a crime can temporarily detain and question the individual. Moreover, if they reasonably suspect that the detainee is armed and dangerous, they can frisk (pat down) that person. The combination of this limited detention and search for purposes of guaranteeing public safety is known as a "stop and frisk."

Reasonable Suspicion and the Origins of Stop and Frisk. Fourth Amendment doctrine establishes "probable cause" as the threshold of information that police officers need to make arrests, conduct warrantless searches, and obtain search warrants. But effective investigation of crime requires that they have the power to question individuals even when they lack probable cause to believe that an individual has done anything wrong. In the case of *Terry v. Ohio* (1968), the U.S. Supreme Court interpreted the Fourth Amendment in a way that allows police officers who lack probable cause to detain individuals while protecting themselves from attack.

With *Terry v. Ohio*, the Court threw three substitutes into the Fourth Amendment game. The substitutes were these:

- A lesser threshold of "reasonable suspicion" replaced the higher threshold of probable cause.
- A lesser level of intrusiveness called a "detention" replaced the higher level of intrusiveness of an arrest.
- A lesser level of invasiveness called a frisk or a pat-down replaced the higher level of invasiveness of a search.

The upshot of these substitutions is that police officers who reasonably suspect that an individual is guilty of a crime can detain and question the individual. Moreover, police officers can protect themselves by frisking detained individuals who are potentially dangerous for weapons. To satisfy judges that they reasonably suspected an individual of criminal involvement, police officers have to identify "specific and articulable facts" in support of their suspicion.

Invalid Stop: Lack of Concrete Facts. A police officer testifies that he pulled over a car driven by Russell because "Russell just looked like a troublemaker to me." The detention is invalid because the police officer didn't identify concrete facts that reasonably suggested that Russell had committed a crime. As a result, any search that the police officer carried out following the stop would also be invalid.

Valid Stop and Frisk: Reasonable Suspicion. A police officer has information from an anonymous tipster that drivers in a particular neighborhood where drug deals often take place signal their desire to purchase illegal drugs at night by driving slowly with their lights off. Patrolling in the neighborhood, the police officer testifies that he observed Russell, who was driving slowly with lights turned off, pull over to the curb, engage in a brief meeting with a known drug dealer, and drive away quickly. The police officer pulled the car over and questioned Russell. The detention is valid because concrete facts allowed the police officer to reasonably suspect that Russell possessed illegal drugs. The anonymous tip is hearsay, but hearsay information can support a police officer's reasonable suspicion.

"It Felt Like a Weapon to Me." Once police officers detain individuals, officers can protect themselves by conducting a brief search for weapons called a frisk or a pat-down. If a frisk reveals an object that an officer reasonably believes is a weapon, the officer has the power to seize it. The seized object is admissible in evidence even if it turns out to be something other than a weapon.

Valid Stop and Frisk: Possible Weapon. After a police officer detains Russell (see the previous example above), Russell refuses to obey the police officer's command to keep both hands on the steering wheel, where the officer can see them. Fearful that Russell might reach for a weapon, the officer orders Russell out of the car and pats down his clothing. The officer feels a long flat object resembling a knife in Russell's rear pants pocket. The

S

officer removes the object, which turns out to be a hard plastic container filled with illegal drugs. The police officer's reasonable fear that Russell was dangerous justified the pat-down search. The object's resemblance to a knife justified the police officer's removing it from Russell's pocket. As a result, the frisk and the seizure of the object were valid and the container of drugs is admissible in evidence.

Invalid Stop and Frisk: No Danger. In the previous example assume that the police officer testifies that he thought that the object in Russell's rear pants pocket was a key. Nevertheless, the police officer seized it because he had a hunch that the key might unlock a box in the car's trunk containing contraband or evidence of a crime. The police officer ordered Russell to open the trunk, and found burglary tools inside. The police officer then arrested Russell for possession of the burglary tools. The arrest is invalid and the tools are not admissible in evidence. The police officer had no right to remove the key from Russell's pocket because there was no reason to believe it was a weapon. Moreover, since the police officer had no articulable facts giving rise to a reasonable suspicion that the trunk contained contraband or evidence of a crime, the trunk search was illegal.

Racial Profiling. The confrontations between police officers and individuals who may have done nothing wrong are at the heart of the racial profiling controversy. Racial profiling refers to the charge that police officers are prone to detaining individuals for no reason other than discriminatory beliefs that the individuals belong to racial groups whose members have a propensity to commit crimes. Racial profiling is illegal if a police officer substitutes group-based assumptions for situation-specific circumstances giving rise to a reasonable suspicion that a particular individual is engaged in criminal activity. Perhaps Chief Justice Warren anticipated the racial profiling controversy when he wrote in *Terry v. Ohio*, "We would be less than candid if we did not acknowledge that this case thrusts to the fore difficult and troublesome issues regarding a sensitive area of police activity."

For example, one of the most common forms of alleged racial profiling is called DWB which refers to "driving while black (or brown)." The charge is that police officers are far more likely to stop and investigate drivers of color, especially if they happen to drive an expensive car in an upscale neighborhood. Political leaders decry racial profiling and police chiefs tend to deny its existence. Members of minority groups have provided numerous accounts of unjustified police stops, but the actual extent of racial profiling is unknown.

 Legal Authority Examples

Fourth Amendment. "The right of the people to be secure in their persons, houses, papers, and effects, against unreasonable searches and seizures, shall not be violated, and no Warrants shall issue, but upon probable cause, supported by Oath or affirmation, and particularly describing the place to be searched, and the persons or things to be seized."

Related terms: search and seizure; *Terry* searches; warrantless searches; probable cause.

strict liability crimes

Strict liability crimes are those in which people are punished for their actions regardless of their intent, purpose, or knowledge. The notion underlying strict liability crimes is that society's interest in deterring and punishing certain actions sometimes outweighs the policy that people are deserving of punishment only if they act with *mens rea* and are therefore morally blameworthy. The punishment for committing a strict liability crime is usually a fine rather than confinement, and states often define strict liability offenses as infractions or regulatory violations rather than misdemeanors.

S

Retreating From Strict Liability. Based on an evolving belief that strict liability laws may unfairly punish morally innocent people, the number of strict liability offenses has diminished in recent years. Especially when criminal laws impose substantial fines and the possibility of imprisonment, conviction usually requires proof of *mens rea*. For example, a federal law makes it illegal to transport films depicting minors engaged in sexual conduct across state lines. People are guilty of violating the law only if they know or reasonably should have known that the performers engaged in the sexual conduct were minors. See *U.S. v. X-Citement Video* (U.S. Sup. Ct. (1994)).

Statutory Rape. Statutory rape is a strict liability crime in many states, meaning that anyone who engages in sexual intercourse with a minor is guilty of it. Some states, including California, don't follow this rule; instead, they provide that defendants aren't guilty if they reasonably believe that an underage sexual partner is old enough to legally consent.

Drug Offenses. Many drug offenses were formerly strict liability crimes, in that people who possessed or sold illegal drugs were guilty regardless of their knowledge of a substance's content. That policy has been abandoned and guilt requires proof that a wrongdoer "knows or reasonably should know" that a substance is an illegal drug.

EXAMPLE: Mary is charged with possession of an illegal quantity of marijuana. She concedes that the baggie she had in her purse contained marijuana, but claims that she thought the drug was an ordinary herb that a colleague at work gave her because it was delicious in omelets. Mary is not guilty unless the prosecution proves that she knew or reasonably should have known that the baggie contained marijuana.

 Legal Authority Examples

Texas. The negligent sale of tobacco products to someone younger than 18 years old is a Class C misdemeanor. A seller is not guilty if the person to whom the tobacco product was sold presented apparently valid proof of identification to the seller. A Class C misdemeanor is punishable by a fine not to exceed $500.

Related terms: *mens rea*; statutory rape.

strikes

See three strikes laws.

suspended sentence

See sentencing (punishment options).

syndrome evidence

Syndromes are groupings of posttraumatic stress reactions that victims of certain types of violent crime tend to experience. Forensic experts may provide syndrome evidence when criminal charges involve child sexual abuse and female survivors of rape and domestic violence, as those are the primary contexts that have been studied by medical and psychological researchers.

Limited Admissibility. Disagreements exist about the reliability of syndrome evidence for distinguishing crime victims from non-victims. Thus, some judges may not admit syndrome evidence at all. Judges who do admit it generally do not allow prosecutors to offer it as proof that a defendant committed a charged crime. Instead, judges almost always limit its admissibility to preventing jurors from deciding cases based on mistaken beliefs about the common behavior and psychological conditions of victims of previous abuse. For example, in a domestic violence case, a prosecutor would be barred from offering evidence from a battered woman syndrome expert that a husband was abusive to his wife. However, if the husband claims that the wife would have moved out of the home had he been abusive, the judge might allow the prosecutor to call a battered woman syndrome expert to explain why the wife may have stayed with the husband even though he was abusing her.

S

Child Sexual Abuse Accommodation Syndrome. The child sexual abuse accommodation syndrome resulted from research into the behavior and psychological condition of children who were sexually abused over a period of time. The syndrome includes the following potential reactions:

- Children do not report the sexual abuse to others.
- Children feel so helpless and trapped that they accommodate to an abuser's demands.
- When abused children do report abuse, their claims are usually long-delayed and unconvincing.
- Children retract their abuse claims.

EXAMPLE: Abe is charged with continual sexual abuse of his six-year-old stepdaughter Penny. Abe's lawyer claims that Penny's delayed reporting and ultimate retraction of the abuse claim, and the loving attitude that Penny displayed toward Abe during family outings, proves that Abe never sexually abused Penny. The prosecutor responds by calling a forensic expert to testify that children who are sexually abused over a period of weeks or months often suffer from posttraumatic stress and as a result behave in a fashion very similar to Penny. However, the forensic expert cannot testify, "Based on Penny's reactions, my opinion is that Penny was sexually abused." And the prosecutor cannot tell the jurors during closing argument, "The expert testimony establishes that Abe is guilty of sexually abusing Penny." But the prosecutor can properly argue, "The expert testimony demonstrates that Penny's behavior is in no way inconsistent with her having been subjected to weeks of sexual abuse by Abe."

Rape Trauma Syndrome. Rape trauma syndrome experts testify to the posttraumatic stress reactions that rape survivors tend to experience. Common reactions include depression, anxiety, relationship problems, health problems, and substance abuse. Rape trauma syndrome evidence is typically only admissible in rape trials when a defendant claims that a rape complainant consented to sexual intercourse. As with other forms of syndrome evidence, rape trauma syndrome testimony is not admissible to prove that a rape took place. Instead, the admissibility of the syndrome evidence is limited to countering a defendant's claim that a rape complainant's behavior is inconsistent with her having been raped. So, for example, rape trauma syndrome evidence is not admissible when a defendant in a rape case offers an alibi defense. On the other hand, if a defendant tries to cast doubt on the rape claim by offering evidence that the victim didn't go to the police until two days after the alleged rape, a prosecutor can call a forensic expert to testify that as a result of experiencing rape trauma syndrome, rape survivors often delay reporting what happened to them.

Battered Woman Syndrome. Battered woman syndrome testimony is most often offered into evidence by women who are charged with murdering their abusers, to show that they acted in self-defense. As a result of long-term abuse, women who suffer from battered woman syndrome often believe themselves to be physically and economically trapped by their abusers, and they become hypervigilant to signals indicating incipient abuse. Thus, abused women may perceive the need to resort to deadly force to save their lives in situations in which nonabused women would not.

> EXAMPLE: Marta is charged with murdering her live-in boyfriend Stewart. Marta claims that she shot and killed Stewart in self-defense. Stewart had not begun to attack Marta at the time of the shooting. However, Stewart had often threatened to kill Marta if she ever tried to leave him. On the day of the killing, Stewart came home drunk. When he saw that Marta had packed a suitcase, he started cursing at her in a way that preceded many other violent attacks. Testimony from a battered woman syndrome expert can explain why under the circumstances, Marta reasonably believed that she needed to kill Stewart to save her own life.

Real-Life Illustration

In a 1995 criminal trial that was watched live by millions of people around the world every day, former football star and actor O.J. Simpson was charged with brutally murdering his ex-wife Nicole Brown Simpson and her companion, Ron Goldman. The prosecution offered evidence that Simpson had repeatedly abused Nicole. During his opening statement, lead defense lawyer Johnnie Cochran promised the jurors that he would call Lenore Walker, the researcher who developed the concept of battered woman syndrome, as a defense expert witness. Cochran told the jurors that Walker would testify that Nicole had not displayed symptoms consistent with spousal abuse before her death, and that therefore Simpson had not abused her. Despite Cochran's promise, Simpson's defense team never called Walker to testify. Nevertheless, the jury found Simpson not guilty. (In a subsequent civil trial, a second jury decided that Simpson had murdered Nicole and Goldman, and awarded huge damages to their survivors.)

 Legal Authority Examples

California Evidence Code: In criminal cases, expert testimony regarding intimate partner battering (battered woman syndrome) and its effects, including how it affects a victim's beliefs and perceptions, is admissible. However, the testimony cannot be offered to prove that a defendant charged with spousal abuse committed the crime.

Kansas: Rape trauma syndrome evidence is admissible when a defendant charged with rape claims that a rape complainant's behavior demonstrates that she consented to sexual intercourse. (*Hauser v. Lowe* (1996))

Related terms: abuse excuse; child sexual assault; rape; alibi; self-defense; forensic science.

terrorism

Terrorism encompasses crimes of violence that are carried out in ways that are likely to cause indiscriminate injury and widespread fear. While acts of terrorism typically violate the laws of the state in which they occur, they also violate federal laws. This means that the far greater resources of the federal government are involved in the apprehension and prosecution of the perpetrators. People who carry out (or conspire or attempt to carry out) acts of terrorism are subject to increased punishment, up to and including the death penalty.

While no single definition of terrorism exists, terrorist crimes typically have one or more of these elements:

- Use of a weapon of mass destruction, such as an explosive device.
- Targeting government representatives or government property.
- Using or interfering with means of interstate commerce, such as the mail system or railroad lines.
- Causing serious injury or death, or the risk of such injury or death.

EXAMPLE: Fred Letterday sends ricin-laced letters to legislators in a number of states who have voted for laws that he disagrees with. Ricin is a potentially deadly powder, and Fred hopes that legislators will open his letters and be killed or seriously injured. Fortunately, postal officials intercept the letters before they can be opened. Nobody is hurt. Fred's actions constitute a federal terrorism offense because he used the mails in an attempt to seriously injure or kill government officials.

Real-Life Illustration

In 2013, brothers Tamerlan and Dzhokhar Tsarnaev allegedly set off homemade explosive devices near the finish line of the Boston Marathon. Three spectators were killed and over 250 people suffered severe injuries, including the loss of limbs. Tamerlan was killed during a gunfight with police officers. Dzhokhar was captured and charged with crimes of terrorism, which are punishable by death.

 Legal Authority Examples

18 United States Code § 2332a: A perpetrator who (using or affecting a means of interstate commerce) illegally "uses, threatens, or attempts or conspires to use a weapon of mass destruction" against any person inside the United States, or against a U.S. national who is out of the country, can be imprisoned for up to life and if a victim dies, is subject to the death penalty. Use of a weapon of mass destruction against property owned by the federal government, wherever in the world it is located, also constitutes terrorism and is punishable by imprisonment for up to life or, if a victim dies, by death.

terrorist threats (criminal threats)

People often associate the word "terrorism" with seemingly random acts of violence inspired by religious or political beliefs. But the term "terrorist (or criminal) threat" can apply to all kinds of threats, verbal or physical, express or implied. If a defendant makes a threat in a way that places a victim in reasonable fear of injury and the defendant intends to create that fear, the crime is complete regardless of whether the defendant actually intends to carry out the threat.

> EXAMPLE: Rosencrantz tells Guildenstern, "I'm done participating in your illegal schemes; I'm going to come clean to

the cops." Guildenstern pulls out a gun and replies, "One word from you to the cops and you're a dead man." Guildenstern's response constitutes a terrorist threat.

EXAMPLE: In the same circumstances, Guildenstern responds to Rosencrantz by saying, "If you do that, someday you'll pay." This response is too vague to constitute a terrorist threat.

EXAMPLE: Walking home with his buddy Guildenstern, Rosencrantz cries out when he sees that his front yard has been covered with toilet paper. When Guildenstern laughs hysterically, Rosencrantz says, "Darn you Guildenstern. I could kill you for this." Rosencrantz's remark wasn't intended to and, given the circumstances, wouldn't reasonably cause Guildenstern to fear harm. Thus, no terrorist threat has occurred.

Terry searches

The U.S. Supreme Court case of *Terry v. Ohio* (1968) allows a police officer to detain someone if the officer "reasonably suspects" that the person is involved in criminal activity. The officer can also frisk the person if there is reason to believe that the person is armed and dangerous. The purpose of the "stop and frisk" process is to allow police officers to conduct brief investigations safely, even if they lack probable cause to conduct a full search or make an arrest.

Related terms: search and seizure; stop and frisk.

theft

The following table lists, defines, and classifies common theft crimes. For information about a particular offense, see the corresponding term in this book.

Theft Crimes		
Crime	**Definition**	**Type of Crime**
Shoplifting	Taking merchandise with a value lower than a statutory amount, often less than $500	Misdemeanor
Petty Larceny	Taking the property of another with a value lower than a statutory amount, often less than $500	Misdemeanor
Grand Larceny	Taking the property of another with a value in excess of a statutory amount, often more than $500	Felony
Burglary	Unauthorized entry into a building with the intent to commit a crime	Felony
Robbery	Taking property from another person by means of force or fear	Felony
Fraud	Making false representations to take possession of or title to the property of another person	Misdemeanor or Felony, depending on the value of the property
Identity Theft (Identity Fraud)	Stealing a victim's personal identifying information in order to acquire property	Felony

three strikes laws

Three strikes laws, also called habitual offender laws, increase prison sentences for repeat offenders who have been convicted of committing serious felonies. The most publicized case that led to the enactment of these laws was the brutal 1993 California murder of 12-year-old Polly Klaas by Richard Allen Davis. Davis was a sex offender with a long history of criminal convictions, yet was free on parole when he murdered Klaas.

Bawls and Strikes. The details of three strikes laws vary from one state to another. Most states' laws identify the felonies that can

374

constitute the first two strikes. In general, these felonies involve either violence or serious harm. In states that have enacted three strikes laws, defendants with two of the enumerated serious felonies on their record who suffer a third conviction may be given a far lengthier sentence than the conviction would otherwise produce. In some states, a third strike must itself be a conviction for a serious or violent felony. In other states, a conviction for any felony can constitute the third strike. Prosecutors generally have discretion over whether to seek a third strike sentence.

 Real-Life Illustration

Andrade was convicted of petty theft for stealing less than $50 worth of video equipment from a retailer. The conviction is a felony under state law because Andrade had previously been convicted of petty theft. Prior to the petty theft conviction, Andrade had been convicted of two crimes that constitute strikes under the state's three strikes law. Under that law, Andrade was sentenced to 25 years to life in prison for the theft of the videotapes. The sentence did not violate the Eighth Amendment's prohibition of cruel and unusual punishment. (*Lockyer v. Andrade*, U.S. Sup. Ct. (2003).)

Forms of Strikes. Convictions for serious felonies in one state can constitute strikes for purposes of another state's three strikes law. Conviction for juvenile offenses can also qualify as strikes, sometimes even if a judge has ordered the offenses sealed. For example, if a defendant has committed two serious felonies in Maine, a state that does not have a three strikes law, and then commits a third serious felony in Washington, a state with a three strikes law, the Washington prosecutor has discretion to seek a third strike sentence.

Most Unfair Three Strikes Sentence Ever? Three strikes sentences remain controversial because they may result in low-level criminals receiving harsher punishment than convicted murderers. Consider the example of Gregory Taylor, a homeless individual who was convicted of attempting to break into a church's food pantry to steal food. Taylor had previously been convicted of purse snatching and attempted theft of a wallet, two offenses that constituted strikes under the state's three strikes law. Taylor was given a third strike sentence of 25 years to life for stealing food from the church. After Taylor had begun serving the sentence, a judge later set it aside and ordered Taylor's release.

Risks and Benefits. By targeting offenders with a past history of serious or dangerous crimes, three strikes laws are designed to protect society by incarcerating potentially dangerous people for longer periods, and sometimes for life. A potential disadvantage is that indiscriminate use of three strikes laws results in lengthy warehousing in prisons at great expense of people who pose little risk of serious harm.

 Legal Authority Examples

Federal Law: Conviction of a serious violent federal felony constitutes a third strike that carries a mandatory sentence of life in prison without possibility of parole if an offender has (1) previously been convicted of two or more prior serious violent federal or state felonies or (2) previously been convicted of one or more serious violent federal or state felonies and one or more serious drug-related federal or state felony.

California: A third strike is a felony conviction incurred by anyone who has previously been convicted of two or more specified serious or dangerous felonies. Violent felonies include murder or manslaughter, rape, mayhem, continuous sexual abuse of a child, and the commission of any felony in which a gun was used or which resulted in great bodily injury. Serious felonies include robbery, kidnapping, arson, burglary of an inhabited dwelling, and aggravated assault. A third strike is punishable by 25 years to life in prison.

Related terms: sentencing (punishment options).

time served

This refers to punishment that is limited to the time in jail that a convicted defendant has already served. (To paraphrase author Lewis Carroll in *Alice in Wonderland*, "first comes the punishment, then comes the conviction.") Time served is a typical sentence for defendants who spend a night or two in jail and then plead guilty to a low-level misdemeanor such as "drunk in public" or "malicious mischief."

Related terms: sentencing (punishment options).

tort

Tort law refers to the body of law covering intentional or negligent injuries of people and businesses. (The word tort is French for "wrong," and its usage continues to reflect the French origins of William the Conqueror and his 1066 conquest of England.) It includes a range of injuries such as battery, assault, theft of property ("conversion"), negligence, false imprisonment ("kidnapping"), fraud, trespass, infliction of emotional distress, defamation ("libel"), invasion of privacy, product liability, strict liability, and nuisance.

Torts and Crimes. As you can see from the list above, many torts can also be categorized as crimes. The primary difference between torts and crimes is that in the case of a tort, the lawsuit is between private parties and the remedy is almost always money damages. People charged with a crime are being prosecuted by the state, not by a private party, and punishment often entails loss of freedom (incarceration), although it may also include payment of a fine and other punishments.

Related terms: civil lawsuit.

trespassing

Trespassing, a misdemeanor, occurs when one person intentionally enters or remains on someone else's property without permission. Momentary incursions do not constitute trespassing; the entrant has to remain on the property for a substantial period of time. So, for example, trespassing does not occur if someone walks onto property marked "Restricted," and immediately leaves. When property appears to be open to the public, property owners have to post notices denying authority to enter for the crime of trespassing to arise. The fact that the owner is not available for permission—for example, a foreclosed home—does not provide a defense. A variation of trespassing occurs when people who enter property with an owner's permission remain on the property despite the owner's demand that they leave. So, for example, a customer who refuses to leave a business establishment may be a trespasser.

Willfulness. Trespassing is illegal only if people intentionally enter or remain on another's property without permission.

> EXAMPLE: Hy stops to rest while walking through undeveloped and unfenced countryside. Unknown to Hy, the path he is following has taken him from public lands onto private property owned by Jean. Hy is not a trespasser, because he lacked the intent to enter another's property without permission. However, if Jean tells Hy that he has entered private property and that he has to leave, Hy becomes a trespasser if he refuses.

Related Offenses. When trespassers enter property in order to commit other crimes, the penalties become more severe. For example, unauthorized entry with intent to steal converts a trespasser to a burglar; unauthorized entry with intent to vandalize does the same.

 Legal Authority Examples

California: Entering or remaining on another's property without permission is a misdemeanor punishable by up to 30 days in jail and/or a fine of up to $1,000.

North Dakota: Hunters may enter property that is posted No Trespassing in order to recover game that was shot on land where the hunter had a lawful right to hunt.

Related terms: burglary; vandalism.

trial by jury (jury trial)

The Sixth Amendment guarantees the right to trial by jury. However, states have the right not to provide for jury trials for defendants whose maximum punishment is no more than six months in jail. (*Lewis v. United States*, U.S. Sup. Ct. (1996).)

Historical Antecedents. During the Middle Ages, English jurors shared case-related information among themselves and carried out their own investigations when necessary to expand upon their preexisting knowledge. By the time of American Independence, jurors had evolved into neutrals who had little or no preexisting knowledge about a case and decided cases based on evidence presented to them by witnesses and legal instructions given to them by judges.

Jury Numbers. While 12-person juries are the norm in criminal cases, in noncapital cases (non-death-penalty cases), juries can consist of as few as six people. With 12-person juries in noncapital cases, states can provide that as few as nine persons must agree for a valid verdict to result. (*Johnson v. Louisiana*, U.S. Sup. Ct. (1972).) When juries consist of as few as six people, verdicts require unanimity.

Jury Selection. *Voir dire* (literally, "to speak truth") refers to the process of selecting jurors. The judge and both parties question prospective jurors, and based on their answers can excuse jurors by exercising challenges for "cause" and peremptory challenges. The typical reason that prospective jurors are removed for cause is that their answers indicate that they are partial to one party or the other—for example a juror in a marijuana possession case states that she believes all laws prohibiting marijuana should be struck down. Parties can exercise a limited number of peremptory challenges against prospective jurors who are legally eligible to serve, but who they think might be unfavorable jurors. Parties may not exercise a peremptory challenge based on a prospective juror's race or gender.

> **EXAMPLE:** Ida is charged with aggravated assault on a former boyfriend. Ida's defense is that the boyfriend's history of violence toward her led her to believe that he was about to attack her again and that she needed to protect herself. A prospective female juror indicates that her daughter had once been physically abused by a boyfriend, but also says that she can give both sides a fair trial. If the defense lawyer challenges the prosecutor's attempt to exercise a peremptory challenge against the prospective juror, the prosecutor will have to satisfy the judge that the challenge is based on the prospective juror's past experience with abuse and not on her gender.

Juror Misconduct. Jurors have to base verdicts on the evidence that parties present to them. They cannot conduct independent investigations. Once a verdict is entered, however, it cannot be set aside unless it is a product of prejudicial information that comes from a source *outside* the jury. So, for example, if a juror bases his decision on a personal prejudice, the verdict would not be set aside. However, if the judge is informed about the juror's prejudicial remarks prior to rendering a verdict, the juror could be removed from the jury. At the same time, if a juror Googles information about DNA investigations during a trial, Google search results constitute an outside source that might lead the judge to set aside the verdict.

> **EXAMPLE:** In the classic film *12 Angry Men*, a young man is accused of stabbing his father to death. To convince the other jurors that the knife's design was not nearly as unusual as the prosecutor argued, Juror No. 8 buys a nearly identical knife at a shop close to the courthouse and displays it to the other jurors during deliberations. Juror No. 8 conducted an improper investigation that if reported to the judge by other jurors would result in his removal from the jury.

Jury Nullification. As the ultimate conscience of the community, juries have the inherent power to nullify the law by acquitting defendants no matter how obvious their guilt (a principle known as "jury nullification"). Jury nullification is a controversial practice in that if a defendant is in fact guilty the jurors disregard the judge's instructions and their oath. Jury nullification became prominent during Prohibition when many juries refused to convict those who violated anti-alcohol laws. Once entered, not guilty verdicts are final and irreversible. Rarely if ever do judges inform jurors of their nullification power, and defense attorneys commit misconduct if they do so.

 Legal Authority Examples

Excerpt from Sixth Amendment to the U.S. Constitution: "In all criminal prosecutions, the accused shall enjoy the right to a speedy and public trial by an impartial jury of the State and district wherein the crime shall have been committed."

Excerpt from Federal Rule of Evidence 606(b): Upon an inquiry into the validity of a verdict, a juror may testify about whether extraneous prejudicial information was improperly brought to the jury's attention or whether any outside influence was improperly brought to bear upon any juror. A juror may not testify as to any matter or statement occurring during the course of the jury's deliberations.

Florida: The prosecutor and the defense each get ten peremptory challenges if an offense is punishable by death or life in prison; six peremptory challenges if an offense is punishable by more than 12 months in prison but is not punishable by death or life in prison; and three peremptory challenges in all other cases.

trial phases (trial cycles)

The phases of trial unfold in a predictable and generally accepted order. These phases—choosing a jury, opening statements, direct and cross-examination, closing arguments, jury instruction, jury deliberation, and verdict—are so well established that many states do not include the order of these phases in statutes or court rules. Judges have some space and power to customize these phases.

Opening Statement. Opening statements function as road maps. They provide an overall picture that may help judges and jurors understand the significance of evidence as attorneys elicit it in piecemeal fashion from different witnesses. Prosecutors normally precede their cases-in-chief (see below) with an opening statement. Defendants may offer their own opening statements immediately afterwards, or they may delay an opening statement until their turn to present a case-in-chief, or they may remain silent. Opening statements should not include argument; they are confined to explanations of what the evidence will show. Opening statements are not evidence—they cannot be relied upon as proof of any fact.

> **EXAMPLE:** In the film *Suspect* (1987), prosecutor Charlie Stella tells the jurors in his opening statement, "I've tried 43 murder cases, and this one is the most senseless and indefensible." Stella's remarks are improper because his experience and the comparison to other cases are irrelevant to the defendant's guilt.

Case-in-Chief. After a jury is chosen, and opening statements have been made, prosecutors commence the trial by presenting their case-in-chief. A case-in-chief consists of the sum total of a prosecutor's (or a defendant's) evidence. A prosecutor's case-in-chief must include evidence sufficient to constitute proof of guilt beyond a reasonable doubt. For this reason, prosecutors present cases-in-chief first. Defendants, who have a constitutional right to remain silent, may or not offer evidence.

> **EXAMPLE:** Angie is charged with insurance fraud. The prosecutor's case-in-chief consists of live witness testimony and numerous documents. Angie's attorney cross-examines the prosecution witnesses and contests the authenticity of some of the documents. When the prosecution's case-in-chief concludes, Angie

382

rests without presenting a case-in-chief. Angie may nevertheless argue that the prosecutor has failed to prove beyond a reasonable doubt that she is guilty.

Direct Examination. Attorneys elicit evidence from witnesses in a question-and-answer format. Evidence rules require attorneys to steer a path between overly broad, vague questions and leading questions that tell witnesses exactly how to respond. Below are some examples:

- **Improper: Leading Question.** In a murder case, the crucial dispute concerns the killer's identity. The prosecutor asks an eyewitness, "Is the defendant seated over there the man you saw holding the gun?" The question is improperly leading.
- **Improper: No Boundaries on Answer.** In a murder case, the defense attorney asks the defendant's alibi witness, "What can you tell us about you and the defendant?" The question is improper because it sets no boundaries on an answer's scope and subject matter.
- **Proper: Eliciting Chronology.** In a murder case, after the defense alibi witness testifies that he met up with the defendant at about 6 p.m. on the night of the killing, the defense attorney asks, "And then what happened?" This is a standard form of proper question that elicits evidence chronologically and one step at a time.

Cross Examination. Like direct examinations, cross-examinations unfold in question-and-answer format. The difference is that evidence rules allow and effective advocacy encourages attorneys to use leading questions when cross-examining witnesses. Leading questions permit cross-examiners to limit witnesses' responses to specific details that the attorneys hope will advance their positions.

EXAMPLE: Alonzo testifies for the prosecution in a drug trafficking case. He admits to accompanying the defendant on some illegal transactions, but testifies that the defendant controlled the operation. To attack Alonzo's credibility without allowing him to repeat damaging testimony, the defense attorney asks the leading question, "The prosecutor has dismissed charges against you in exchange for your testimony against my client, correct?"

The possibly apocryphal "Nose Story" illustrates the risk of putting nonleading questions to adverse witnesses. In the Nose Story, a defendant is charged with mayhem for biting off a chunk of a victim's nose. Cross-examining the prosecution's eyewitness, the defense attorney successfully leads the witness into admitting that the witness did not actually see the victim bite off the victim's nose. The defense attorney then asks the fatal nonleading question, "Then how can you possibly testify that my client bit off the victim's nose?" The witness responds, "Because I saw him spit it out."

Closing Argument. Closing argument is the most free-form phase of trial. But attorneys' references to applicable law and evidence must be accurate. And lawyers (especially prosecutors) cannot appeal to jurors' passions and prejudices rather than their reason or ask judges or jurors to rely on factors that are outside the scope of trial. But in the tradition of the adversary system, rhetorical flair is appropriate in closing arguments.

EXAMPLE: Based on the notorious 1924 Leopold and Loeb murder prosecution, the film *Compulsion* (1959) incorporates excerpts from defense attorney Clarence Darrow's actual closing argument for his clients to be sentenced to life in prison rather than death. Darrow responded to the clamor to mete out the same punishment to his clients that they did to their victim, 14-year-old Bobby Franks, by arguing, "If our state is not kinder, more human and more intelligent than the mad act of these two sick boys, then I'm sorry I've lived so long." Concluding his argument, Darrow told the judge, "If you hang these boys, you turn back to the past. I'm pleading for the future … I'm not pleading for these two lives but for life itself." The judge sentenced Leopold and Loeb to life in prison. Loeb died in prison after another inmate stabbed him to death. Leopold became a model prisoner and was released after serving 33 years of his sentence; his prosecutor submitted a letter supporting his release. After his release, Leopold married, moved to Puerto Rico, and wrote a book, *Birds of Puerto Rico*.

Attorneys can refer to history, popular culture, everyday experience, folk wisdom, and virtually any aspect of general human experience that they believe will persuade a judge or jurors of the credibility and legal merit of their arguments. There are limits, though. Below are two examples.

- **Improper Argument: Sending a Message.** A prosecutor argues that a jury should convict a defendant charged with possession of child pornography "in order to send a message to the community that sex offenders are not welcome here." The argument is improper because a verdict's message is an irrelevant consideration. A guilty verdict sends the same message regardless of the defendant's actual guilt.
- **Improper Argument: Appealing to Prejudices.** A prosecutor refers to a defendant charged with selling illegal drugs as "filthy vermin, a lower-order beast who is too disgusting to exist in society." Over-the-top rhetoric such as this is improper because it portrays a defendant as less than a human being and appeals to jurors' prejudices.

 Legal Authority Examples

Federal Rule of Evidence 611(c): Leading questions should not be used in the direct examination of a witness except as may be necessary to develop the witness's testimony. Ordinarily leading questions should be permitted on cross-examination.

Related terms: burdens of proof; conspiracy; failure of proof; prosecutors; defense counsel (defense attorney); hostile witness.

turncoat witness

See hostile witness.

U

underage drinking

The legal drinking age in most states is 21. A variety of laws punish people who sell or serve alcohol to minors, as well as the minors themselves. For example, in the familiar scenario in which teenagers solicit an adult to buy liquor for them, the teenagers and the adult have violated the law. If the store clerk saw the solicitation, the clerk would also have violated the law by selling the alcohol. At the same time, parents who furnish alcohol to minors are also guilty, and may also be liable for injuries resulting from their inebriated guests' actions. But, in many states parents may legally provide a limited amount of alcohol to their children to drink in the home and under supervision.

 Legal Authority Examples

Texas: Minors who purchase or consume alcohol are guilty of a Class C misdemeanor. A first offense is punishable by a fine up to $500, enrollment in an alcohol awareness class, performance of up to 40 hours of community service, and loss of a driver's license. Sale of alcohol to a minor by either an adult or a minor is a Class A misdemeanor punishable by a fine up to $4,000, confinement in jail for up to a year, or both, and automatic driver's license suspension.

vagrancy laws

See disorderly conduct.

vandalism

Vandalism (also called malicious mischief or criminal mischief) is an umbrella term that encompasses a variety of methods of intentionally destroying or defacing private or public property without the owner's consent. Examples of vandalism include spraying graffiti onto the side of a bridge, sawing parking meters in half, pasting garage sale flyers on telephone poles, keying cars, and egging or "TP-ing" a front yard (unrolling toilet paper). Vandalism is typically a misdemeanor, but factors such as a recidivist's prior record of vandalism or significant damage to property can elevate vandalism to a felony. Artistic merit—for example, high-quality graffiti that has been praised by art critics—is not a defense to vandalism.

Origin of the Term. The term vandalism hearkens back to the Germanic tribe known as the Vandals that sacked Rome in 455 AD. Probably the Vandals were no more destructive than many other groups of medieval pillagers and plunderers. But they were unlucky enough to catch a bad break when British poet John Dryden wrote a late-17th-century poem that included the memorable words "Till Goths, and Vandals, a rude Northern race, Did all the matchless Monuments deface."

Broken Windows Policing. William J. Bratton popularized the "broken windows" approach to policing in the 1990s, first as the head of the New York City Transit Police and then as New York City's Police Commissioner. This approach posited that vandalism laws should be strictly enforced not only because vandals damaged property, but also because if left unchecked, vandalism multiplied and led to more serious criminal activity and the decline of neighborhoods. Critics have attacked the broken windows theory, asserting that a link between greater enforcement of vandalism laws and reduced rates for more serious crimes has never been demonstrated. Critics also argue that greater enforcement of vandalism laws in urban areas leads to overpolicing of minority neighborhoods and can heighten tension between the police and minority communities. The merits of the competing positions aside, the broken windows theory continues to reduce communities' tolerance for vandalism.

Enforcement Issues. Intentionally damaging property technically constitutes vandalism whether the culprit is a prankster playing a joke on a high school classmate or a gang member spraying graffiti to claim a neighborhood as the gang's turf. The primary actors in the criminal justice system, including police officers, prosecutors, and judges, have to enforce the laws with discretion lest too many people be wrongly stigmatized as lawbreakers. Yet the exercise of discretion often produces "selective enforcement" debates, with people in some communities arguing that they are unfairly targeted.

EXAMPLE: Rose plays a secret practical joke on her longtime high school friend Iris while Iris and her family are away for the weekend. Rose digs up Iris's carrot patch and replaces the carrot plants with rutabaga plants, knowing that Iris hates rutabagas. Rose has vandalized Iris's property. But even if Iris or her parents complain to the police, Rose is unlikely to face criminal charges. However, now assume that Rose and Iris are of different ethnicities and that they live in an urban neighborhood that regularly experiences violence between members of the different ethnic groups. The carrots that Rose dug up and replaced with rutabagas were in an urban garden in which an uneasy truce between the ethnic groups existed. If Iris reports Rose's actions to the police, the police and prosecutors might pursue the case in court and a judge might at least order Rose to repair the damage.

Do You Know What Your Children Are Doing? Crime statistics suggest that youths are often responsible for vandalism. Thus, many states try to motivate parents to become more vigilant supervisors of their children's activities by making parents financially responsible for fines when their children are convicted of vandalism. For example, California Penal Code Section 594 provides in part that if a minor is personally unable to pay a fine, "the parent of that minor shall be liable for payment." The amount of the fine can be significant, up to $10,000 if damage to property exceeds $400 and up to $50,000 if property damage exceeds $10,000.

 Legal Authority Examples

Virginia: Intentional destruction, defacement, or damage to property in which the damage is less than $1,000 constitutes a Class 1 misdemeanor. If the damage exceeds $1,000, the crime is punishable as a Class 6 felony. A Class 1 misdemeanor is punishable by up to a year in jail and a fine of $2,500. A Class 6 felony is punishable by up to five years in prison and a fine of $2,500.

New York City: Municipal ordinances make it illegal to write or paint graffiti on any public or private building without consent of the owner; to carry an aerosol spray paint can, broad felt-tipped marker, or etching acid into a public building with the intent to deface it; and to sell these items to anyone who is less than 18 years old.

venue, change of

Venue refers to the place of trial. Venue involves the fairness and convenience of proceeding with a prosecution in a particular locality, as opposed to a court's power to proceed in the first place. Defendants who believe that they cannot obtain a fair and impartial trial in one venue with jurisdiction over the case may file a motion seeking a change to a different venue that also has jurisdiction.

Real-Life Illustration

Johannes Mehserle, a rapid transit police officer, was charged in Oakland, California with murdering Oscar Grant on a train platform in the early hours of New Year's Day 2009. Mehserle claimed that the killing was accidental. Because Mehserle was Caucasian and Grant was African-American, widespread rioting erupted in largely black and racially charged Oakland immediately after the shooting. A video of the shooting was repeatedly shown and analyzed by Oakland media, and speakers at public demonstrations called Mehserle a murderer. Mehserle moved for a change of venue, arguing that he could not receive a fair trial in Oakland. The Oakland judge moved the trial to Los Angeles, where a jury convicted Mehserle of the far less serious crime of involuntary manslaughter. Mehserle was sentenced to a two-year term of imprisonment.

victims' rights laws

Victims' rights laws provide crime victims (and sometimes their families) with limited participation in the prosecution of criminal cases. Victims' rights laws also establish government compensation funds; victims can seek payments from these funds to cushion their financial losses. (Judges often order perpetrators to pay restitution to crime victims, but these orders are practically worthless when perpetrators are destitute.)

Historical Antecedents. Until the late 1700s crime victims had to prosecute perpetrators. Public prosecutors' offices were eventually established. Even so, in the last decades of the 20th century, many crime victims came to believe that the criminal justice system was ignoring their needs and concerns. Pressure from what was known as the Victims' Rights Movement led legislators to enact victims' rights laws.

To Prosecute or Not Is the Question. Prosecutors and not victims decide whether to prosecute alleged wrongdoers and what charges to file. Victims can neither force prosecutors to file charges nor prevent them from doing so. But prosecutors may take into account the victim's (or victim's family's) wishes when plea bargaining or seeking a particular sentence. This can occur, for example, when the family members of a murder victim advise the prosecution whether or not they would like to see the death penalty imposed.

> **EXAMPLE:** Maya reports her ex-boyfriend Joe's violent assault to the police. A few days later, Maya tells the police that she and Joe have reconciled and that she doesn't want to press charges against him. The prosecutor can charge Joe with domestic violence regardless of Maya's wishes.

Victim Impact Statements. Crime victims may be able to attend a sentencing hearing and tell the judge how a crime has affected their lives. In death penalty cases, where jurors often recommend a sentence of life or death, victims' relatives frequently testify about the impact of the victim's loss on their lives.

> **EXAMPLE:** Hannibal is convicted of first degree murder of Dustin Miojo. At the penalty phase, Dustin's family members describe the emotional and financial impact of Dustin's death. The judge also allows the family to show a brief memorial video that consists of photos and digital film clips depicting Dustin at different stages of his life.

Megan's Law. Spurred by parents whose children had been sexually abused, New Jersey passed a statute known as Megan's Law in 1994. The law was passed approximately a month after a previously convicted sex offender raped and murdered seven-year-old Megan Kanka. The federal government and almost all other states have enacted their own versions of Megan's Law, which generally require information about registered sex offenders to be published in newspapers and posted on websites.

See sex offender.

Legal Authority Examples

Alabama: Crime victims can demand that prosecutors notify them of all charges and criminal proceedings as soon as possible. Prosecutors have to confer with crime victims before agreeing to plea bargains. Victims have the right to present evidence, an impact statement, and any information concerning an offense or a sentence during any presentencing, sentencing, or restitution proceeding. Upon victims' request, prisons have to notify them of a prisoner's imminent release or death in prison.

North Carolina: Crime victims may receive compensation from the state only for economic losses, not for noneconomic losses (such as emotional distress). A victim's application for compensation must include information about the crime and the resultant injuries, and the law enforcement agency to which it was reported. The application should also include the total economic losses that a victim suffered. Compensation may be awarded even if a perpetrator is not prosecuted or convicted. Victims have two years after a crime was committed to seek compensation.

Related Terms: death penalty; plea bargaining; restitution.

vigilante

A vigilante is someone (perhaps a crime victim or a family member of a crime victim) who seeks personal revenge against a suspected criminal. Vigilante justice is improper; a person who attacks or in some other way causes harm to a suspected criminal commits a crime. In the film *Young Mr. Lincoln*, Abraham Lincoln eloquently describes the harm of vigilante justice when he addresses a lynch mob: "Trouble is, when men start taking the law into their own hands, they're just as apt in all the confusion and fun to start hanging someone who's not a murderer as someone who is. ... We do things together that we be mighty ashamed to do by ourselves."

voir dire

See trial by jury (jury trial).

warrantless searches

As the name indicates, warrantless searches occur without a warrant—that is, a judge has not officially authorized the search. The Fourth Amendment requires that searches be reasonable and refers to the necessity of probable cause for the issuance of search warrants. What the Fourth Amendment does not say is under what circumstances police officers have to obtain warrants before conducting searches. Taking their cue from the word "reasonable," judges uphold warrantless searches when police officers have probable cause to conduct a search and the lack of a search warrant is reasonable. Below are some common circumstances in which judges generally conclude that warrantless searches are reasonable.

Warrantless Searches Following Arrests. A police officer who makes a legitimate arrest has the right to search both the suspect and the immediate area in which the arrest takes place. Warrantless searches that are "incident to an arrest" are reasonable because they allow officers to protect themselves and to gather evidence pertaining to the crime that led to the arrest. As noted, the arrest must be legitimate for the search to be "incident to arrest." So, if a police officer arrests a suspect without probable cause—for example, the officer knows the suspect has a long rap sheet and simply arrests him for no reason—the resulting warrantless search will be invalid no matter what the officer's search turns up. The same is true if the search is not in the immediate area of the arrest. For example, an officer who arrests a burglary suspect at the scene of a crime cannot then drive to the burglar's home and search it without a warrant.

Consent Searches. An individual's consent to a police officer's request to conduct a warrantless search renders the search reasonable and the results admissible in evidence at trial. The "*Miranda* rules" (in which an officer advises the suspect as to certain constitutional rights) don't apply to searches; police officers do not have to advise people of the right to refuse a search request.

> EXAMPLE: Officer Sephora notices a teenager walking in a fancy shopping area and carrying a large purse. Acting purely on a hunch, Sephora approaches the teenager and asks to look inside the purse. The teenager responds, "Okay, I guess I have no choice." Sephora searches the purse, finds numerous items of cosmetics with the price tags attached, and arrests the teenager for theft. The officer was under no duty to advise the teen that consenting to the search was purely optional. The search is valid.

Plain View Searches. Searches for evidence or contraband are valid and police officers may seize these items when they are openly visible from a place where the officer has a right to be. For example, assume that a police officer, after issuing a speeding ticket, sees what appears to be a packet of illegal drugs on the passenger seat. The officer can seize the packet because it was in the officer's plain view. Of course, if the officer has no right to be some place—for example, the officer has climbed over a fence into a suspect's yard and is peering through a kitchen window—any search will be invalid no matter what the officer sees.

Exigent Circumstances. Judges uphold warrantless searches when the risk that evidence will be destroyed or that a suspect will avoid capture makes it reasonable for police officers to conduct an immediate search.

> EXAMPLE: Police officers interview the patrons of a tavern moments after a fatal stabbing takes place. An officer notices one patron rubbing his fingers together and putting his hands in and out of his pants pockets. Suspecting that the patron might

be trying to rub blood off of his fingers (and therefore having probable cause), the officer immediately tests the suspect's hands for blood residue. The test is legitimate because any evidence would be destroyed if the officer did not act on the spot.

 Legal Authority Examples

Text of the Fourth Amendment. "The right of the people to be secure in their persons, houses, papers, and effects, against unreasonable searches and seizures, shall not be violated, and no Warrants shall issue, but upon probable cause, supported by Oath or affirmation, and particularly describing the place to be searched, and the persons or things to be seized."

Related terms: search and seizure; search warrants; probable cause.

white-collar crime

White-collar crime refers to nonviolent crimes of fraud and theft committed by business people at a distance from victims (as opposed to crimes often committed directly against victims). White-collar criminals may receive lengthy sentences, but often serve them in more comfortable prisons than their violent counterparts. However, white-collar crooks are equally morally guilty. Most criminals simply commit "the crimes that they have the ability to commit," and white-collar crooks have the ability to commit crimes through indirect methods.

White-Collar Crimes		
Crime	**Definition**	**Type of Crime**
Embezzlement	Misappropriating (stealing or wrongly using) the property of another	Misdemeanor or Felony, depending on the value of the misappropriated property
Securities Fraud	Defrauding victims with false or misleading statements about investments	Felony
Insider Trading	Buying or selling shares of stock based on confidential information not publicly available	Felony
Churning	Making stock transactions for the benefit of the trader and not the customer	Felony
Ponzi Schemes	Using money invested by recent victims to fool earlier victims into thinking that an investment is profitable	Felony
Phishing	Sending false electronic statements over the internet in order to induce victims to reveal personal information	Felony

Related terms: cyber-crimes.

wobblers

Crimes that are punishable either as misdemeanors or felonies.

See hierarchy of criminal offenses.

work product rule

A form of a privilege rule that protects an attorney's case-related research and strategies from disclosure to an adversary. For example, a defense attorney has no right to examine a prosecutor's internal memorandum analyzing the strengths and weaknesses of a case.

Related terms: privileges; attorney-client privilege.

writ of *habeas corpus*

A writ of *habeas corpus* is a court order mandating a change in the fact or conditions of an individual's confinement. "*Habeas corpus*" is Latin for "you have the body." State and federal courts issue this writ if they conclude that confinement violates legal rights. Typically, a petition asking a court to grant a *habeas* writ constitutes a "collateral attack" on an existing conviction, as most petitions seek to challenge the constitutionality of confinement after an offender's opportunity to appeal a conviction has ended.

Historical Antecedents. In 17th century England, the Crown's power to arrest and imprison people without justifying its actions in court sparked fierce opposition from Parliament. Parliament prevailed with the enactment of the Habeas Corpus Act of 1679. After U.S. independence, *habeas corpus* was enshrined in the Constitution and acquired the moniker of The Great Writ. During the Civil War Congress authorized President Lincoln to suspend the writ.

Preconviction Petitions. Although most *habeas* petitions are attacks on existing judgments, an individual who is confined can petition for a writ of *habeas corpus* at any stage of a criminal proceeding. For example, a defendant who is required to post a high bail has the right to file a petition for *habeas corpus* claiming that the bail amount is so excessive that it constitutes cruel and unusual punishment in violation of the Eighth Amendment.

Unconstitutionality of Convictions; Retroactivity. A *habeas* petition can base a claim that a conviction violates constitutional rights on either legal or factual grounds. For example, a *habeas* petition might allege that the trial judge made a legally erroneous ruling that led to a prisoner's conviction, or that newly discovered evidence (that could not have reasonably been discovered at the time of trial) proves the prisoner's innocence. However, if the legal rules have changed since the conviction—for example, the Supreme Court has made a new ruling on the matter—those new legal rules don't always apply to prior rulings.

> **EXAMPLE:** Seth was convicted of domestic violence. Since Joan, the target of Seth's abuse, was afraid to testify against him in court, the conviction was based largely on hearsay testimony from a police officer who spoke to Joan shortly after the assault. Two years after Seth's conviction, the U.S. Supreme Court decided in the case of *Crawford v. Washington* (2004) that hearsay statements of nontestifying witnesses are generally inadmissible against criminal defendants. Despite the Court's ruling, Seth's federal *habeas* petition asking that his conviction be set aside based on the new rule will be denied. (However, a state court considering the same *habeas* argument could conceivably apply the *Crawford* rule retroactively.)

Unconstitutionality of Confinement. Prisoners can file *habeas* petitions challenging the conditions of their confinement. For example, a prisoner who is subject to repeated beatings may file a *habeas* petition seeking transfer to a different prison facility on the grounds that his present confinement is illegal because the prison guards look the other way when other inmates physically attack him.

Procedural Wrangling. As great as The Great Writ may be, Congress and the federal judiciary have devoted considerable effort in recent years to putting obstacles in the path of *habeas* petitioners. One reason is the belief of many federal judges that they had been swamped with meritless petitions. Another reason is federal judges' general reluctance to interfere in state criminal processes. *Habeas* procedures are so complex that many prisoners whose petitions are turned down by state court judges are shut out of federal court entirely. For example, an inmate's failure to "exhaust all state remedies"—that is, to make a timely appeal of an adverse state court ruling—may prevent the inmate from filing a *habeas* petition in federal court.

Legal Authority Examples

U.S. Constitution, Article I § 9: "The Privilege of the Writ of Habeas Corpus shall not be suspended, unless when in cases of rebellion or invasion, the public safety may require it."

Excerpt from 28 United States Code § 2254: An application for a writ of habeas corpus by a person in state court custody shall not be granted unless the applicant has exhausted state court remedies ... or unless a state court's decision involved an unreasonable application of clearly established Federal law ... or resulted in a decision that was based on an unreasonable determination of the facts. A determination of a factual issue made by a state court is presumed to be correct.

Related terms: bail; confrontation of prosecution witnesses; domestic violence; three strikes laws; appeals.

NOLO *Bestsellers*

The Small Business Start-Up Kit

A Step-by-Step Legal Guide

$29.99

How to Write a Business Plan

$34.99

The Executor's Guide

Settling a Loved One's Estate or Trust

$39.99

Every Landlord's Legal Guide

$44.99

Patent It Yourself

$49.99

Make Your Own Living Trust

$39.99

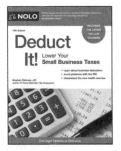

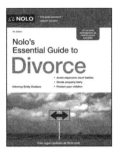

Nolo's Essential Guide to Divorce

$24.99

Tax Savvy for Small Business

$39.99

Get It Together

Organize Your Records So Your Family Won't Have To

$24.99

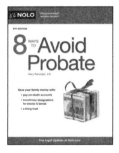

8 Ways to Avoid Probate

$21.99

Nolo's Essential Guide to Buying Your First Home

$24.99

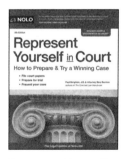

Represent Yourself in Court

How to Prepare & Try a Winning Case

$39.99

Effective Fundraising for Nonprofits

Real-World Strategies That Work

$29.99

Credit Repair

$24.99

Solve Your Money Troubles

Debt, Credit & Bankruptcy

$24.99

First-Time Landlord

Your Guide to Renting Out a Single-Family Home

$24.99

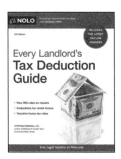

Every Landlord's Tax Deduction Guide

$39.99

IRAs, 401(k)s & Other Retirement Plans

Taking Your Money Out

$34.99

NOLO® *Online Legal Forms*

Nolo offers a large library of legal solutions and forms, created by Nolo's in-house legal staff. These reliable documents can be prepared in minutes.

Create a Document

- **Incorporation.** Incorporate your business in any state.
- **LLC Formations.** Gain asset protection and pass-through tax status in any state.
- **Wills.** Nolo has helped people make over 2 million wills. Is it time to make or revise yours?
- **Living Trust (avoid probate).** Plan now to save your family the cost, delays, and hassle of probate.
- **Trademark.** Protect the name of your business or product.
- **Provisional Patent.** Preserve your rights under patent law and claim "patent pending" status.

Download a Legal Form

Nolo.com has hundreds of top quality legal forms available for download—bills of sale, promissory notes, nondisclosure agreements, LLC operating agreements, corporate minutes, commercial lease and sublease, motor vehicle bill of sale, consignment agreements and many more.

Review Your Documents

Many lawyers in Nolo's consumer-friendly lawyer directory will review Nolo documents for a very reasonable fee. Check their detailed profiles at **Nolo.com/lawyers**.